IMAGES
of America

CHERRY VALLEY

I0806167

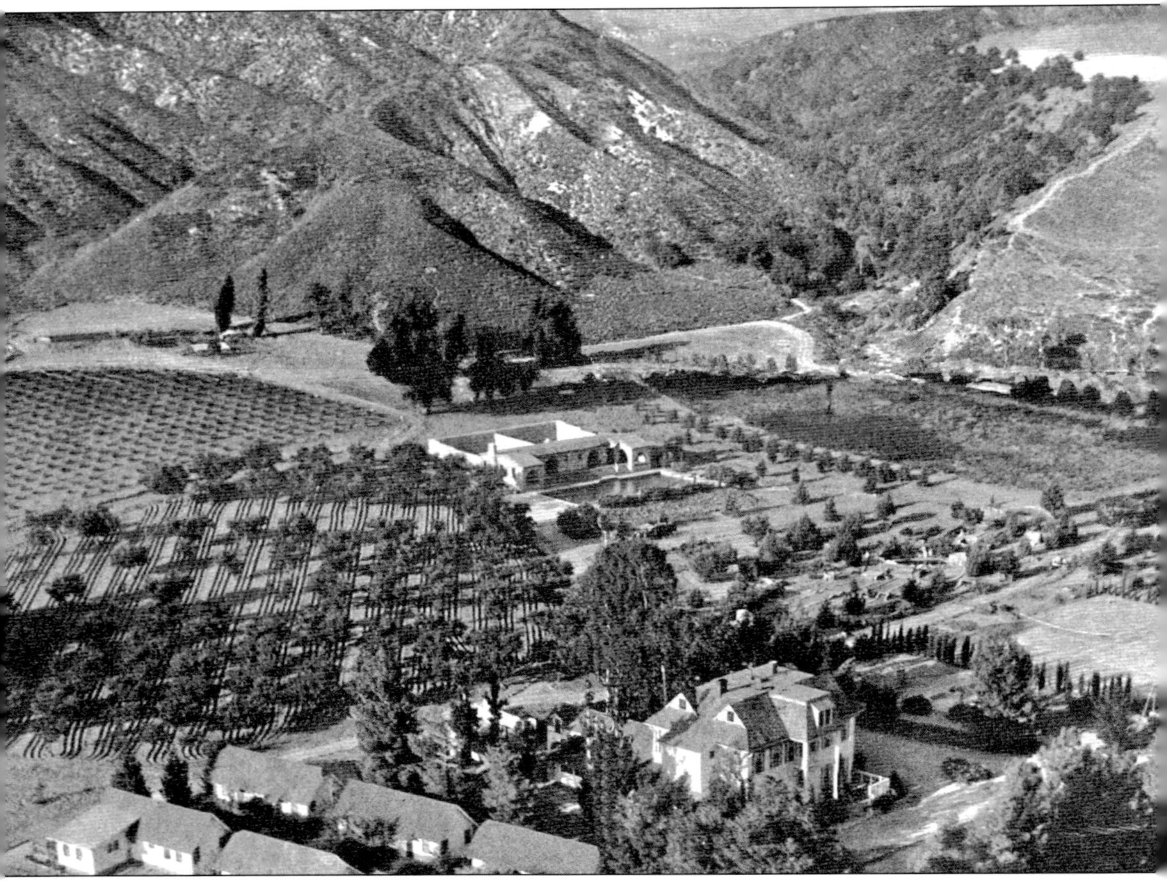

This early aerial view of Highland Springs shows the Highland Home in the foreground with several cottages at the left. In the center is the old swimming pool that was so popular during this era. At left, near the center, are a fruit orchard and a grape vineyard near the foothills in the rear. (Courtesy of Steve Lech.)

ON THE COVER: This mid-1950s photograph was taken in Cherry Valley during a Cherry Festival celebration of that time. It was customary to highlight the festival during this event with pictures of exotic cars, cherry trees, and beautiful girls associated with the festival; most importantly, the Cherry Festival queen. (Courtesy of SGPHS.)

IMAGES
of America

CHERRY VALLEY

Kenneth M. Holtzclaw and Tom Chong

ARCADIA
PUBLISHING

ISBN 978-0-7385-5952-0

Published by Arcadia Publishing
Charleston SC, Chicago IL, Portsmouth NH, San Francisco CA

Printed in the United States of America

Library of Congress Catalog Card Number: 2008928310

For all general information contact Arcadia Publishing at:
Telephone 843-853-2070
Fax 843-853-0044
E-mail sales@arcadiapublishing.com
For customer service and orders:
Toll-Free 1-888-313-2665

Visit us on the Internet at www.arcadiapublishing.com

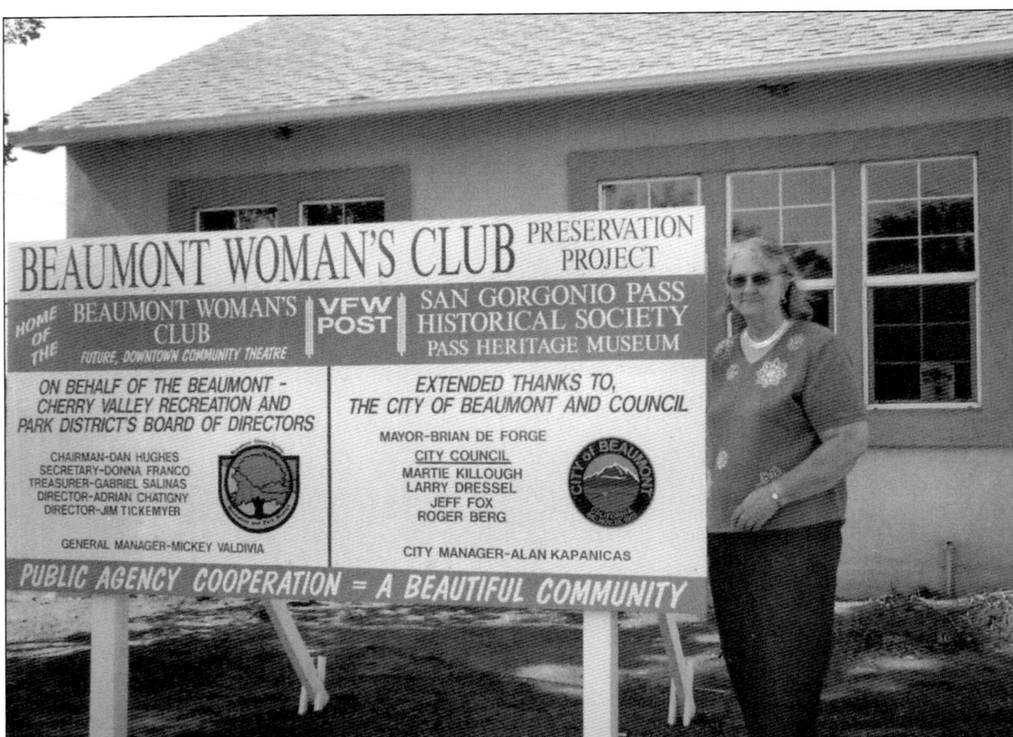

Virginia Ross, president of the San Gorgonio Pass Historical Society, stands beside a temporary sign in front of the Beaumont Woman's Club. The sign has been placed there as a token of thanks for all engaged in the renovation effort of the 100-year-old structure, which will be the home of the Beaumont Woman's Club, VFW Post, Pass Heritage Museum, and San Gorgonio Pass Historical Society. (Courtesy of Margaret Holtzclaw.)

Contents

ACKNOWLEDGMENTS

Many of the pictures obtained for this book came from the San Gorgonio Pass Historical Society (SGPHS), and thanks are given to them for their contribution. Each picture obtained from this society is acknowledged by its SGPHS abbreviation. The Edward Dean Museum and Gardens (EDM&G) provided most of the photographs from their archives for chapter four and each acknowledgment includes their EDM&G abbreviation. Grateful thanks are given to Joan Coombs for many of the pictures in chapter five and all are acknowledged there.

There are others who contributed to the book, helping to make it a success, and all are kindly thanked: Bahjit Toor, Steve Lech, Marilyn Vonderheide, Judy and Roy Polman, Connie and Ben Stevenson, RaLana Gurney, Mike Iorio, Teresa Gallaven, Blanch Sambera, Brandon Keith, Joe Lyneis, Virginia Ross, Evelyn Hawkins, and Margarito Arreola. Pictures in the book without courtesy lines are, by default, courtesy of the author.

INTRODUCTION

Cherry Valley has an interesting history, predating even the Native American habitation of the area. The first white settlers of the San Gorgonio Pass arrived near the end of that era. They lived in Cherry Valley and formed the oldest settlement established in the San Gorgonio Pass. It was not until the early 1820s that Spanish explorers discovered the pass area. In the early 1800s, friars had migrated over from the San Gabriel Mission located to the west and established an outpost mission in Cherry Valley. It was headquartered near the center of the heart of Cherry Valley, near Fire Station No. 22. There is a monument standing just a few yards to the east of the fire station. Placed there by local firemen, it denotes the location of the original adobe.

After the friars arrived at Cherry Valley on March 9, 1823, they named their mission San Gorgonio Rancho, in honor of St. Gorgonius. The date later became known as St. Gorgonius Day. They held in awe the high, snowcapped mountain to the north, and it soon acquired the name of Mount San Gorgonio. Cherry Valley is cradled between Mount San Gorgonio and the San Bernardino Range of Mountains to the north and Mount San Jacinto and the San Jacinto Mountains to the south. Both peaks are over 10,000 feet in height. The seasonal snowcapped mountain peaks portray the picturesque beauty of Cherry Valley, towering high above its community floor. Cherry Valley lies in the San Gorgonio Pass, the deepest pass in the continental United States, and exceeds the Grand Canyon by 2,000 feet.

Allegedly, the San Gorgonio Rancho was abandoned by the friars and a scout and mountain man named Pauline Weaver was granted the deed to the rancho by Pio Pico, the governor of Mexico. Weaver lived in the San Gorgonio Rancho with his Native American wife and worked for a man named Daniel Sexton at a lumber mill located in Edgar Canyon, north of Cherry Valley. Dr. William Edgar had a ranch there, raised grapes, and established a winery. The first U.S. Post Office in this area was established at his winery in 1868, with Mark Garrett as the postmaster. This canyon was named in honor of the early pioneer, Dr. Edgar, and Edgar Canyon today is a great source of water for the Beaumont/Cherry Valley Water District. The American flag was flown for the first time in 1843 in California at Cherry Valley, celebrating Independence Day with the local Native Americans.

Throughout the years, the population grew slowly in and around Cherry Valley, and it was in 1907 that Claredon Eyer and Kenneth Smoot purchased Edgar and Noble Canyons to use as water sources. Water was desperately needed when they established the Apple Valley Water Company. At the time, apples were chiefly grown here, instituting the name Apple Valley. It did not become Cherry Valley until cherries later replaced apples as the major crop, spurring apple growing in nearby Oak Glen to the north.

Dr. Isaac Smith obtained property from Pauline Weaver and built his home where Highland Springs Resort is located today. He operated a stage stop there. The San Gorgonio Pass soon became a major east-west route for the stagecoach lines. In 1856, Martha Smith married James Gilman at her home in Highland Springs. That same year, Emily Smith became the first white baby born in Cherry Valley. In 1859, Oliver M. Smith became the first white male born there.

When Oliver Smith grew up, he extended the Highland Springs ranch operation to include Whitewater, where he and his partner, Robert Coombs (Bert), dry farmed and raised cattle. In the heat of summer, they herded their cattle to Big Bear Valley and grazed them there, living during this time in the family's lodgings there. Meanwhile, passenger travel by stagecoach as well as freighting through the San Gorgonio Pass continued in significant quantity until the late 1870s, when the Southern Pacific Railroad completed the extension of its track from Los Angeles to Fort Yuma, Arizona. With the introduction of passenger railroad in 1876, traffic through the area began to increase. In 1884, a Los Angeles company purchased the Highland Springs property and built a three-story structure on the site. Although the building, named the Highland Home, later burned down, the area is still a well-known landmark in Cherry Valley. Today it is home of Highland Springs Resort and Conference Center. Upon its acreage, large fields of lavender are grown and a Lavender Festival is held each year; this year representing the fourth consecutive one to be staged.

One

Round about Town

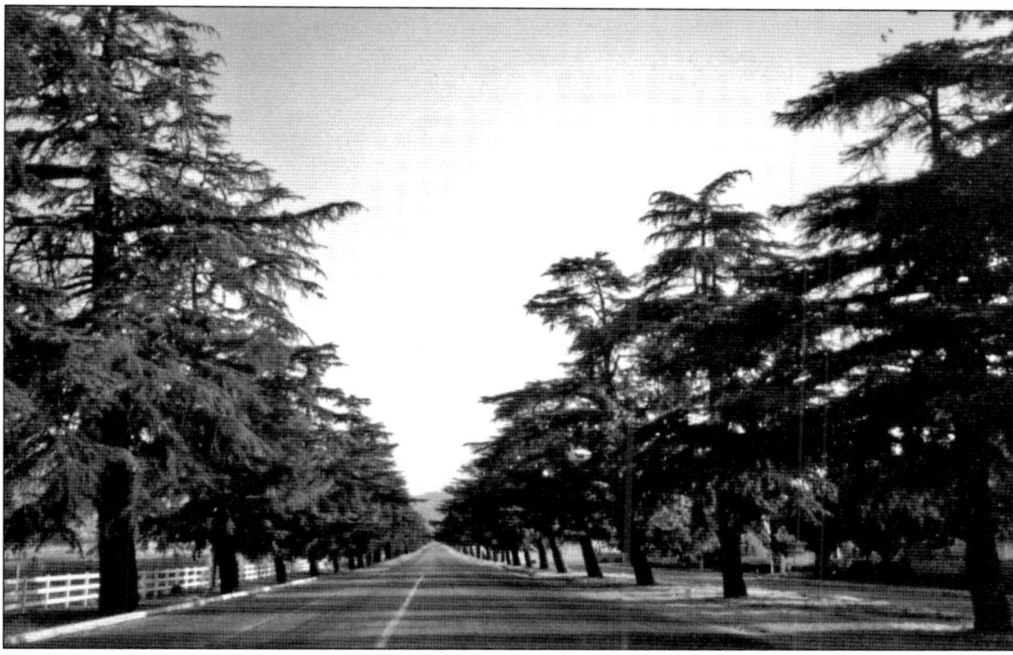

Beaumont Avenue enters the vicinity of Cherry Valley from the south. The trees that align the avenue are East Indian cedars, known as deodar trees. The road serves as a corridor for travel through Cherry Valley, connecting to Cherry Valley's adjoining neighbor, Oak Glen, which rests above in a beautiful mountain area. Native Americans, mostly Cahuilla, were the first residents of Cherry Valley. In the early 1820s, Spanish explorers discovered the San Gorgonio Pass and around the mid-1800s, friars from the San Gabriel Mission established a mission outpost here, which they named San Gorgonio Rancho. Its center was an adobe building located in today's Cherry Valley.

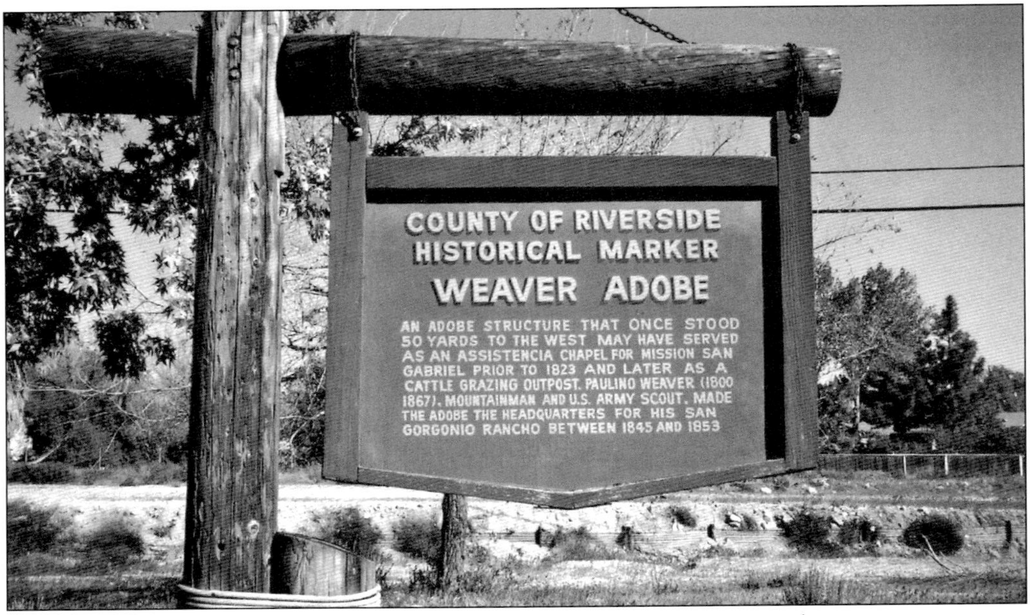

After the mission was eventually abandoned, Pauline Weaver, a scout and mountain man, was granted the deed to the rancho in 1844 by Pio Pico, the governor of Mexico. Weaver lived in the adobe at the San Gorgonio Rancho with his Native American wife, working for Daniel Sexton at his lumber mill north of the adobe. This Riverside County historical marker now designates the Weaver adobe's site, which stood 50 yards to the west of the marker.

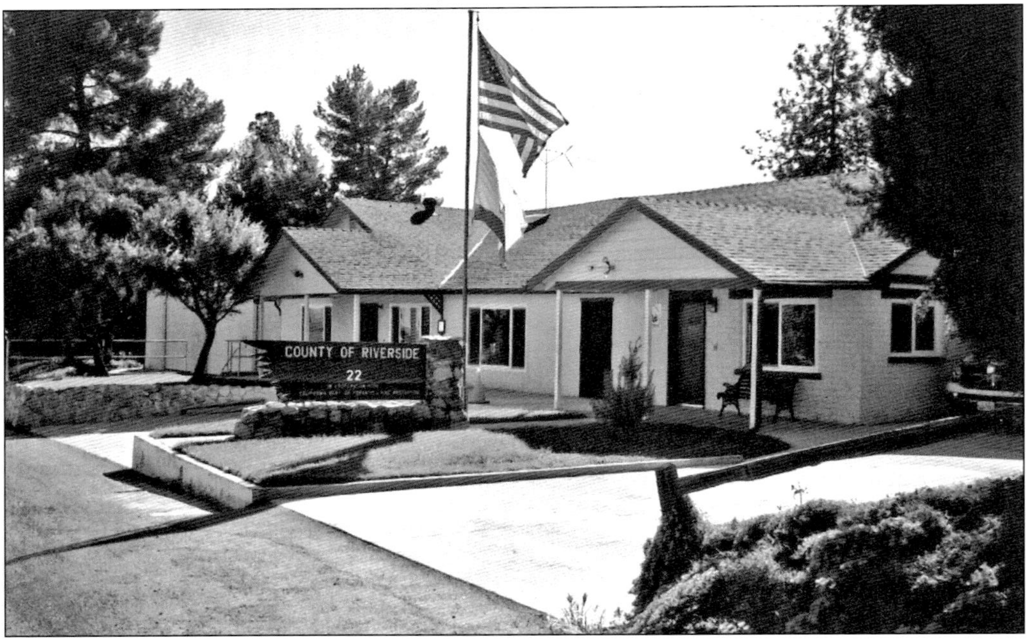

Fire Station No. 22 stands just west of the County of Riverside historical marker, near the location of the original Weaver adobe. It is one of many fire stations that comprise the Riverside County Fire Department, which is one of the largest regional fire service organizations in California. The department is staffed with approximately 952 career and 1,100 volunteer personnel.

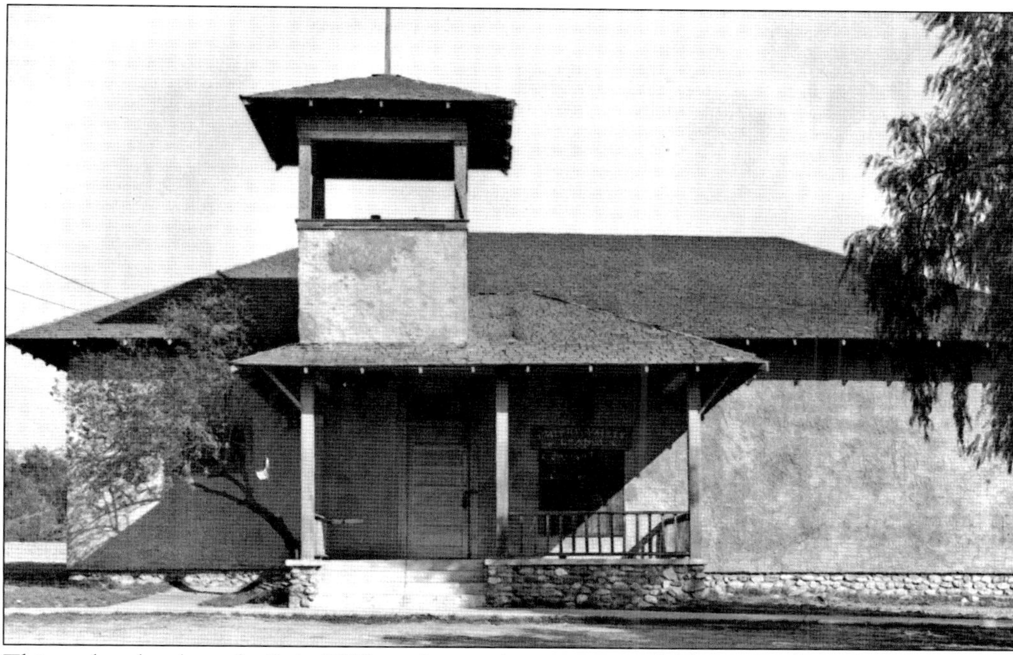

This early school was built in 1905 on the northeast corner of Cherry Boulevard and Beaumont Avenue. The organization, the Grange, began in 1867 after the Civil War to protect against dangers on the western frontier. By 1950, the Grange had bought this vintage schoolhouse, which would become its meeting place. Today the building is known as the Cherry Valley Grange and acts as a meeting hall for various functions. (Courtesy of SGPHS.)

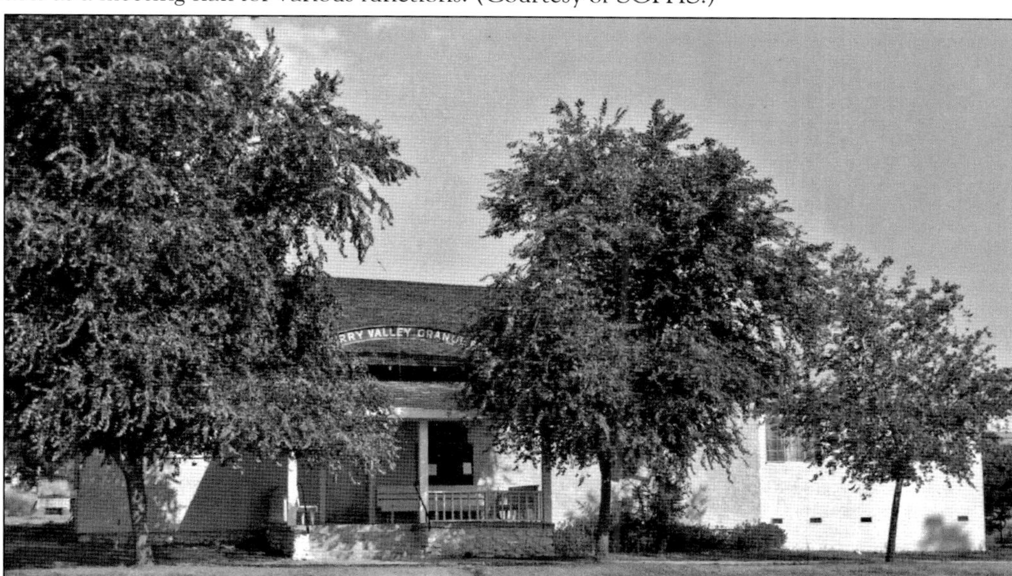

The Cherry Valley Grange No. 586 building was constructed in 1905 as a small schoolhouse with outside restrooms. According to some historians, it once had a bell tower. The Grange building has been a landmark in Cherry Valley for many years and continues to be so today. (Courtesy of Ros Otero.)

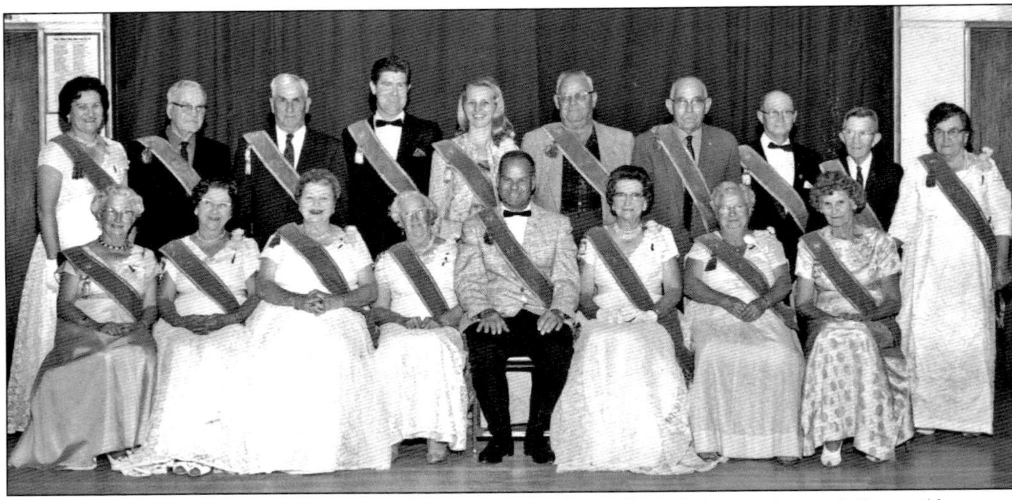

The 1968 Cherry Valley Grange officers are pictured here, from left to right, as follows: (first row) Trudy Haueter, treasurer; Florence Walker, ceres; Ivy Nelson, chaplain; Berth Vlasek, lecturer; Chick Hoover, master; Anna Schmidt, lady assistant steward; Martha Engel, flora; and Mayme Hayes, pianist; (second row) Annie Endres, promoter; John Vlasek, one-year executive; Jack Stark, two-year executive; Terry Speers, overseer; Linda Hoover, secretary; Oscar Huckfeldt, gatekeeper; Chuck Walker, three-year executive; Luther Ward, assistant steward; Clarence Hurt, steward; and Stella Hammer, WAC chairman. (Courtesy of Ros Otero.)

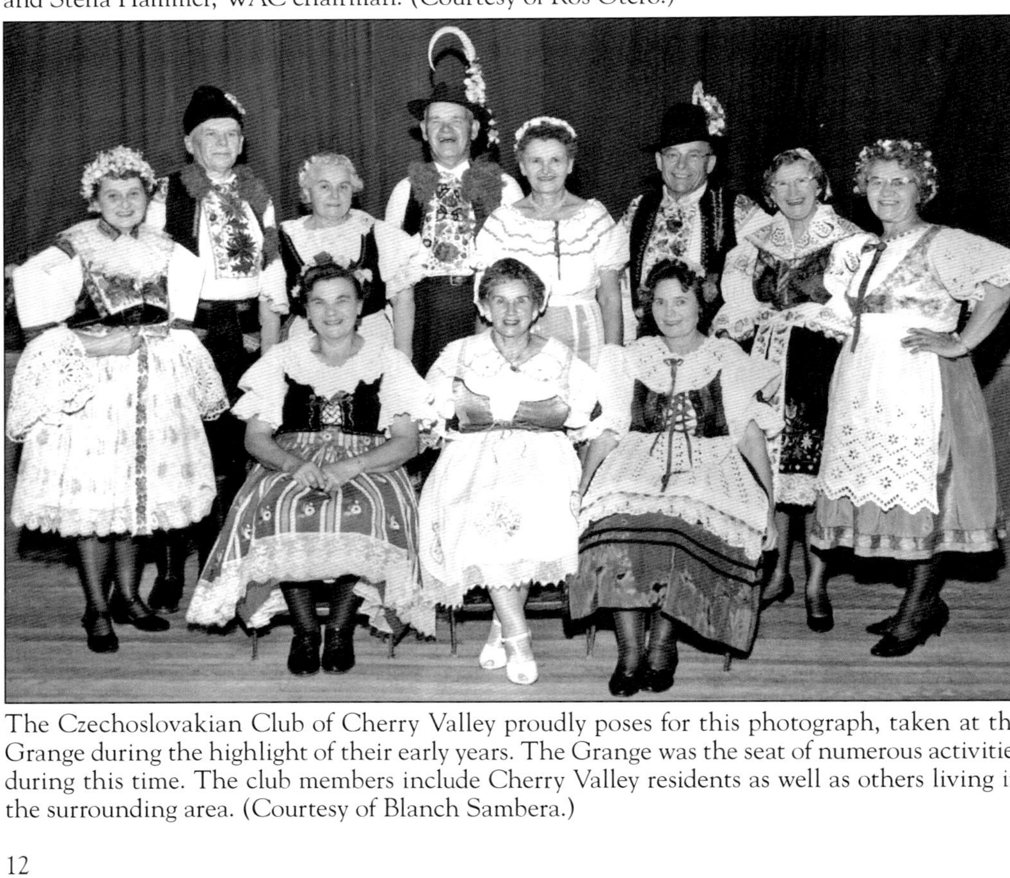

The Czechoslovakian Club of Cherry Valley proudly poses for this photograph, taken at the Grange during the highlight of their early years. The Grange was the seat of numerous activities during this time. The club members include Cherry Valley residents as well as others living in the surrounding area. (Courtesy of Blanch Sambera.)

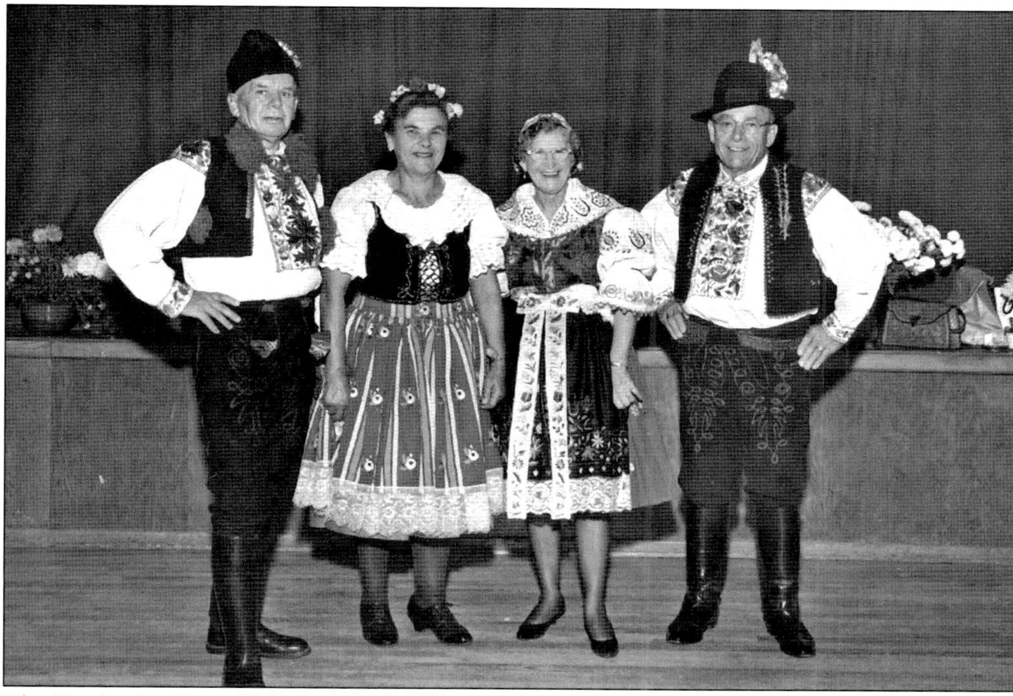

The Czechoslovakian Club of Cherry Valley used the Grange as their primary meeting headquarters and often conducted activities there. These dancers, a Czechoslovakian dance quartette with their regalia of fancy trappings, were always a delight to watch during a dance presentation at the club's activities. (Courtesy of Blanch Sambera.)

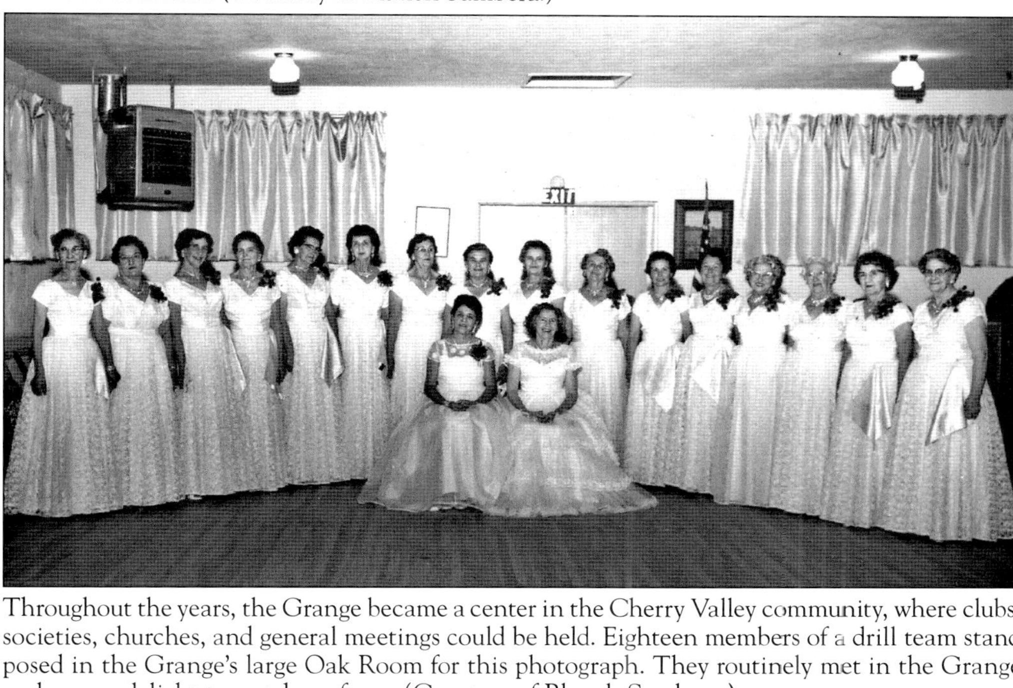

Throughout the years, the Grange became a center in the Cherry Valley community, where clubs, societies, churches, and general meetings could be held. Eighteen members of a drill team stand posed in the Grange's large Oak Room for this photograph. They routinely met in the Grange and were a delight to watch perform. (Courtesy of Blanch Sambera.)

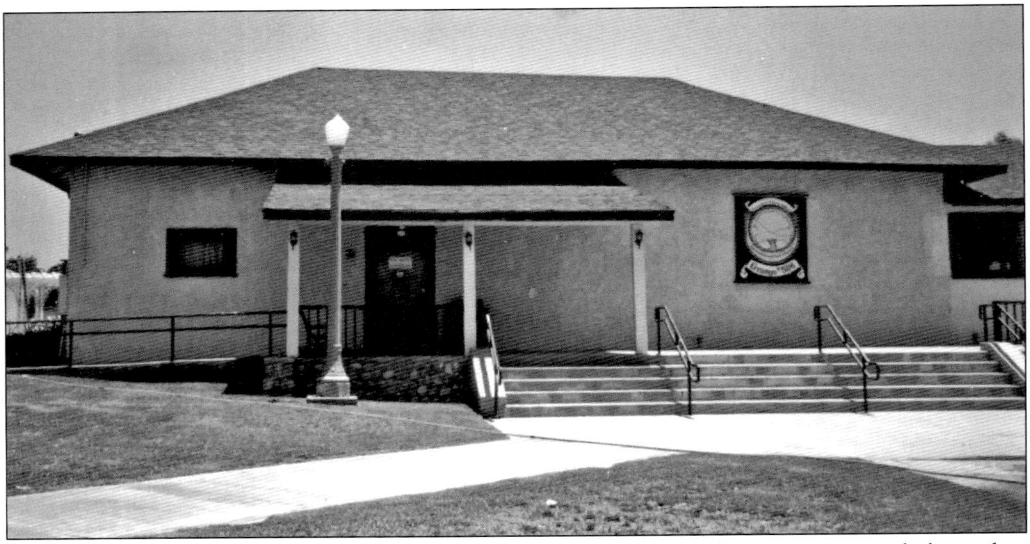

The 100-year-old Grange is viewed after its renovation in 1997. The property was dedicated to the Beaumont-Cherry Valley Parks and Recreation District in August 1988, because Grange membership had dropped so significantly that they could no longer maintain the building. It is still known as the Cherry Valley Grange but now functions as a meeting hall for other various activities as well.

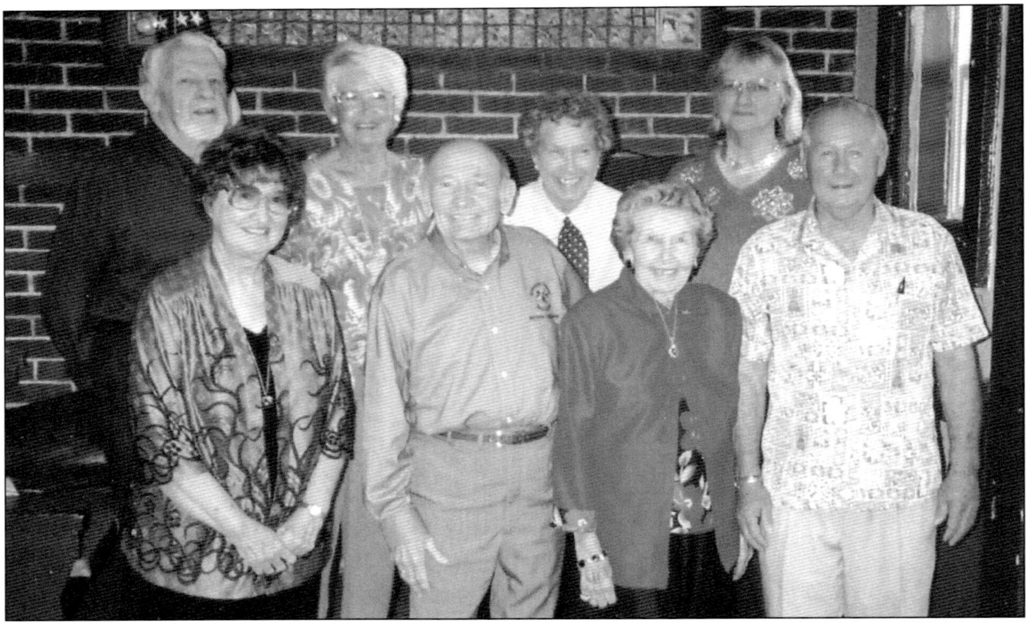

Pictured are the officers and board of directors of the San Gorgonio Pass Historical Society. From left to right are (first row) Rose Cunningham, director and secretary/treasurer; Jerry Cody, vice president; Claire Broyles, director and chairman; and Ken Holtzclaw, director; (second row) Bill Furbush, director; Betty Warren, director; Margaret Holtzclaw, director and historian; and Virginia Ross, director and president. Not pictured is Bud Mathewson, historian. For years, the society has held meetings in the Grange in Cherry Valley but now has moved to their new home in the Woman's Club in Beaumont.

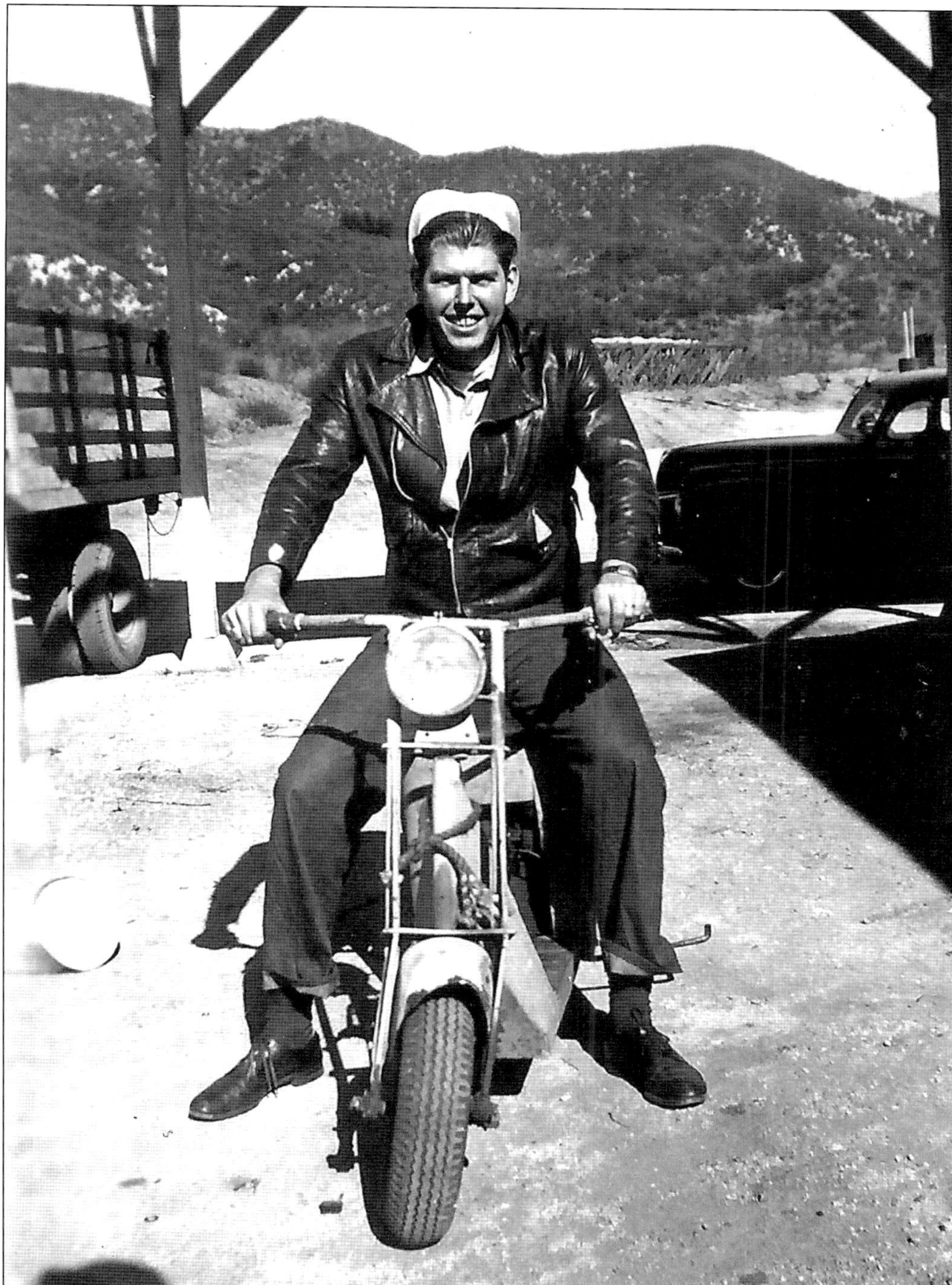

Homer Shockey sits on his scooter around 1945. He was one of 30 navy corpsmen who came to Cherry Valley to renovate and convert General Patton's deserted army hospitals in Banning and Cherry Valley into navy hospitals. Today Homer lives in nearby Banning with his wife, Margaret. He recalls fond memories at the hospital. (Courtesy of Homer Shockey.)

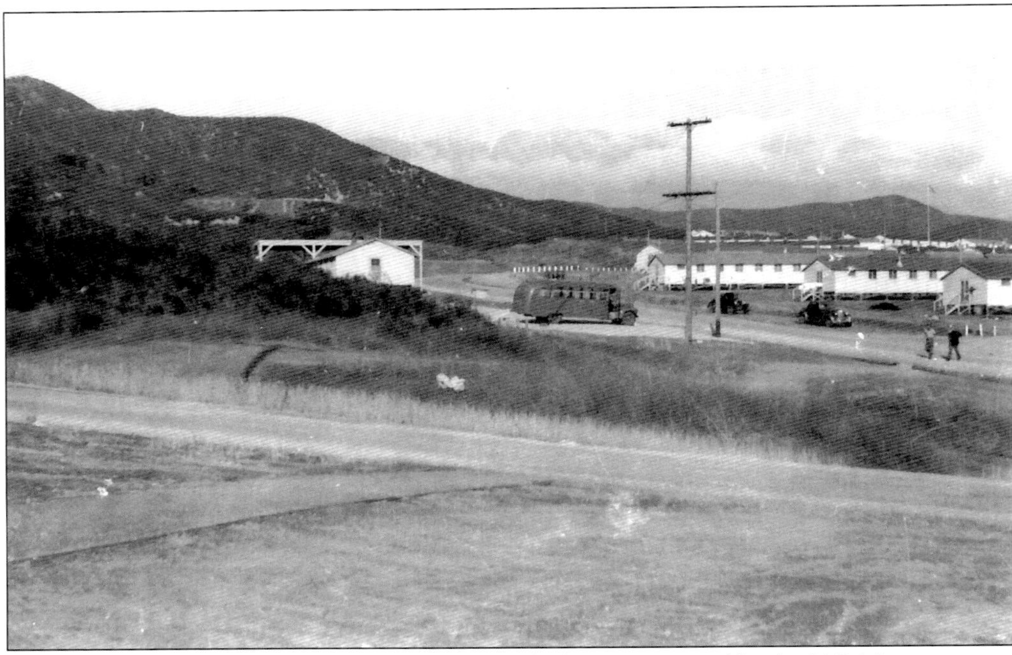

This is a 1944 view of General Patton's hospital, which was renovated by the U.S. Navy corpsmen after Patton abandoned it to begin his North African campaign. The hospital compound covered some 100 acres, reaching into the foothills of Cherry Valley, north of Orchard Street. (Courtesy of Homer Shockey.)

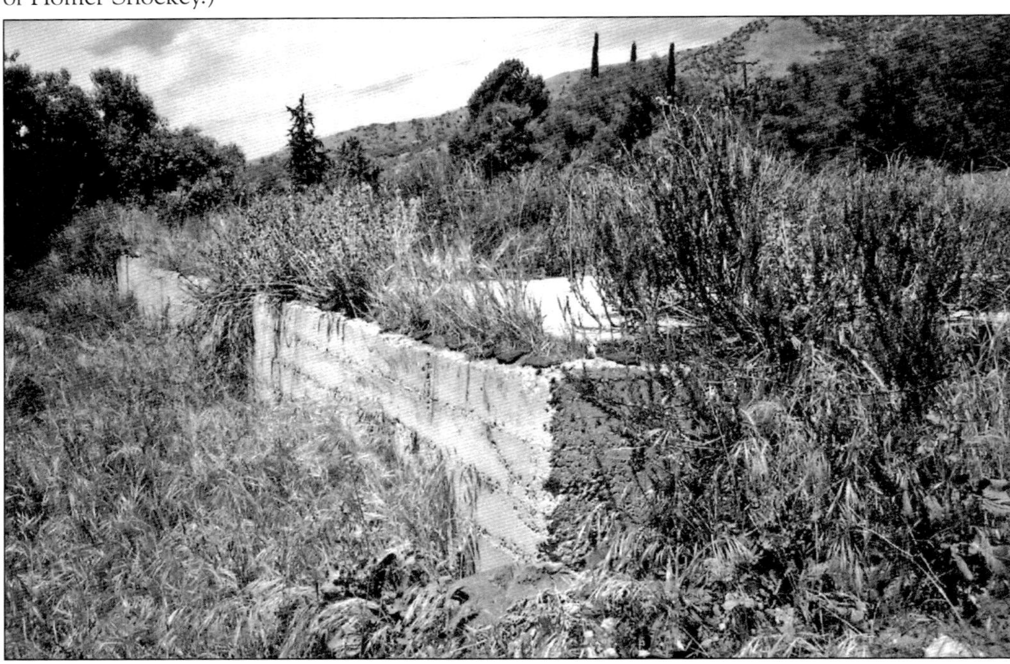

There is not much left of the navy hospital that once stood proudly in Cherry Valley other than this foundation of one of its buildings, the administration building flag pole, and a water reservoir, still used today by a local water company.

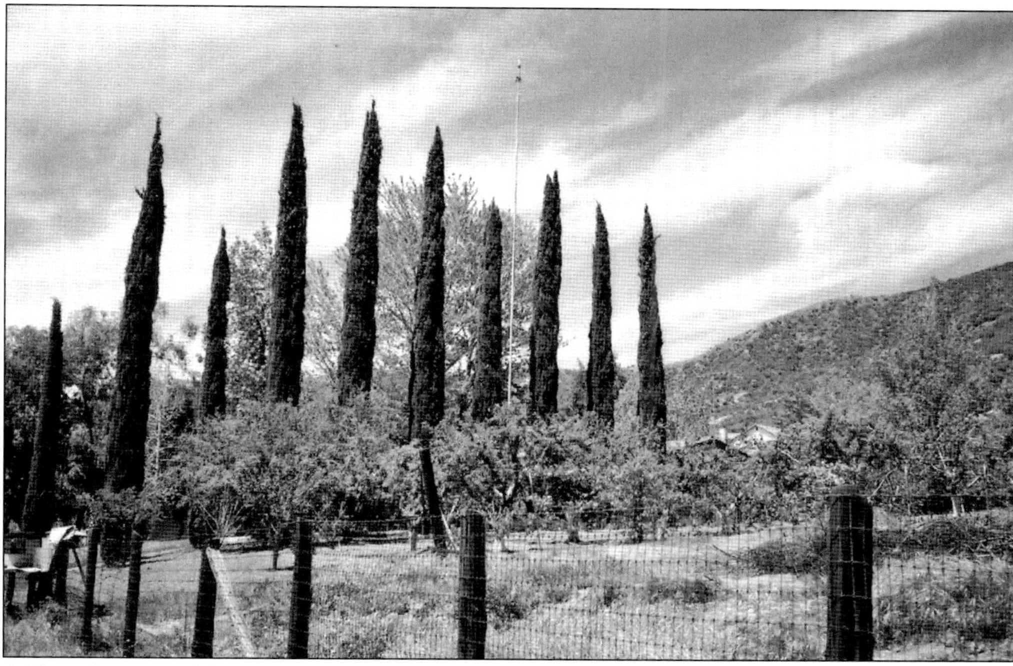

Although removed from its original site in front of the naval hospital in Cherry Valley, the flagpole is a reminder that the hospital once stood nearby. The hospital cared for wounded militia brought in from the Pacific campaign of World War II. It was a vital facility during that time.

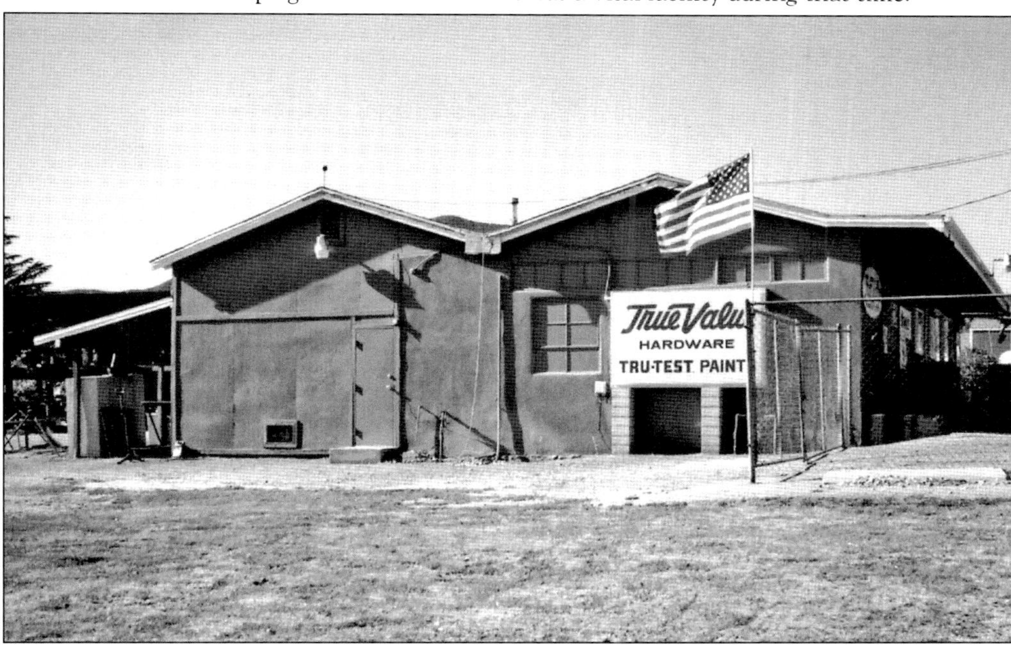

This photograph exemplifies one extent to which some of the barracks taken from the hospital compound were commercially utilized. In this case, two of the barracks were incorporated to form a True Value hardware store, owned today by Chris Hogan. Other barracks were converted into businesses, houses, or apartments, some of which still stand today.

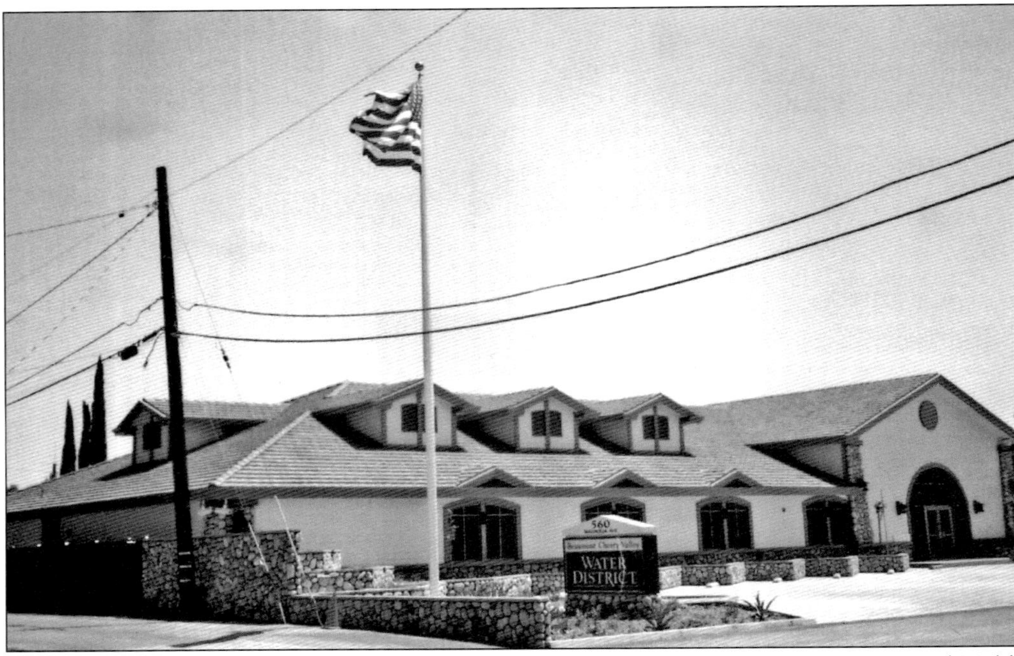

The Beaumont/Cherry Valley Water District covers a large area in Edgar Canyon and Noble Creek, where they maintain a number of water-producing wells that supply water to Beaumont and Cherry Valley. Pictured here is the new Beaumont/Cherry Valley Water District building, quite a renovation from their past headquarters.

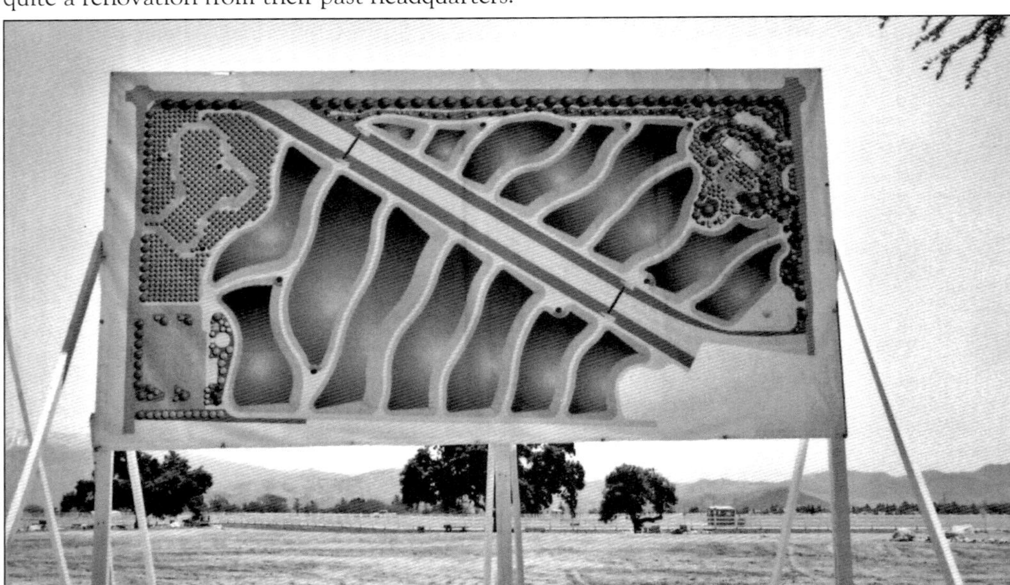

This pictorial depiction was placed on the southeast corner of Beaumont Avenue and Cherry Avenue to portray the 16 water-holding ponds that have been excavated there. The purpose of each pond is to collect rainwater, and at certain intervals, California state water from the State Water Project, so that the water can drain down through the soil and increase water content in the aquifer below.

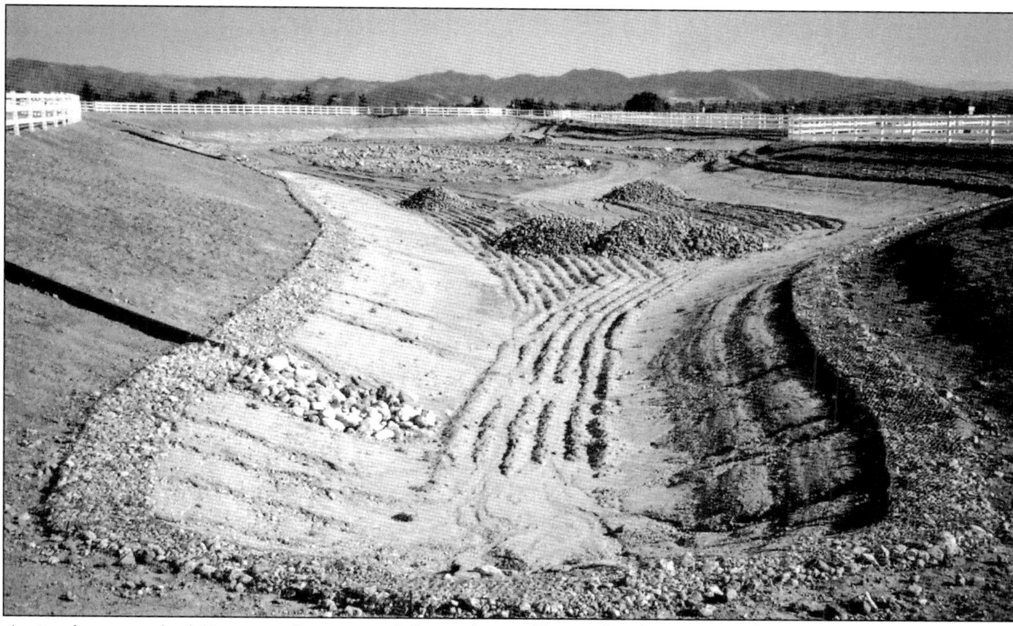

A single water-holding pond is viewed from the walkway leading around the pond. It is dry at this point, but with rain or the input of water from the State Water Project, the pond can accumulate large amounts of water and competently supply it to the aquifer below ground. The agency sells this water to local water suppliers to reduce groundwater overdraft. One pond was recently filled with state water and a fishing contest was held at the pond. The water dissipated through the soil and into the aquifer soon after that event.

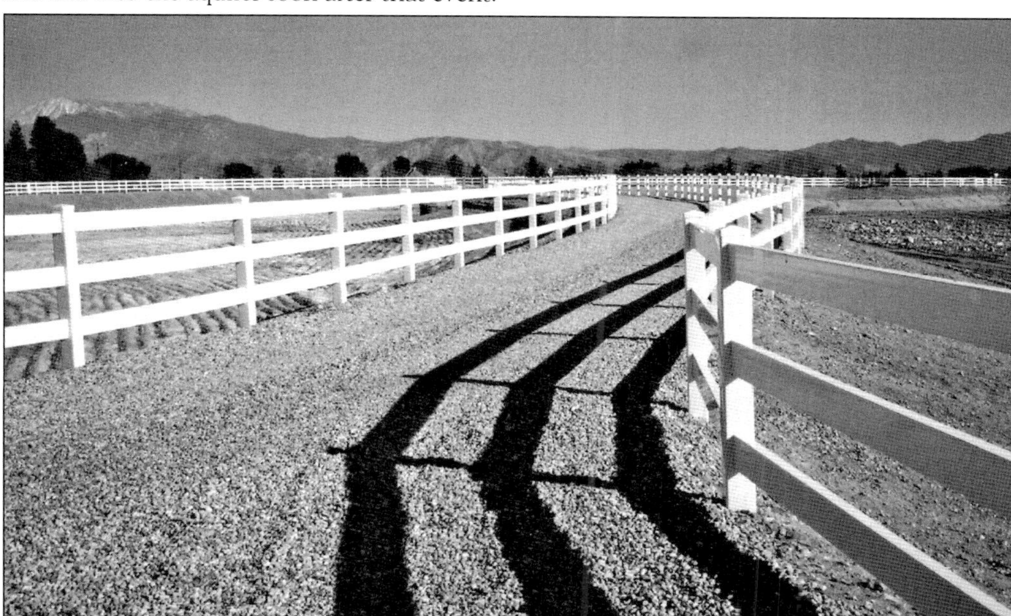

A view of the walkway around the water-holding ponds can be seen here. The continuous, winding walkway includes rest stops where one can stop and rest. These rest stops are used by people who come not only to walk, but to enjoy the picnic area-like rest stops as well.

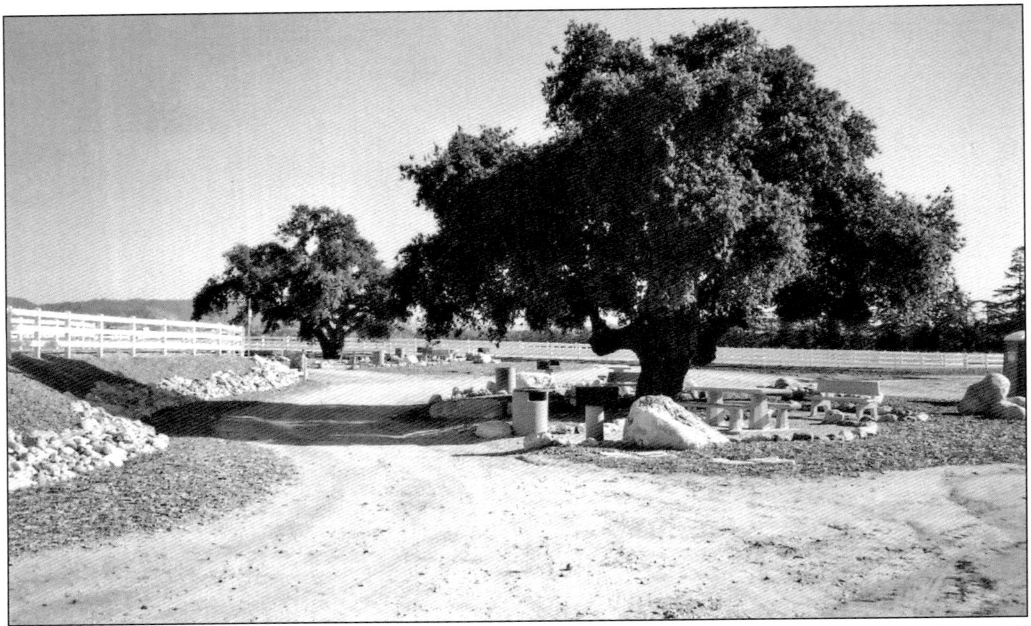

A large oak stands near the site of the water-holding ponds. It makes a great canopy for the small park site where Cherry Valley citizens enjoy reprieves during their walks. Some walkers of these trails cannot resist stopping by this inviting site for a short interlude from their walk.

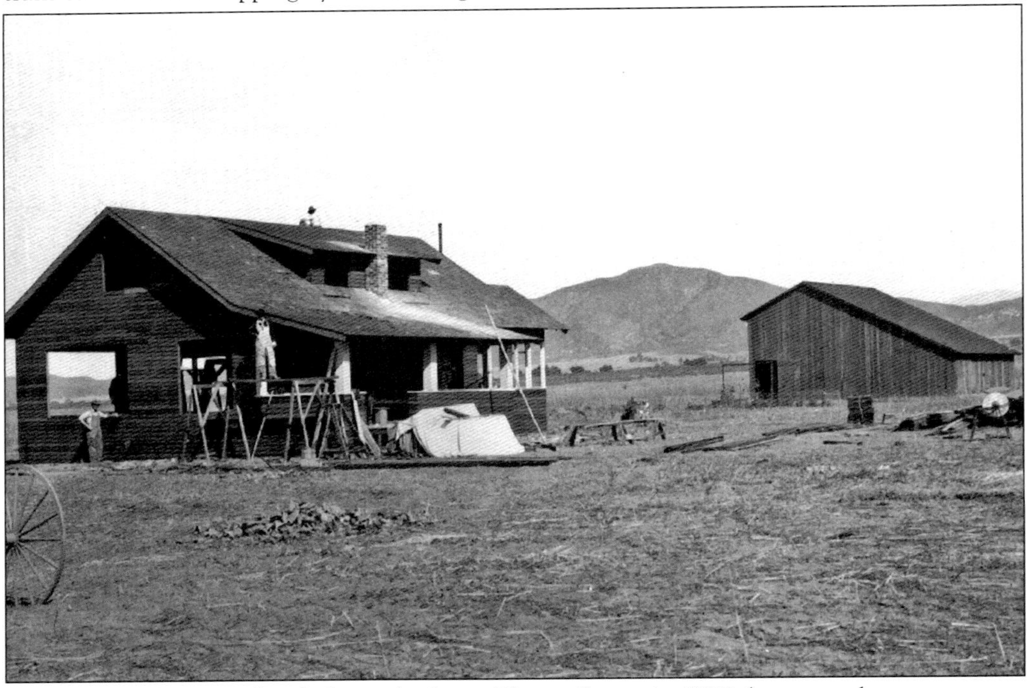

Houses, like the Seitz family home built on Cherry Street in 1909, began to dot open spaces around Cherry Valley as the population grew. This farm comprised a small acreage where fruit trees were eventually planted. Sometime later the house was occupied by Raw Edgar. (Courtesy of SGPHS.)

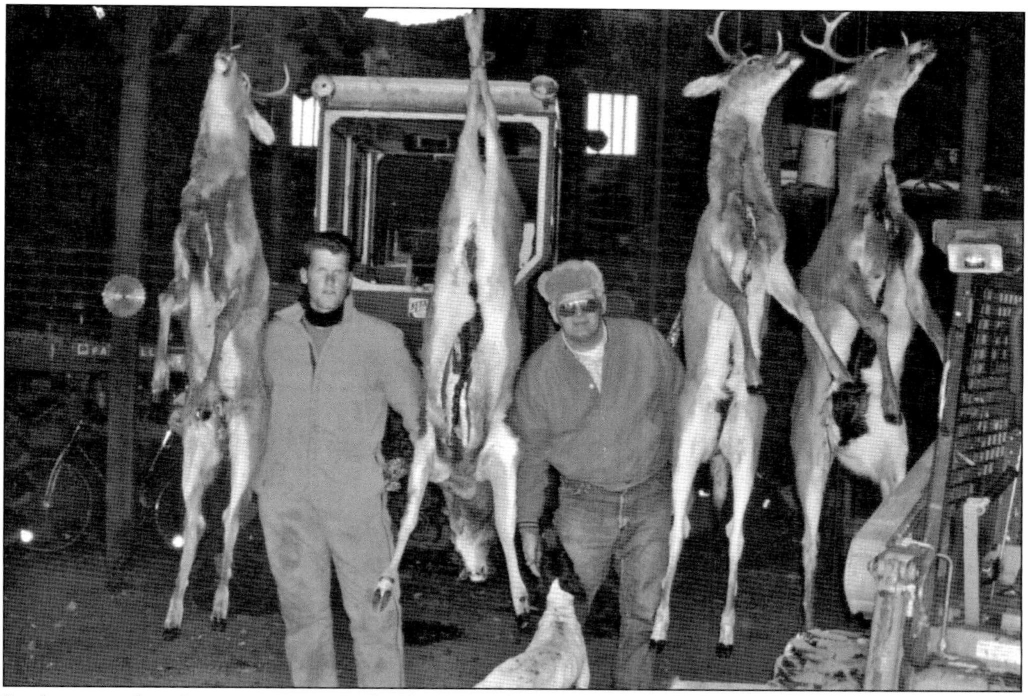

In the past, deer hunting was popular for sports hunters in the surrounding mountains of Cherry Valley. Two unidentified hunters are preparing the four deer that they have shot. In the early days in Cherry Valley, catches like this demanded cold storage space after the animals were butchered. (Courtesy of Joe Lyneis.)

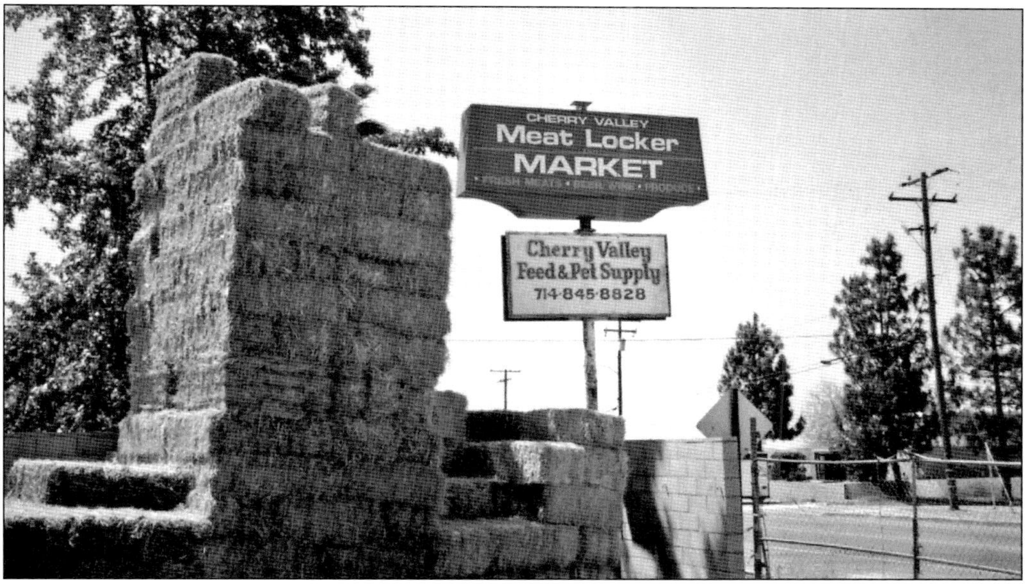

The old Cherry Valley Meat Locker and Market no longer exists, but the sign still stands high on a pole beside the Cherry Valley Feed and Pet Supply. In years past, when home freezers were less common, the meat locker served as a vital facility in which to store meats for hunters as well as local residents that butchered beef, hogs, and goats for their home use. (Courtesy of Joe Lyneis.)

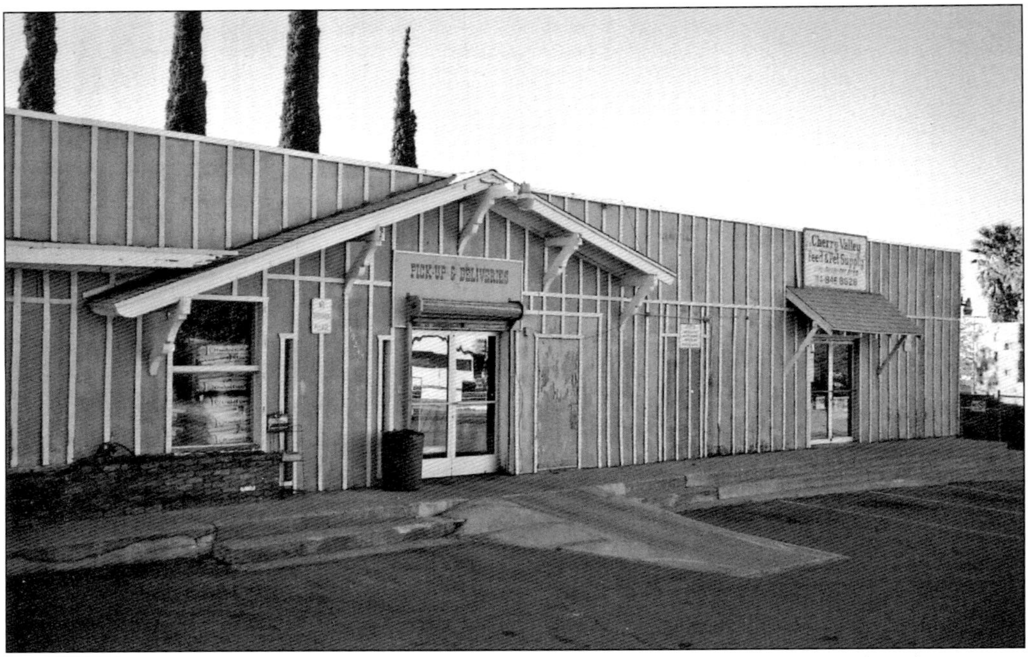

When the meat locker in Cherry Valley was closed and no longer deemed a prudent business, a feed store was established on the grounds. It is pictured here and is now owned by John DeBoer. Because Cherry Valley is a rural community, horses, goats, cows, ponies, and many other animals are raised there. The feed store provides vital supplies for all their needs.

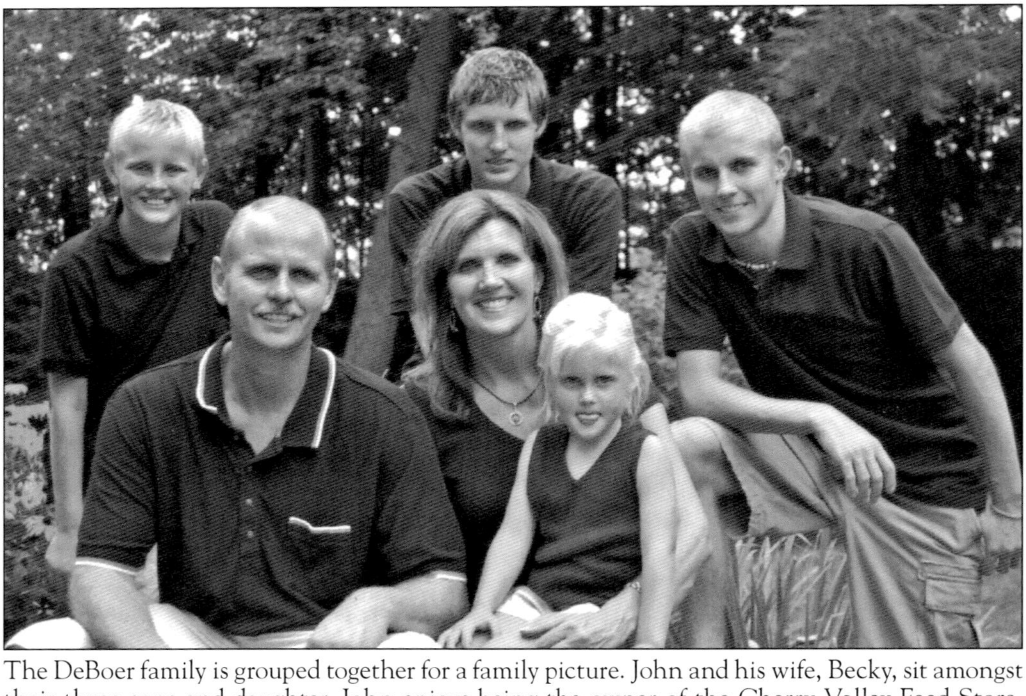

The DeBoer family is grouped together for a family picture. John and his wife, Becky, sit amongst their three sons and daughter. John enjoys being the owner of the Cherry Valley Feed Store, although he no longer resides in Cherry Valley or manages the store. (Courtesy of Joe Lyneis.)

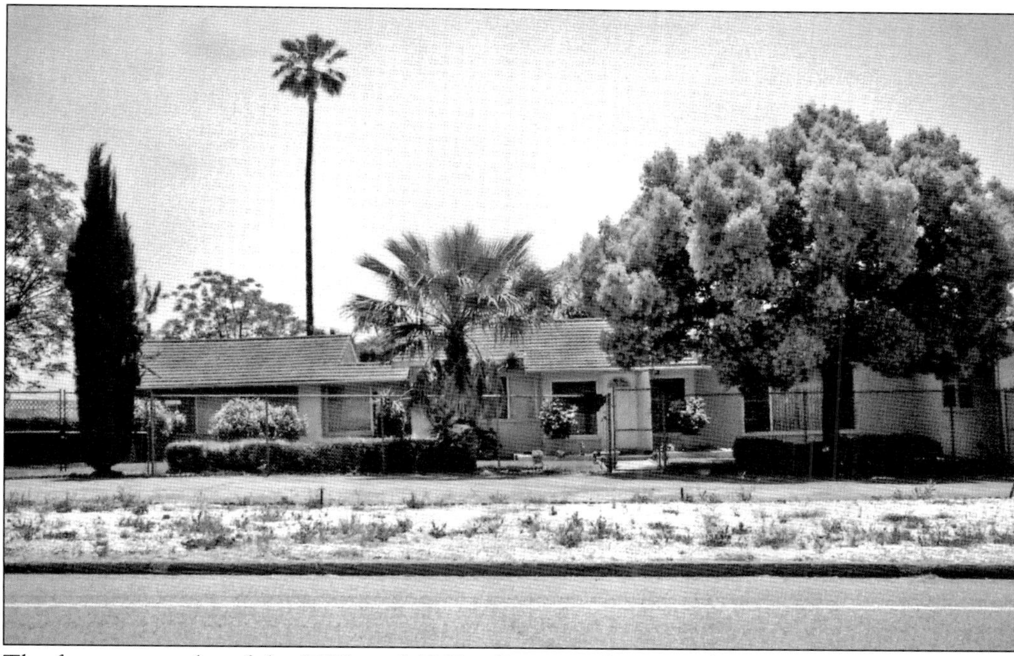

The famous wrestler of the 1950s and 1960s, Gorgeous George, who was born George Wagner, once lived in this house in Cherry Valley. He has been said to have unquestionably changed the sport of professional wrestling. When he lived here, he had a large turkey ranch with purple-painted turkey houses and a purple house of his own. It was quite a spectacle along Cherry Avenue at that time.

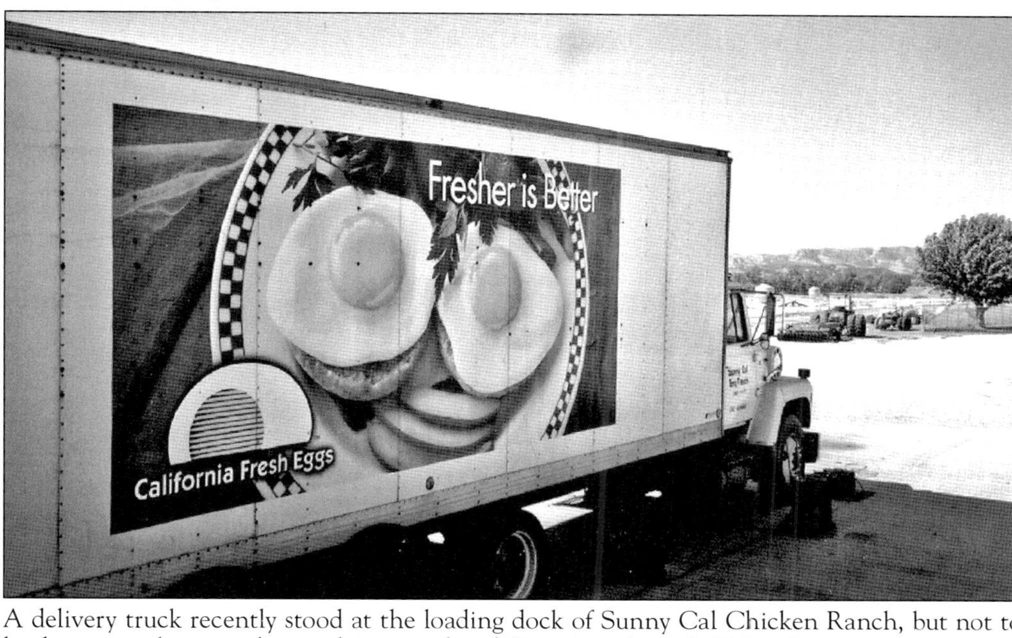

A delivery truck recently stood at the loading dock of Sunny Cal Chicken Ranch, but not to load any eggs, because the ranch is now closed. Remains of razed chicken houses can be seen at right with only the feed tanks still standing. The processing plant at this facility was capable of processing 500 cases of eggs per hour, each containing 30 dozen eggs.

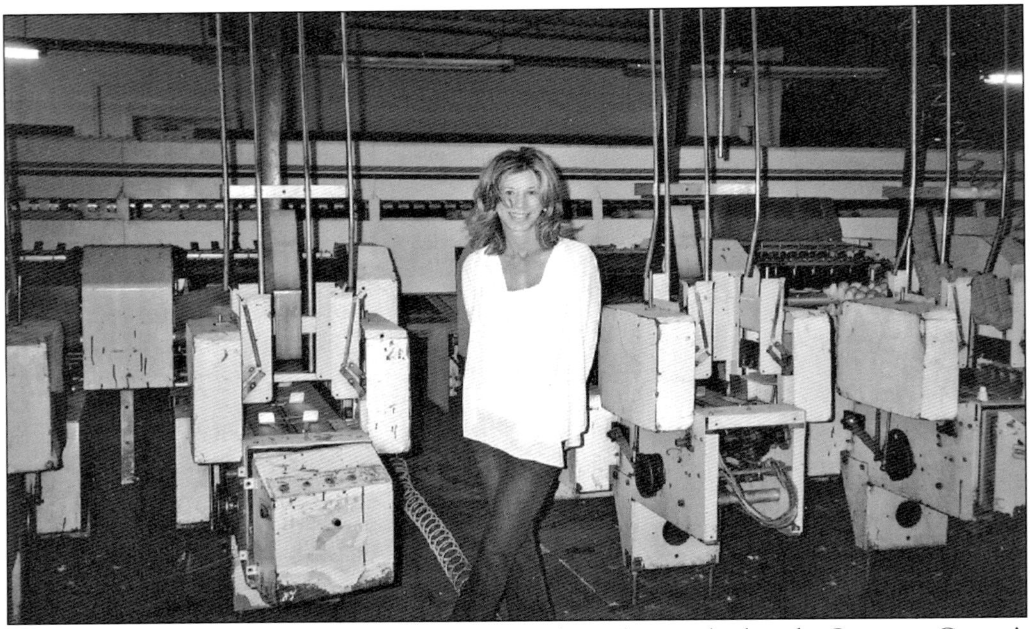

This picture shows Cathy Burham, daughter of Bud Manheim, who bought Gorgeous George's turkey ranch in 1964. Cathy is giving a tour of the egg-processing facility, one of the buildings that still remains after the closure of the ranch. The ranch originally contained 100 chicken houses, which were approximately 400 feet long and contained 15,000 birds each.

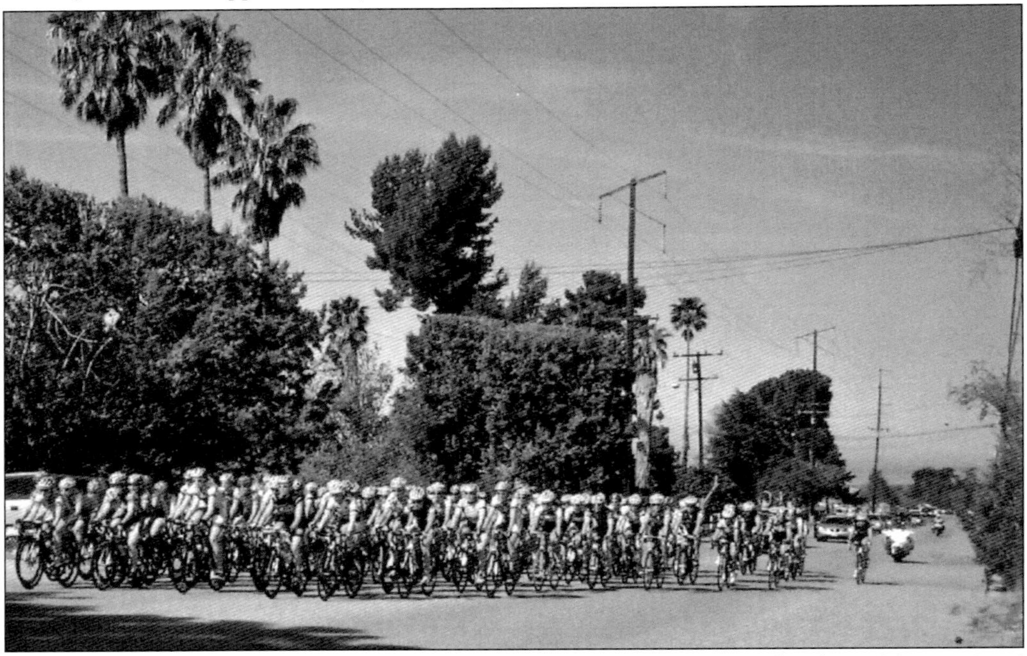

The 24th Annual Bike Classic was a three-stage race, which began in Redlands, California, April 3, 2008. It wound its way up through Beaumont and Cherry Valley to Bogart Park. The women's segment is pictured here, traveling in Cherry Valley along Orchard Street and approaching Beaumont Avenue.

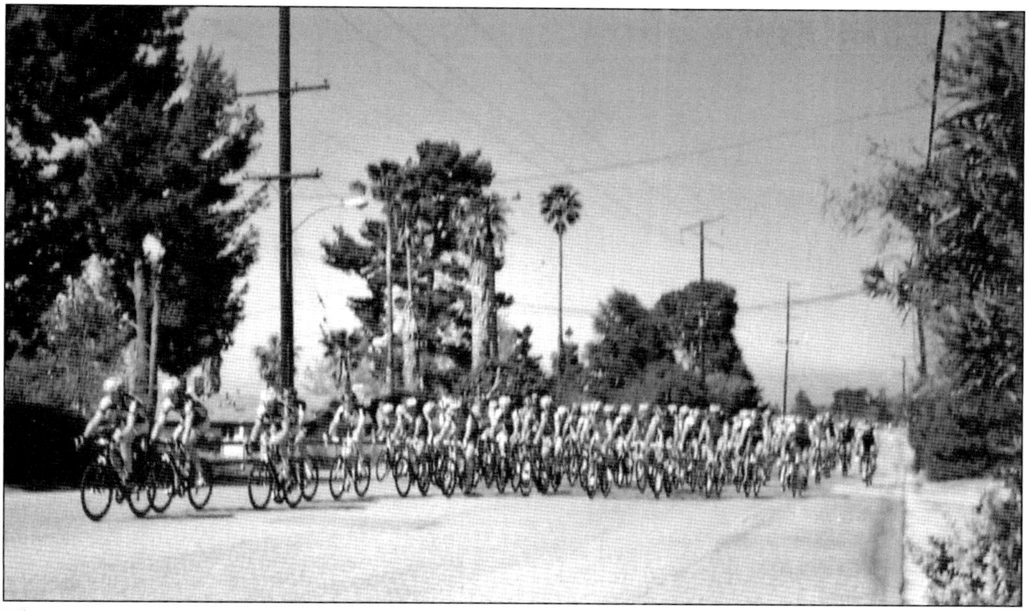

The men's segment of the 24th Annual Bike Classic passes along Orchard Street, following the bike route passed minutes before by the women's cycling group. This is an exciting event where spectators often line the bike path to view the race. It is very popular amongst the citizens of rural Cherry Valley.

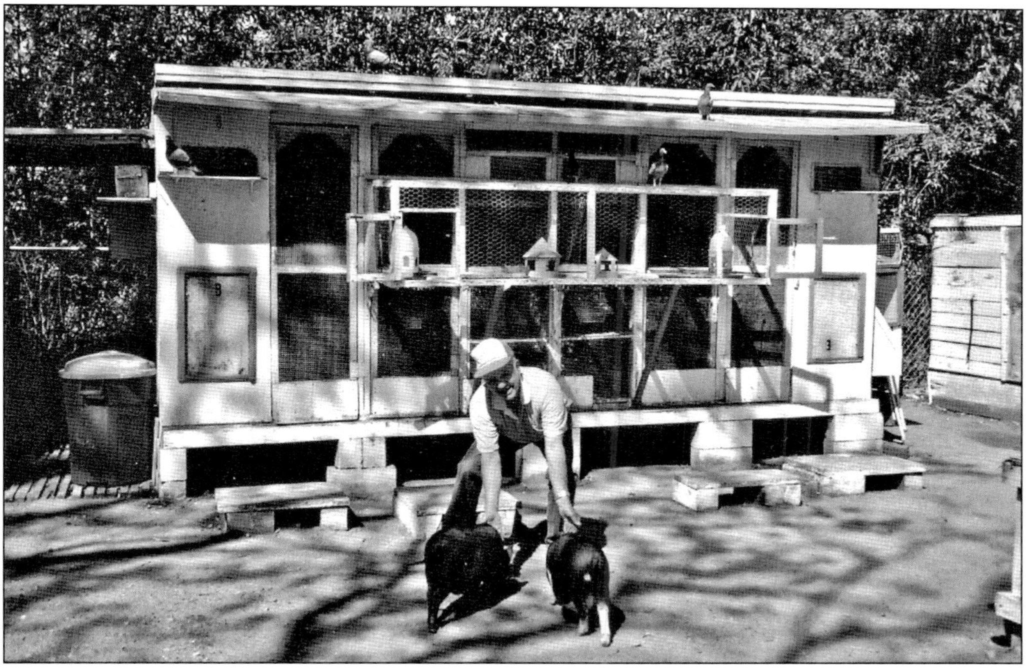

Mike Iorio, longtime Cherry Valley resident, leans down to greet his two potbellied pigs, which are kept as pets by many people. Behind him are his homing pigeons, a variety of domesticated rock pigeon that was selectively bred to find its way home over long distances. Mike is a member of a club that raises homing pigeons.

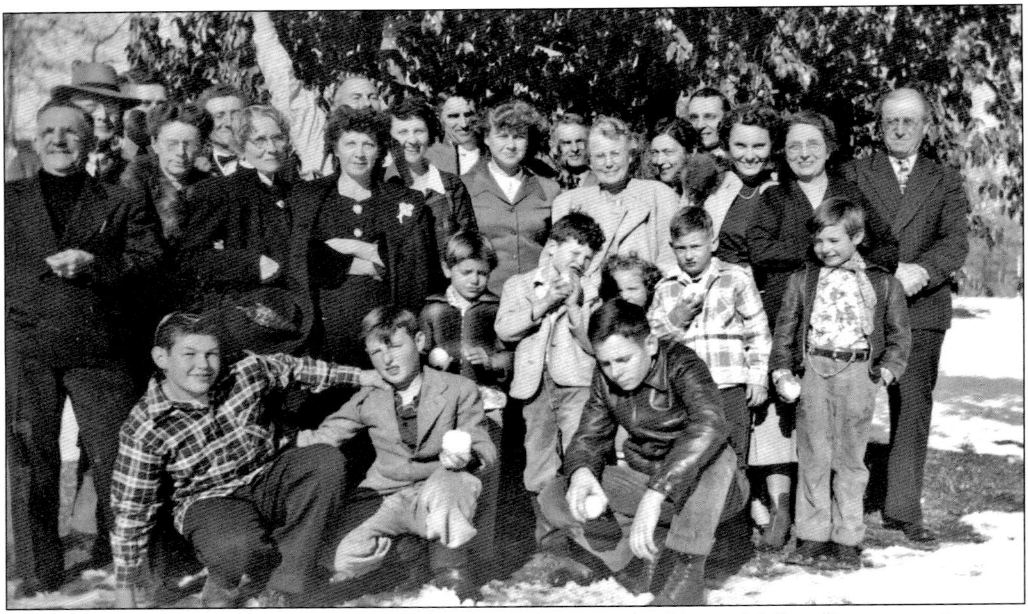

The members of Brethren Church grouped together outside Cherry Valley Grange on January 16, 1949, for this photograph. At the time, there was no Brethren Church building in Cherry Valley; therefore, they met routinely in the Grange for Sunday church services and other related church meetings. (Courtesy of Judy Polman.)

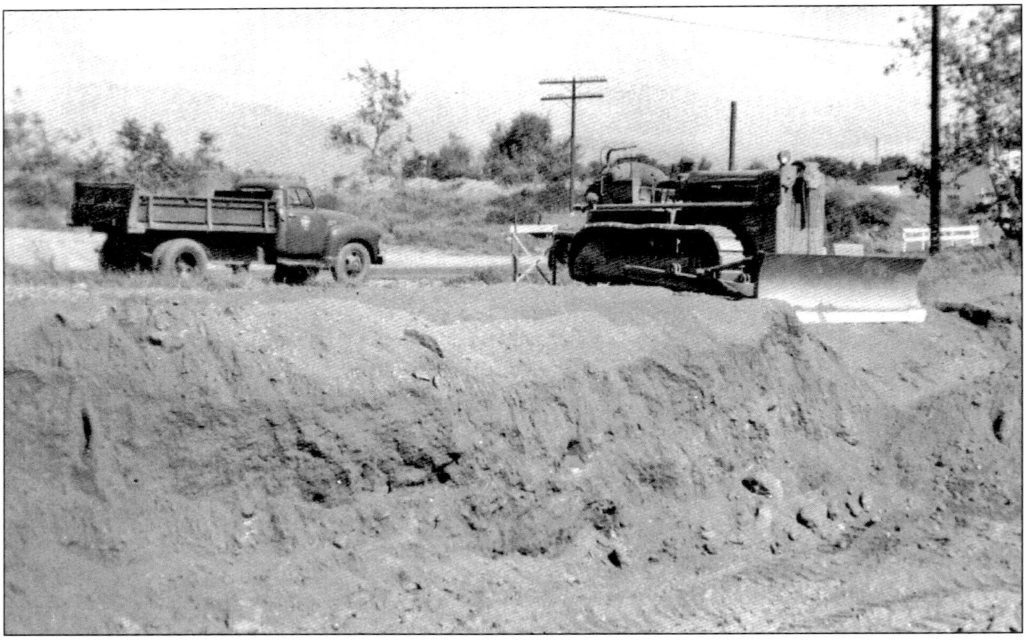

Tractor and truck stand parked following a ground-breaking service on May 18, 1950, and after which excavation of the grounds for construction of the Grace Brethren Church began. Note the corner batten at the rear of the tractor, which defines one corner of the building to be constructed. The site is on the corner of Vineland Street and Beaumont Avenue. (Courtesy of Judy Polman.)

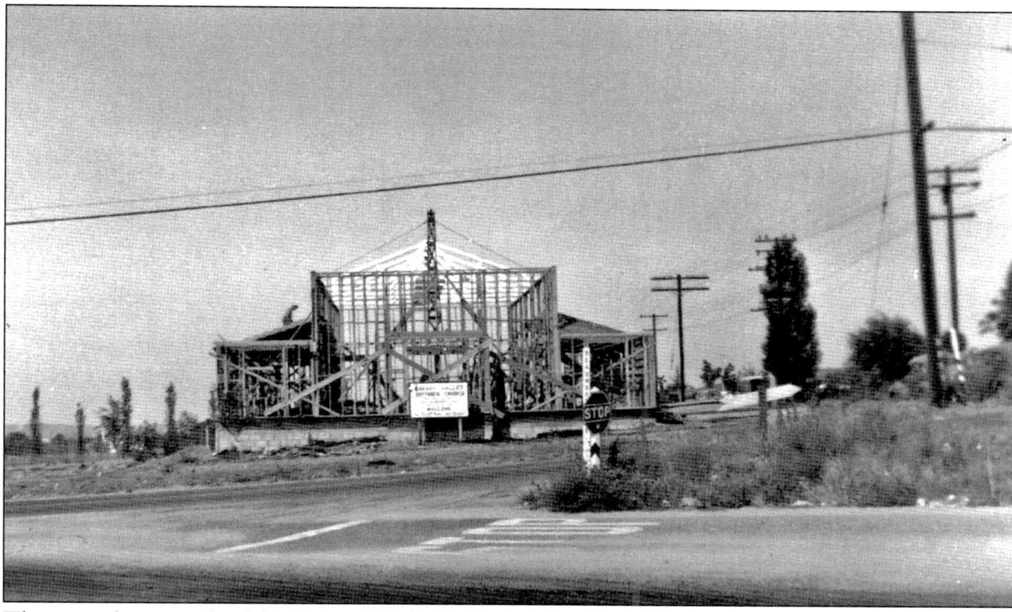

The erect framework of the Grace Brethren Church structure is highlighted in the early 1950s, on the corner of Vineland Street and Beaumont Avenue in Cherry Valley. Members of the church had waited a long time for this moment; now the reality of a new church was forming before their eyes. (Courtesy of Judy Polman.)

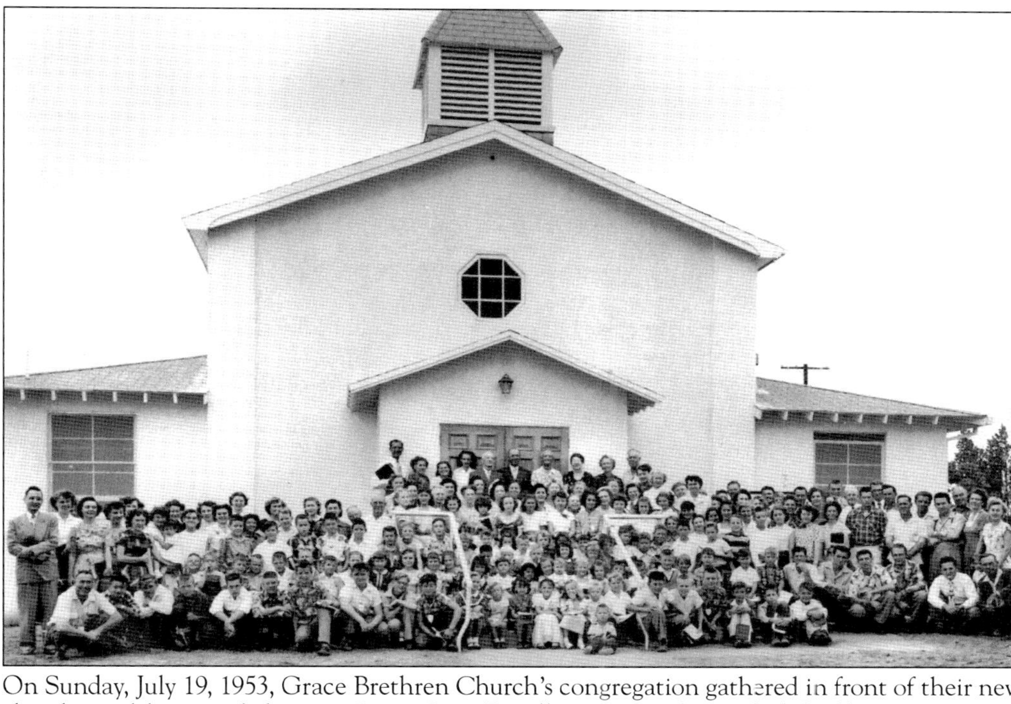

On Sunday, July 19, 1953, Grace Brethren Church's congregation gathered in front of their new church to celebrate its dedication. Pastor Gene Ferrell is seen standing at far left of his congregation. The *c.* 1850 church bell rests in the small, vaulted structure at the top of the church. It came from Stewart McClellan's grandfather's church in Morning Sun, Iowa. (Courtesy of Judy Polman.)

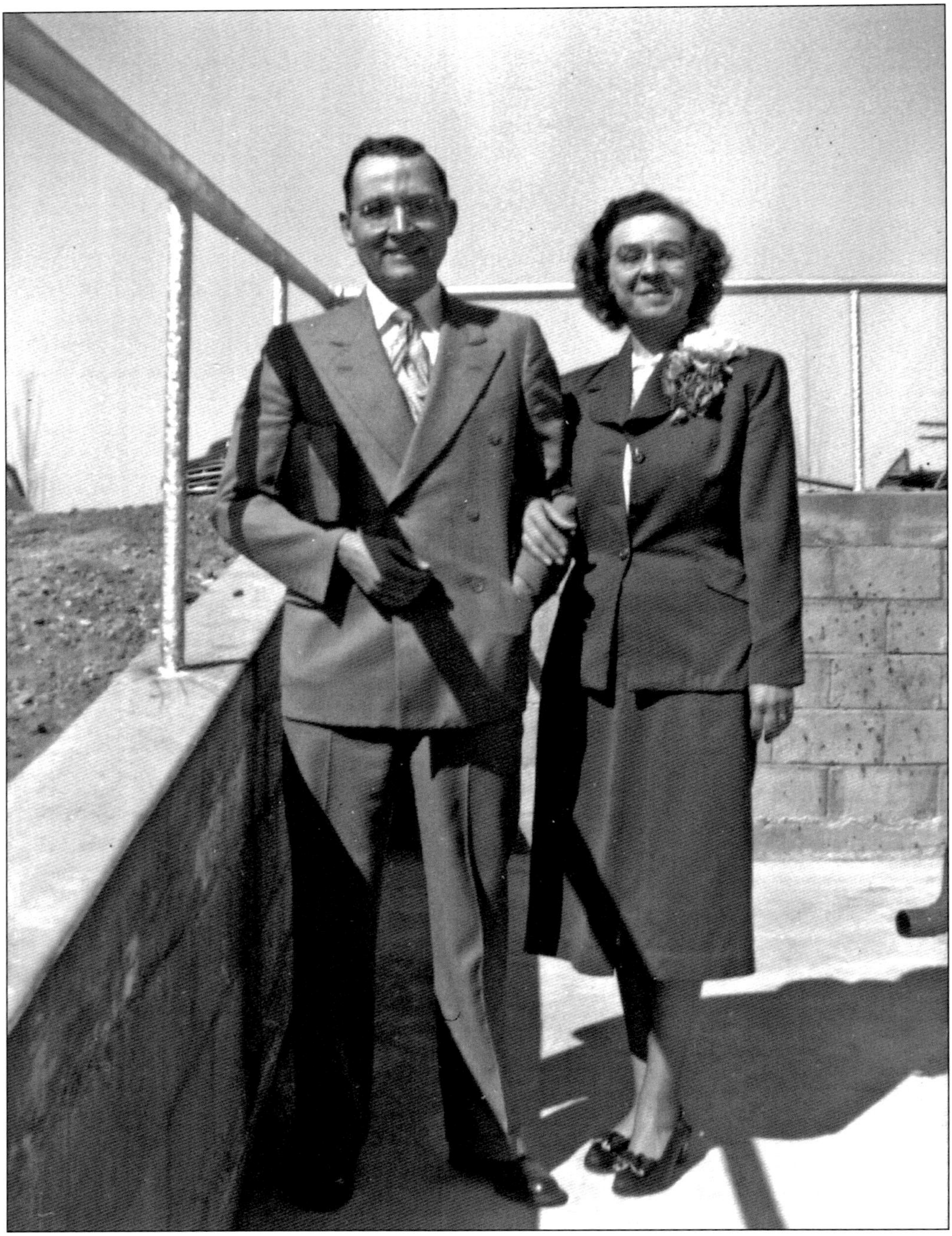

Pastor Gene Ferrell and his wife, Georgia, are pictured during the early years of the Grace Brethren Church in Cherry Valley. The congregation at this time was meeting for Sunday services in the new church, following the few years that they met in the Grange. The membership of the church had by now increased significantly, so the new church was quite welcomed. (Courtesy of Judy Polman.)

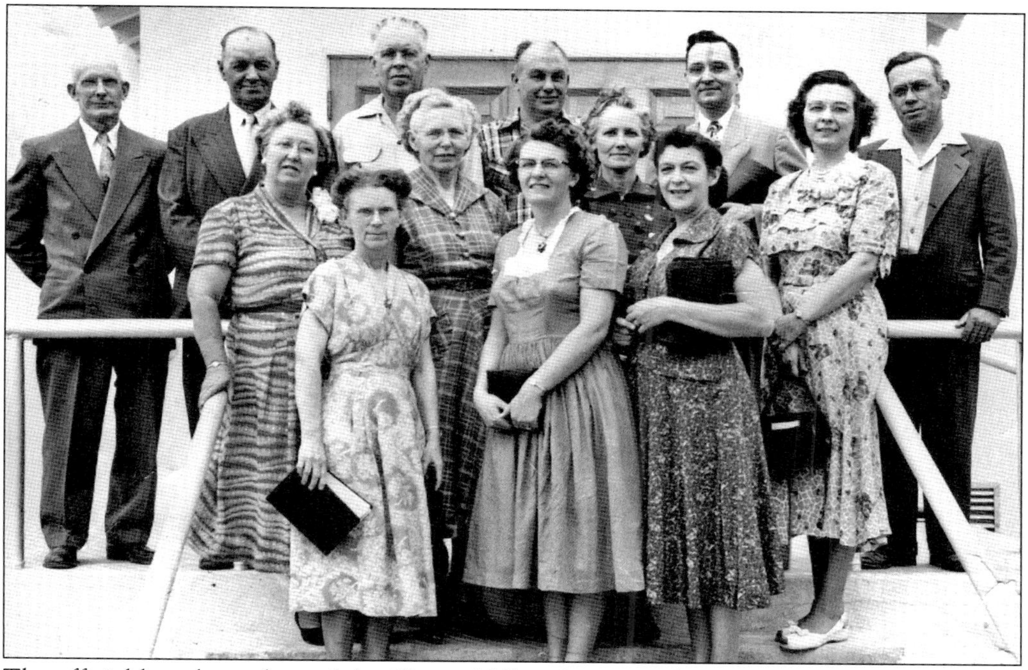

The official board members of the Cherry Valley Grace Brethren Church are represented in this 1953 photograph. Pictured left to right are (first row) Mrs. Liggett, Lois Hanley, and Edna McClellan; (second row) Mrs. Daggett, unidentified lady, Mrs. Rasmussen, and Georgia Ferrell; (third row) Mr. Liggett, Mr. Daggett, Mark Manning, Stuart McClellan, Pastor Gene Ferrell, and Chet Hanley. (Courtesy of Judy Polman.)

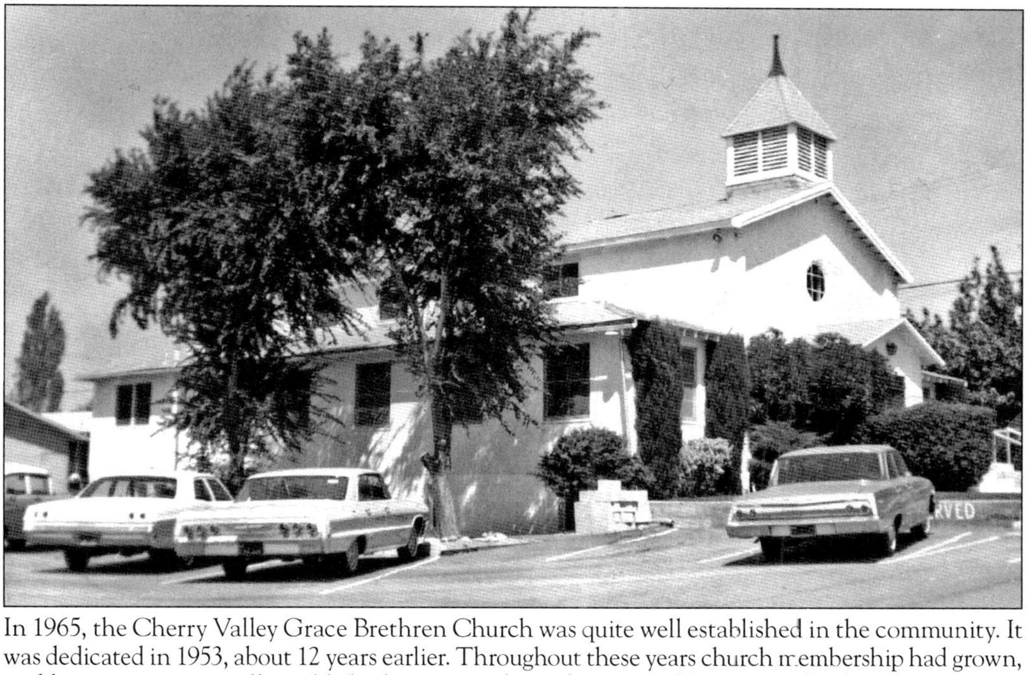

In 1965, the Cherry Valley Grace Brethren Church was quite well established in the community. It was dedicated in 1953, about 12 years earlier. Throughout these years church membership had grown, and by now it was a well-established entity in the community. (Courtesy of Judy Polman.)

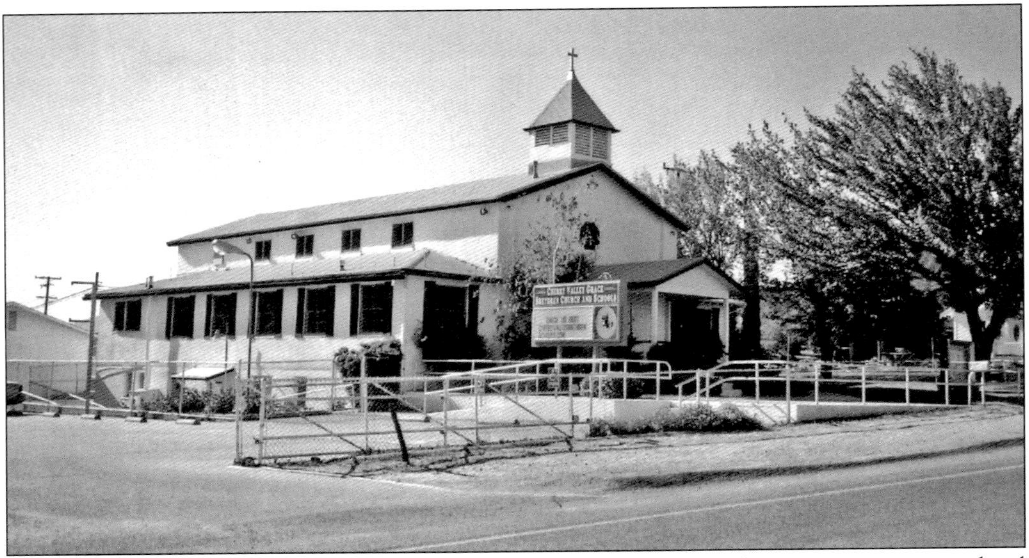

The signboard reads Cherry Valley Grace Brethren Church and Schools. By now, a campus school was incorporated with the church, and it enrolls 61 students. Additionally, there are 23 students in home school and 63 in preschool. Today the Grace Brethren movement is made up of more than 260 churches in the United States and Canada and over 2,000 elsewhere. The Brethren movement began in the 18th century in Germany, founded by Alexander Mack, and was brought to Pennsylvania between 1729 and 1883 to escape persecution elsewhere.

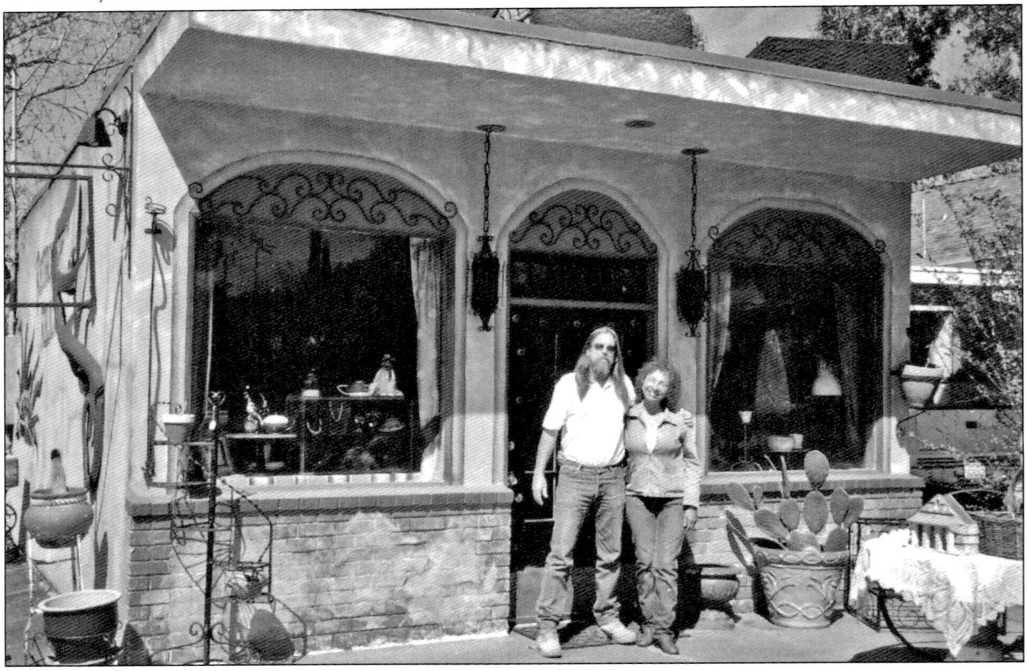

Ben and Irene Stephenson stand in front of their antique store in Cherry Valley. They enjoy doing business in this quiet, rural community, away from the bustle of more populated areas. Within their store, they have a fine collection of antiques, some of which have been acquired directly in Cherry Valley. The perimeter around the store is surrounded with large artifacts.

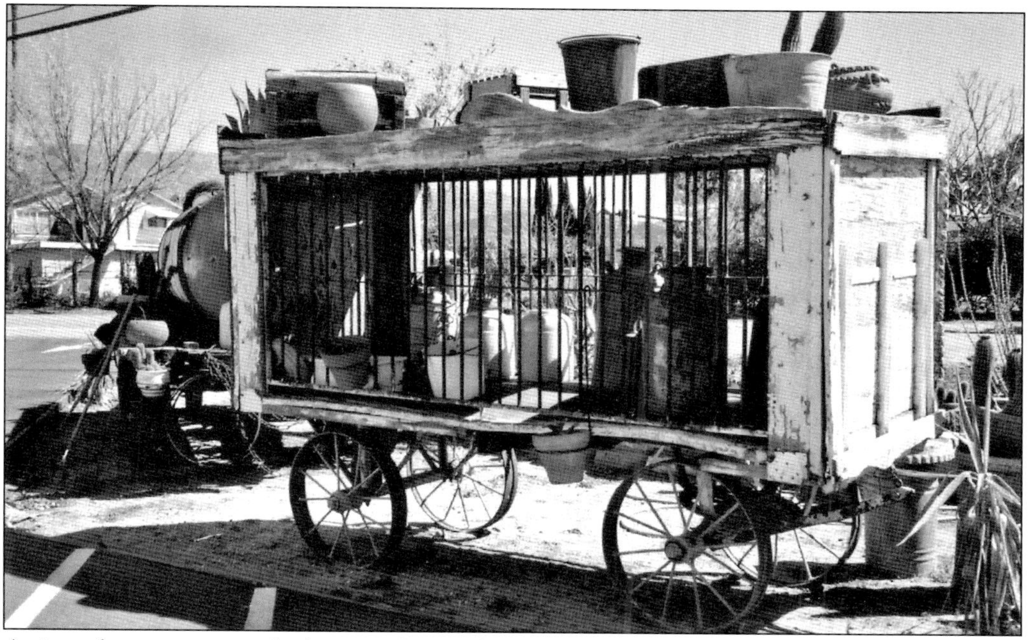

A circus-lion cage sits parked next to Ben and Irene Stephenson's antique store in Cherry Valley. It was purchased locally by them from a local resident in the community and has been added as an attraction on the grounds of their store. They are researching the history of the lion cage to make it a more interesting exhibit.

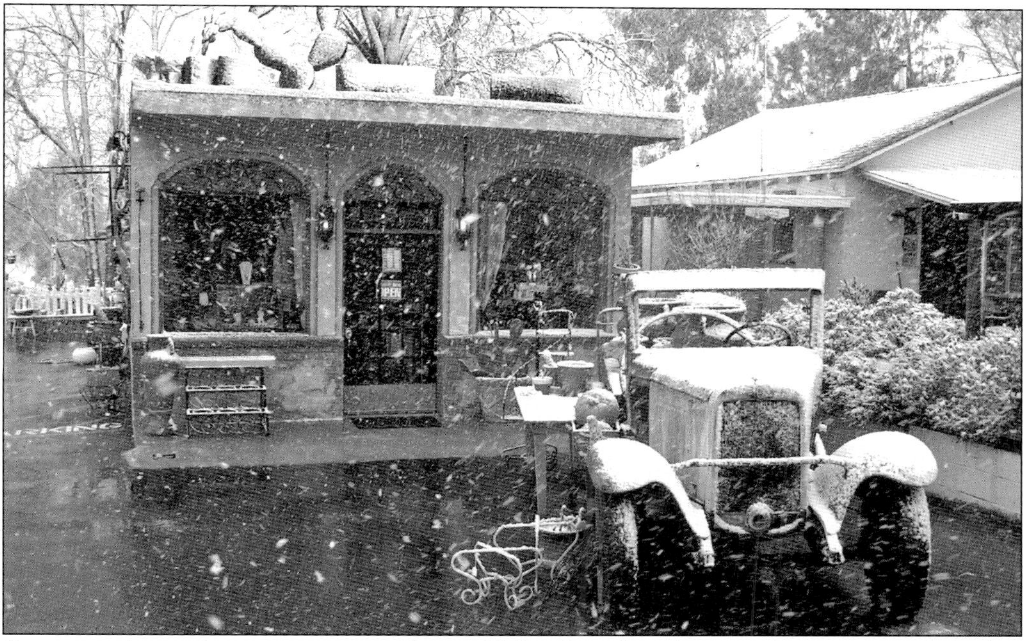

Some say that it does not snow in Cherry Valley, but this photograph appears to defy that conception. A few years ago, snow was photographed at Ben and Irene's antique store in the heart of Cherry Valley. Note the old truck in front that is completely white with heavy snow. (Courtesy of Ben and Irene Stephenson.)

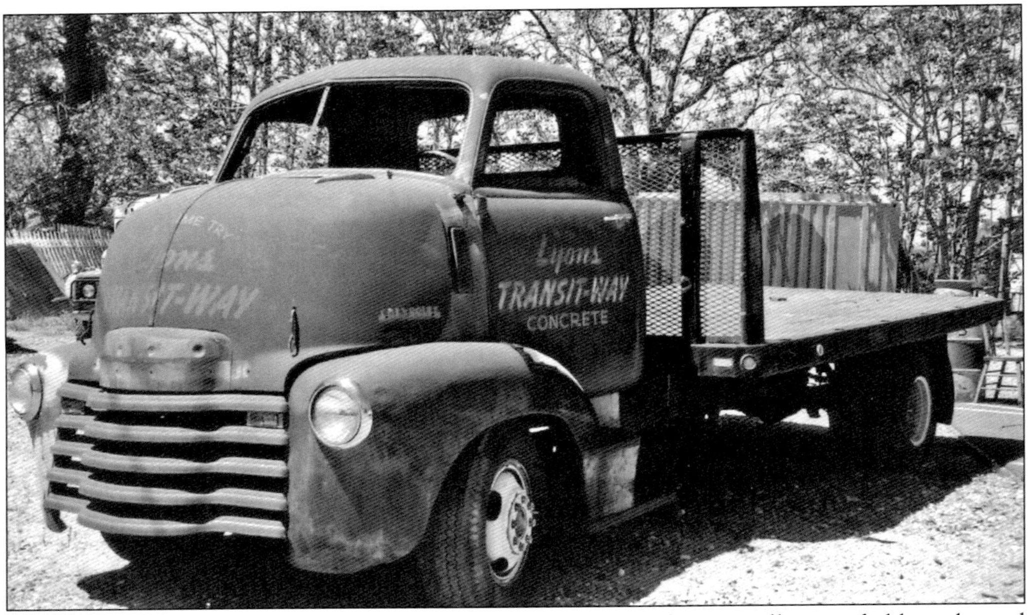

This old Chevy flatbed truck is owned by Ben Stephenson, who is a collector of old trucks and other vintage vehicles. It is a reminder of the meager beginning of the ready-mix industry, which is so prevalent today. The industry began to thrive here during World War II when General Patton's hospital was built here. Since then, the population growth has spurred it along significantly.

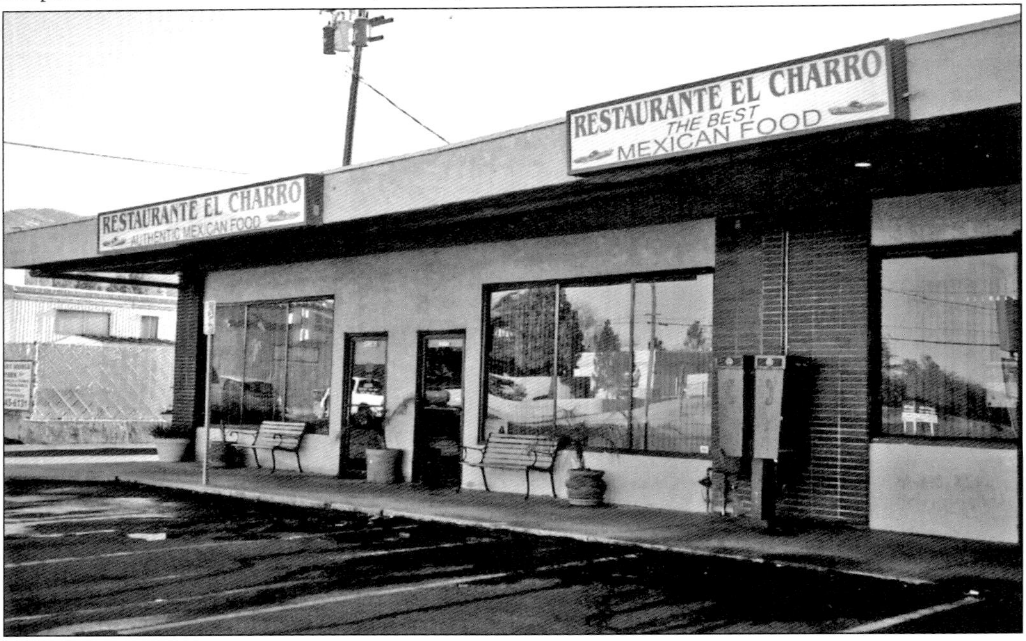

Cherry Valley does not have a large selection of restaurants. However, Restaurante El Charro is within the heart of Cherry Valley and is a popular dining spot for many residents and suburban people. It is owned by Margarito Arreola, a longtime resident and native of a small town in Mexico, Ameca, in the state of Jalisco. The restaurant, formerly known as Casa Maya, has been owned by Margarito and his wife, Lucina, since 2004.

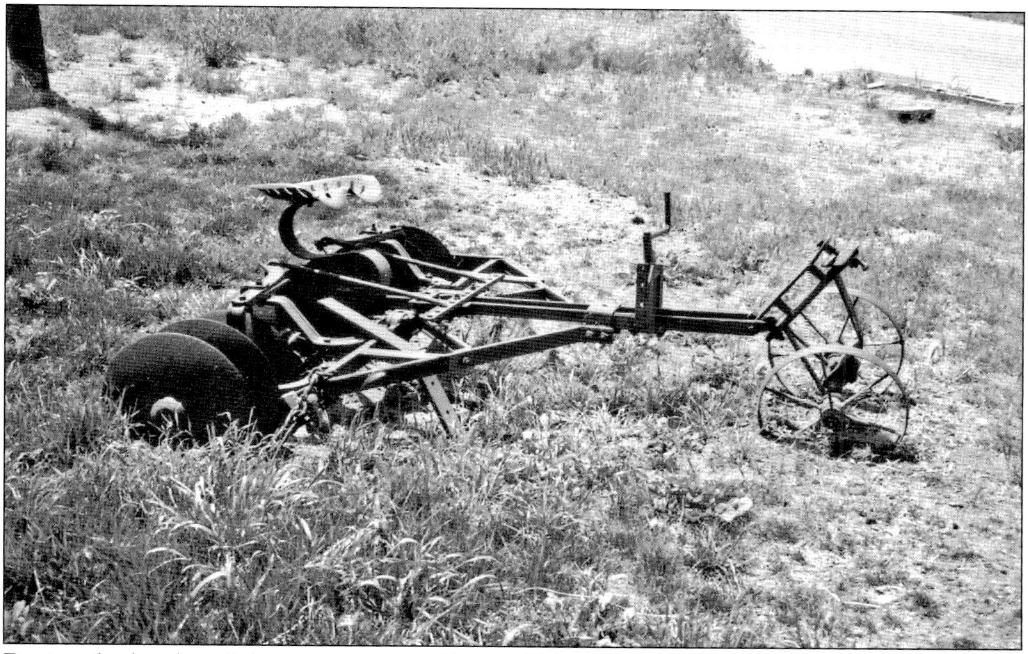

During the heyday of cherry growing in Cherry Valley, there were numerous, small, mom-and-pop–operated orchards, ones that did not even warrant the purchase of a tractor to do the weed disking and cultivation between trees. Alternatively, some used a disk like the one pictured, pulled by a horse or horses and guided by the farmer who sat on the seat above the disk. Today of course, equipment like this is used only for yard or museum exhibition.

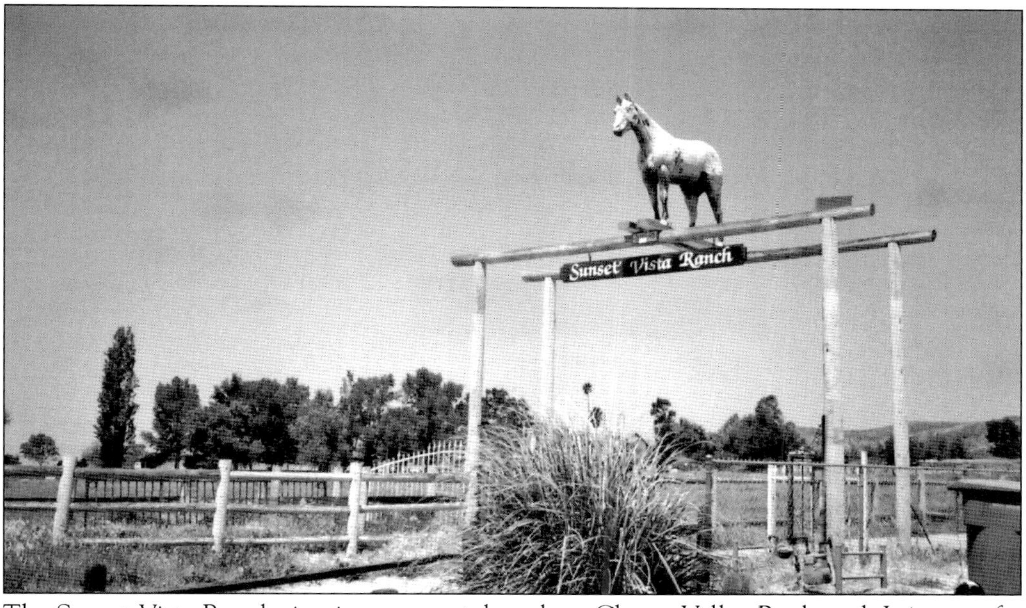

The Sunset Vista Ranch sign is an eye-catcher along Cherry Valley Boulevard. It is one of a number of ranches in the rural surrounding areas of Cherry Valley. Just west of this site, the famous Danny Thomas once owned a ranch of about 300 acres. His house that remained after he sold the ranch has recently been torn down, making room for housing development.

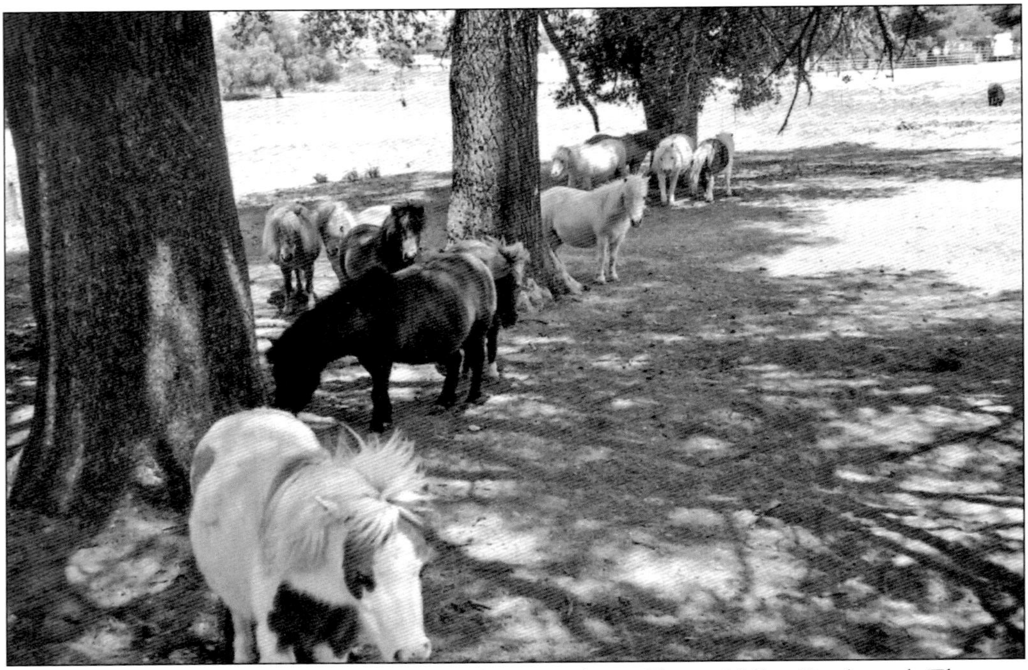

Groups of small ponies like this can often be seen along Cherry Valley Boulevard. They are raised commercially and are an attraction to many who pass by the road. The pony originated from wild-horse prototypes, which developed a smaller stature from living on the margins of uninhabitable land. They are loveable animals to children.

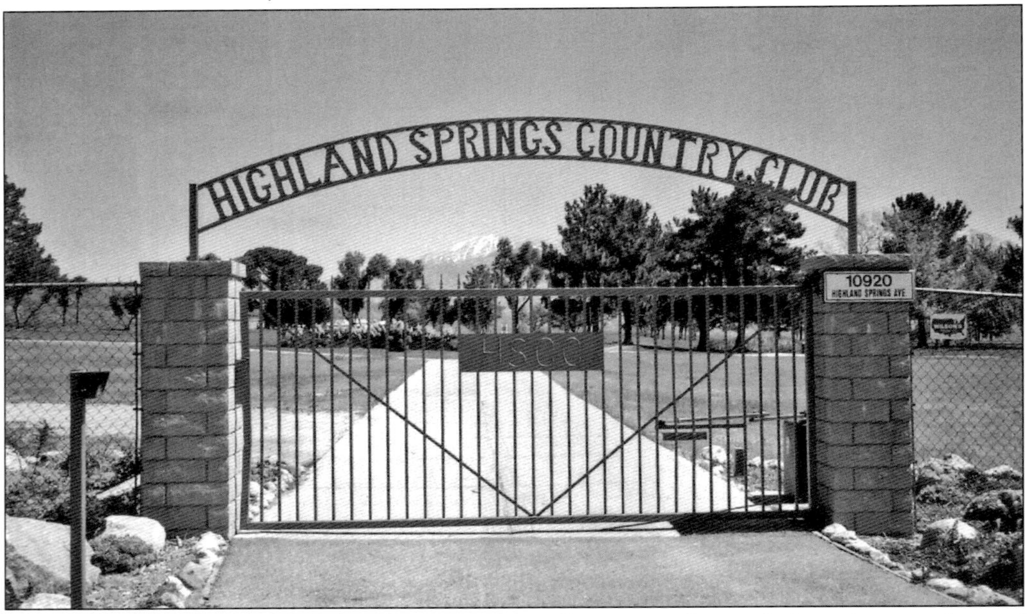

Highland Springs Country Club golf course is a small course with nine holes, where residents of the adjoining country club enjoy playing golf in a rather secluded area. It opened in 1973. There are numerous larger courses around, including a beautiful PGA course. However, some golfers enjoy the serenity that this little course provides.

Laura Mae Stewart sits proudly at the back of this parade car during the Cherry Festival Parade of 1961 approximately 40 years after she was voted its first queen. She is being honored in this gala event along with other prominent citizens. The Cherry Festival Parade is welcomed each year by both Cherry Valley and its neighbor, Beaumont. (Courtesy of SGPHS.)

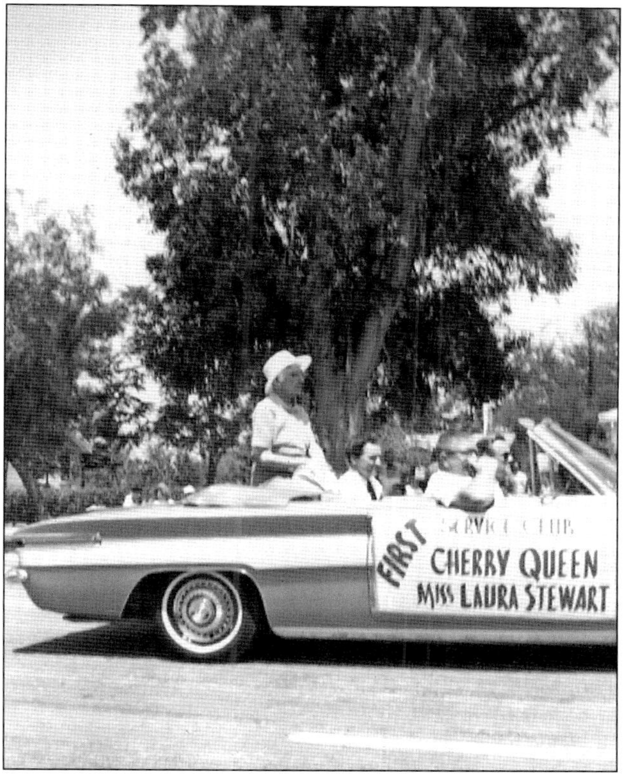

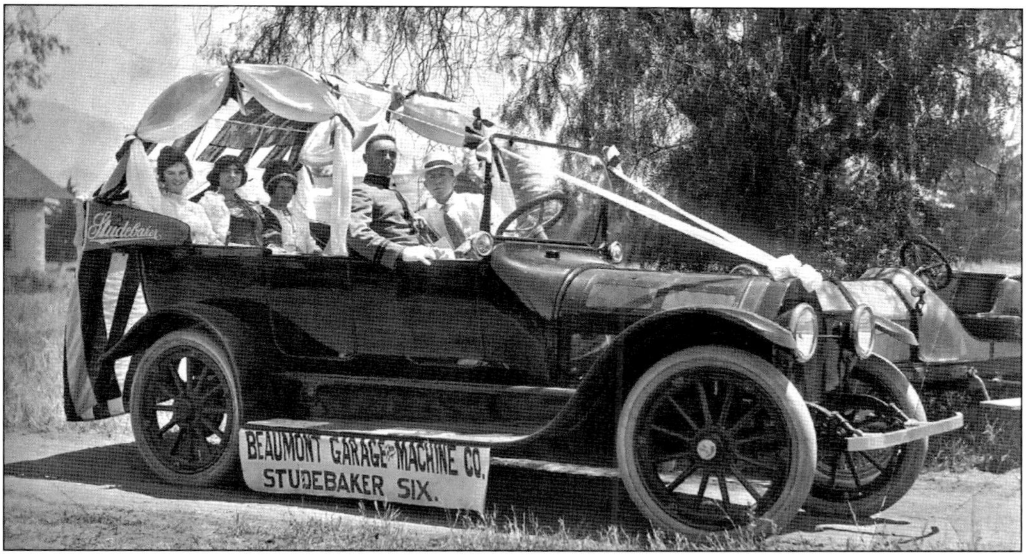

The first Cherry Festival began in 1913 and, along with the following year's festival, was a great success. The Studebaker pictured here was brought out from Los Angeles to carry the festival's first queen during the 1919 parade. Queen Laura Mae Stewart is in the center of the rear seat of the Studebaker, while princesses Lois Behu (right) and Clara Dietrich (left) flank her. Lawrence Rulier, in uniform, is the queen's escort, and E. O. Jones is the driver. (Courtesy of Marilyn Vonderheide and Laura Mae Stewart Foundation.)

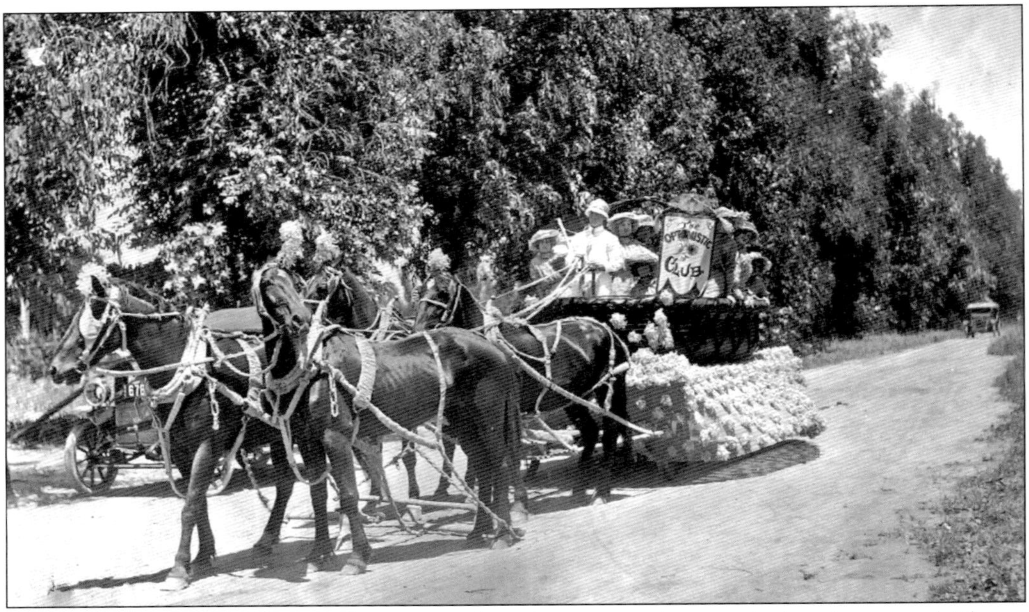

The Optimistic Club's float makes it way along Beaumont Avenue during the second Cherry Festival in 1914. This route would be followed by Cherry Festival parades for years to come. The author recalls a local roller-skating rink's entry in the parade sometime around the early 1960s. The entry included a donkey, sprayed pink with food coloring, set on roller skates. It roller-skated the entire route; of course, the avenue was paved by then. (Courtesy of Marilyn Vonderheide and Laura Mae Stewart Foundation.)

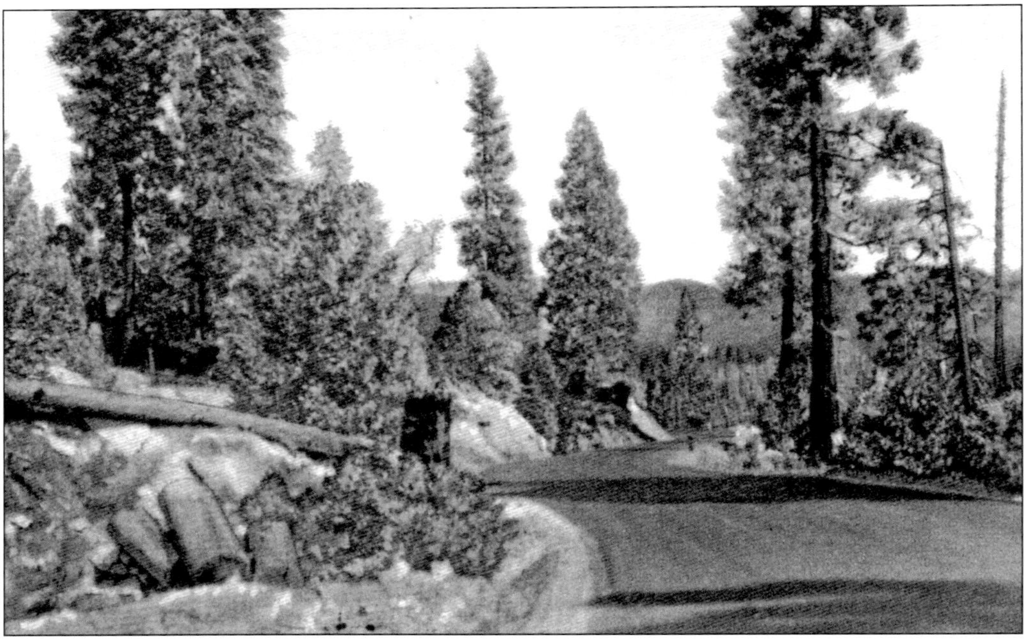

This is a section of the highway leading to the mountains north of Cherry Valley and reaching the apple-growing community of Oak Glen. During apple season, tourists come from afar to purchase apples that are grown there. (Courtesy of Steve Lech.)

Two

Bogart Park

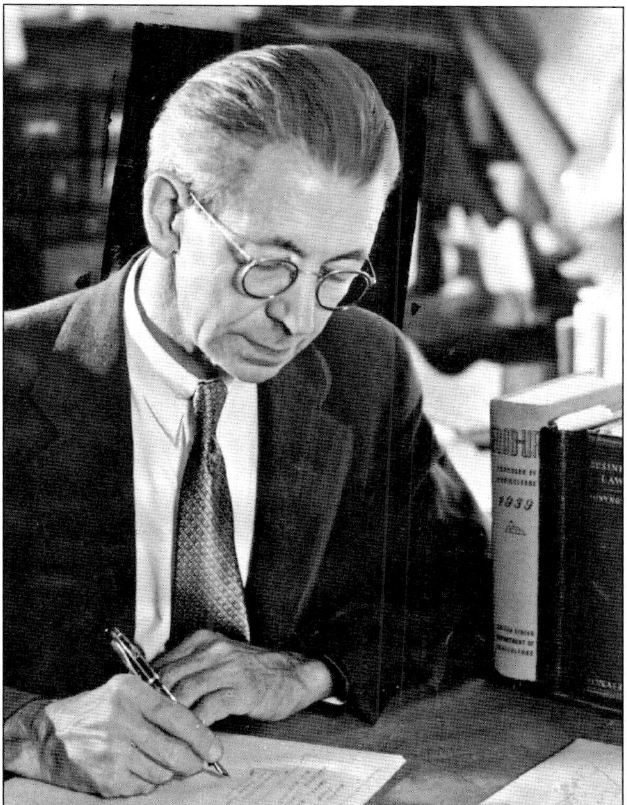

Guy Bogart came from Los Angeles in 1924 to settle in Beaumont. He is remembered as a community builder in the San Gorgonio Pass, especially around Beaumont and Cherry Valley. He immediately went to work to improve the community and developed a great interest in the area. He was successful in numerous endeavors, including becoming Beaumont's mayor at one time. On March 30, 1930, the city of Beaumont and the Beaumont Rotary Club hosted the first official Japanese Cherry Blossom Festival held in the United States. Thirty-two thousand people descended upon Beaumont for this event. Guy Bogart, who was once president of the Beaumont Rotary, found a more suitable location in the vicinity of Noble Creek, north of Beaumont in Cherry Valley. The area and its surroundings eventually became known as Bogart Park; the original park was named International Park. (Courtesy of SGPHS.)

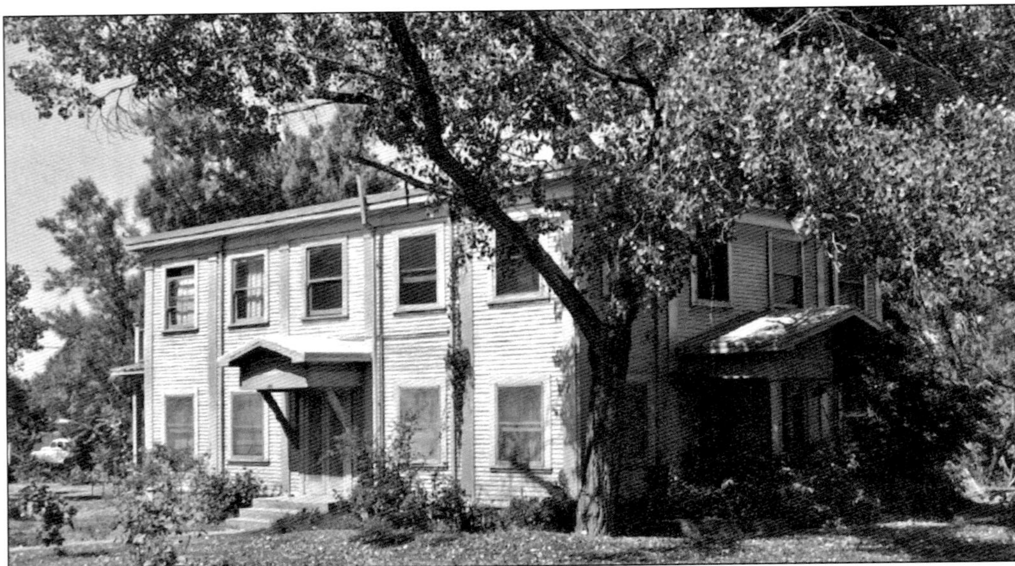

This is the original homesite of Guy Bogart's house in Beaumont on Euclid Avenue, which was built soon after arriving in 1924. Today it is registered on the National Register of Historic Places. William and Deborah Lash recently bought the Bogart House, an example of Colonial Revival architecture, and are now restoring it. (Courtesy of SGPHS.)

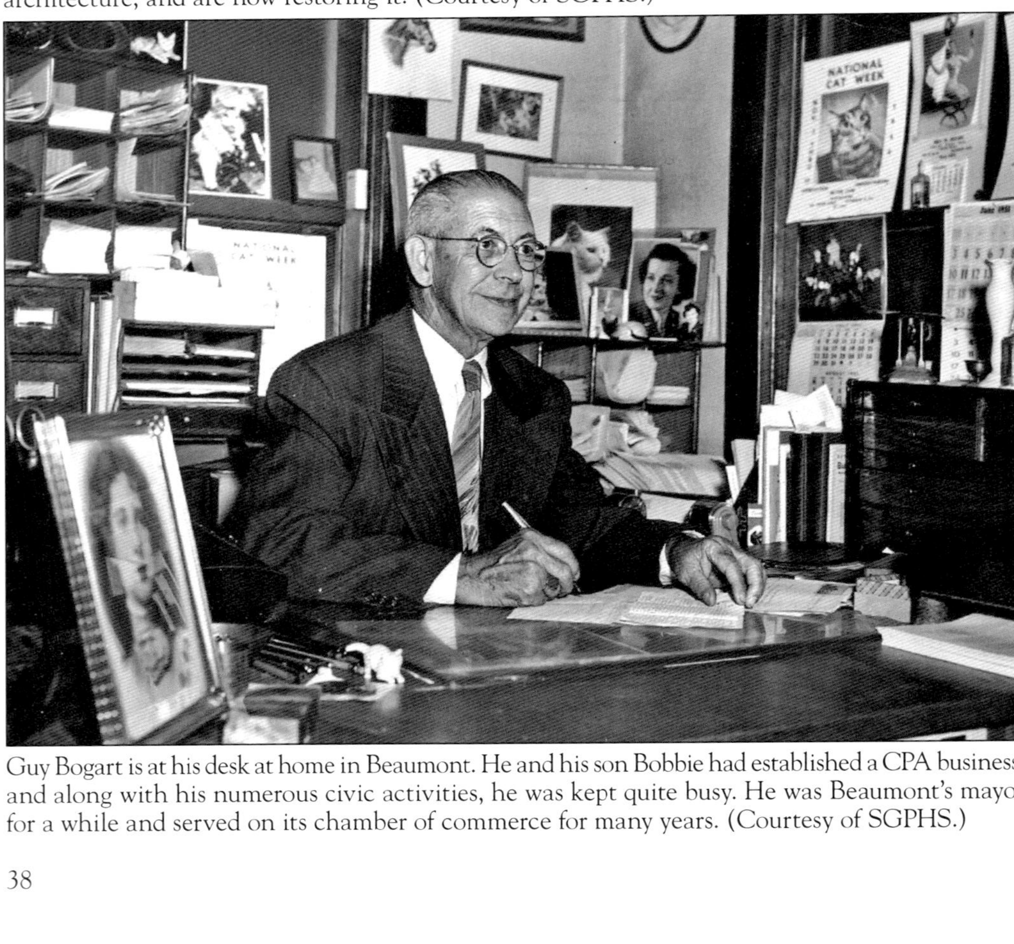

Guy Bogart is at his desk at home in Beaumont. He and his son Bobbie had established a CPA business, and along with his numerous civic activities, he was kept quite busy. He was Beaumont's mayor for a while and served on its chamber of commerce for many years. (Courtesy of SGPHS.)

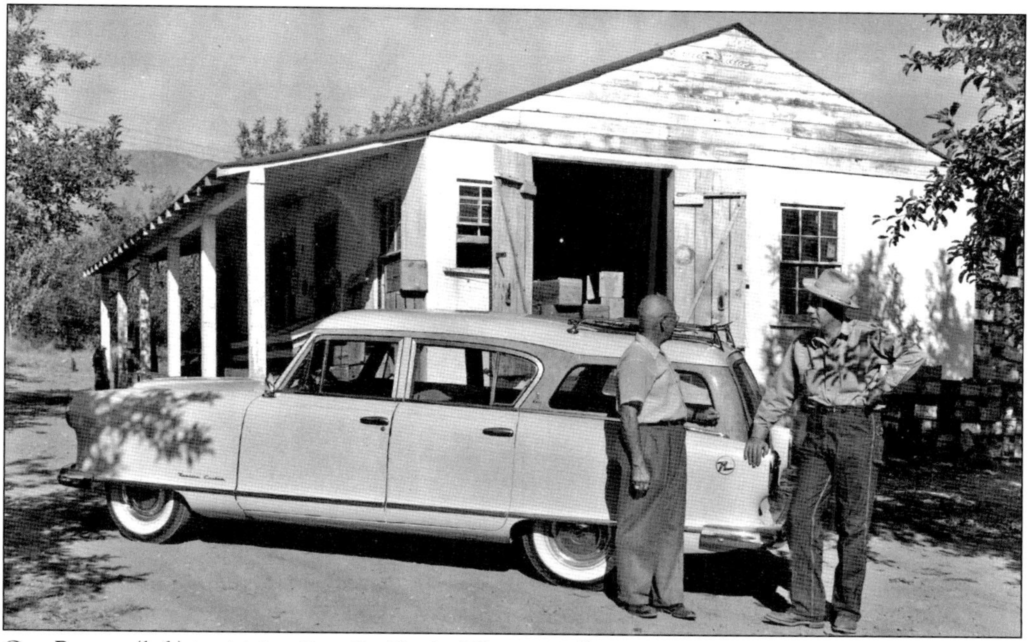

Guy Bogart (left) is visiting Dan Bedford of Sleepy Hollow Ranch at Oak Glen in October 1954. Bogart held an extraordinary, ambassador relationship with not only cherry growers in Cherry Valley but also with fruit growers in the surrounding areas. He was very influential in promoting the best means of fruit production. (Courtesy of SGPHS.)

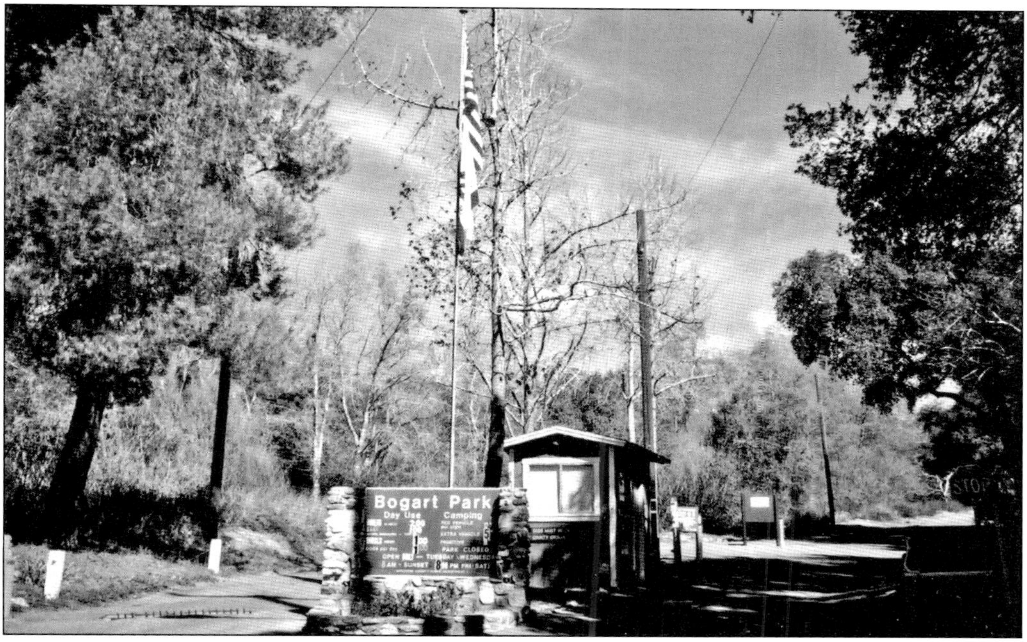

This is the entrance gate to Bogart Park in Cherry Valley, where Cherry Valley meets Noble Creek, at 9600 Cherry Avenue. Today it is owned and operated by the Regional Park and Open-Space District. Facilities include an equestrian campground and a reservation-only, group campground. Also, there are 24 water-only campsites and a picnic area with a small fishing pond.

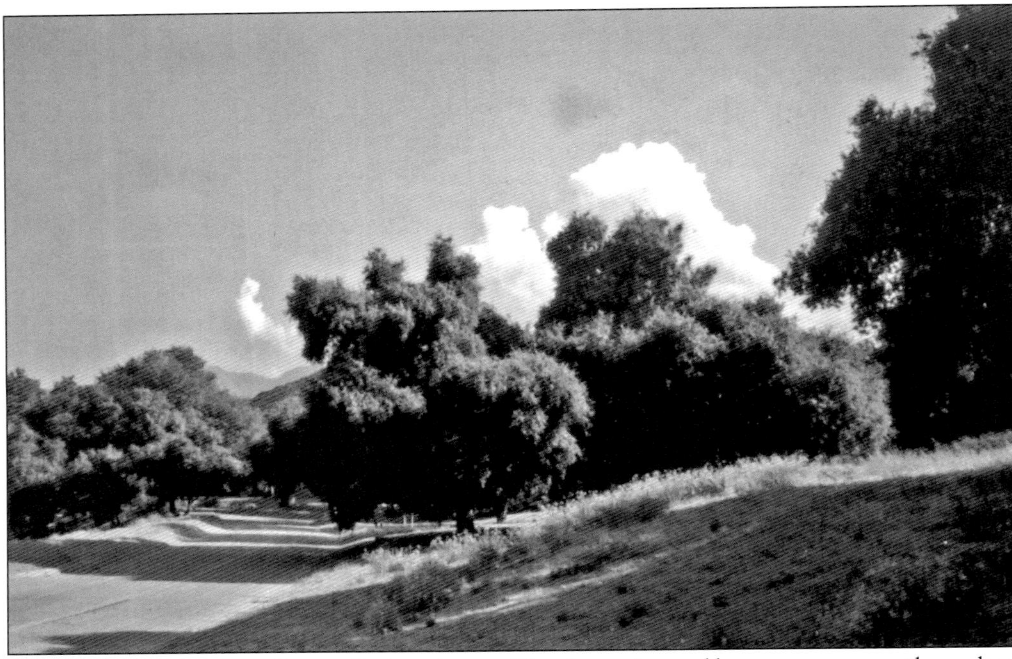

Past the entrance gate to Bogart Park, oak trees like those pictured here are common throughout the park grounds. They provide shade for many of the sites in the park, as well as enhancing the overall beauty of the grounds. Some of these oaks are quite old.

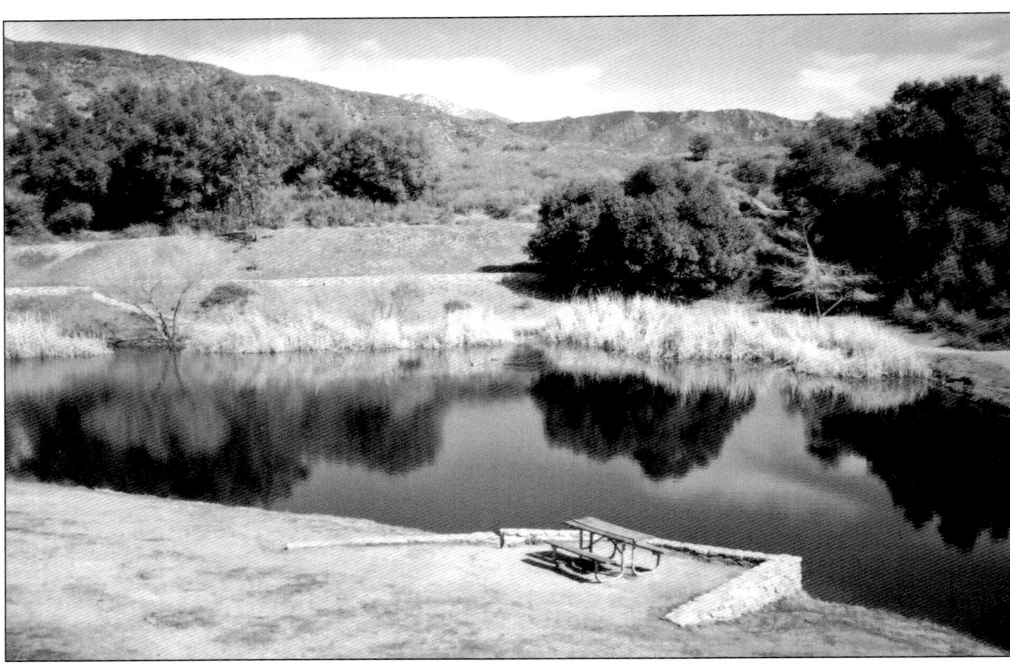

The fishpond at Bogart Park is marked by a peaceful repose where the park visitors come to fish or join the bench beside the pond for a picnic setting. The calm, serene setting lures many here when they visit the park. Snowcapped San Gorgonio Mountain is visible in the distance.

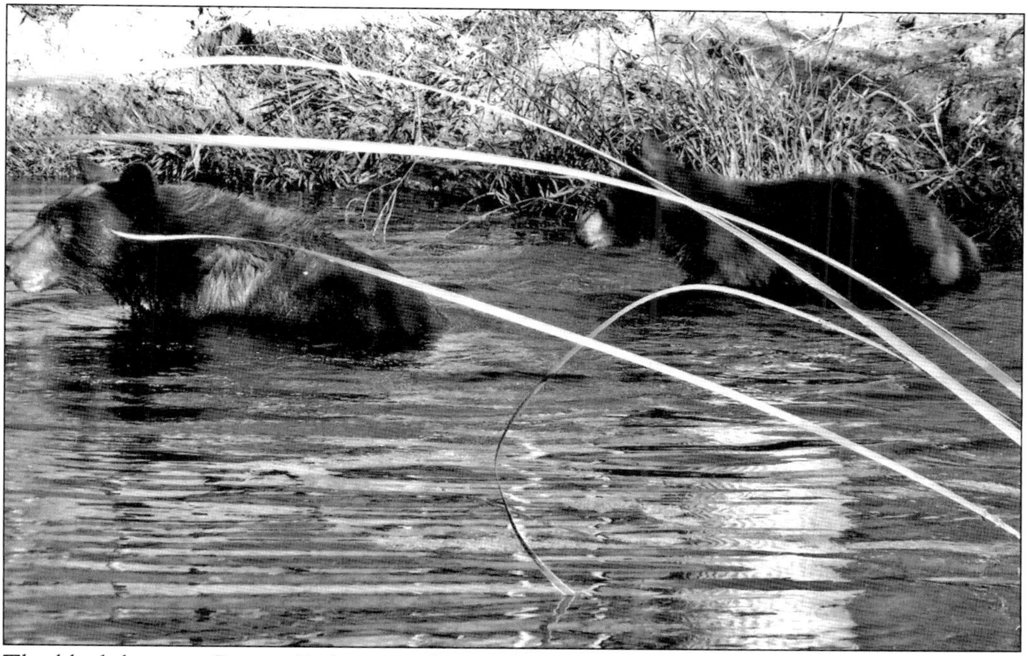

The black bears at Bogart Park enjoy the pond, too. A mother bear and her cub find it most enjoyable to take a swim in the pond in the heat of the day. Black bears are good swimmers. They can swim at least half of a mile in freshwater, but usually just enjoy rambling around and playing in the water. (Courtesy of Tori Beck.)

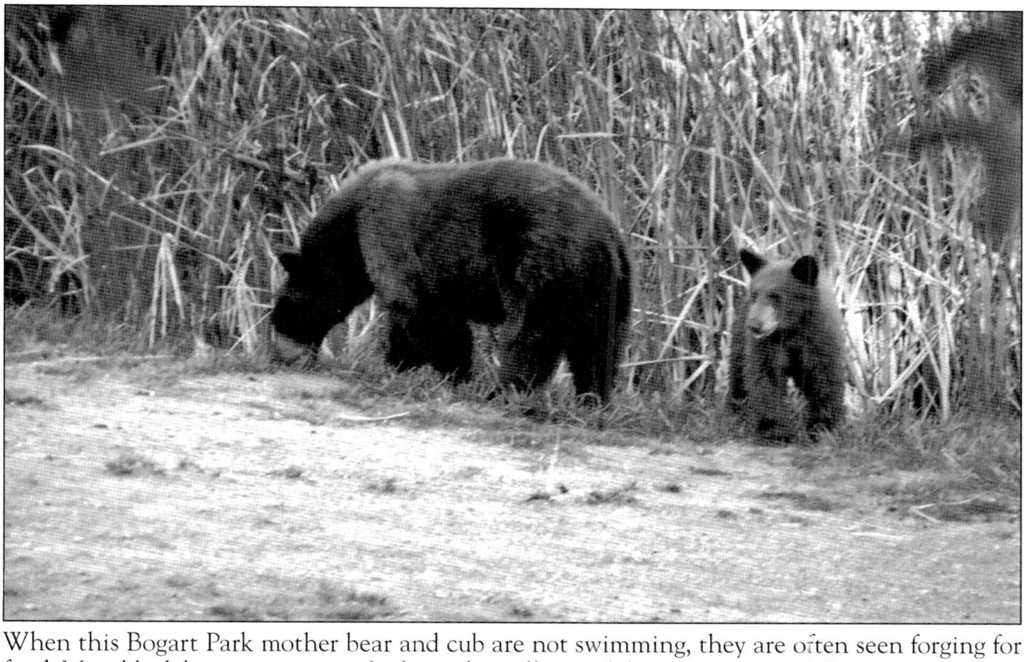

When this Bogart Park mother bear and cub are not swimming, they are often seen forging for food. Most black bears are extremely shy and usually avoid direct contact with humans. Incidents of black bears attacking humans have been reported but are extremely rare. Regardless, caution is advised in the park. (Courtesy of Tori Beck.)

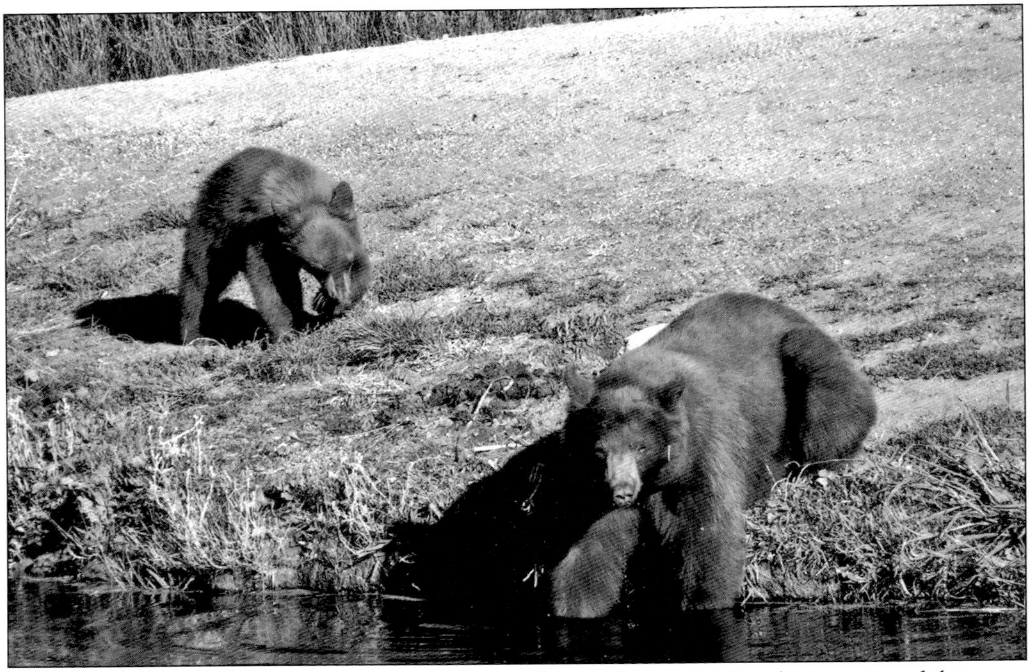

This mother bear and her cub are at the pond at Bogart Park enjoying the serenity of the view. Even though their visit was interrupted by the photographer, they were not deterred. Mother bear appears to be engrossed in soaking her paws in the cool water. (Courtesy of Tori Beck.)

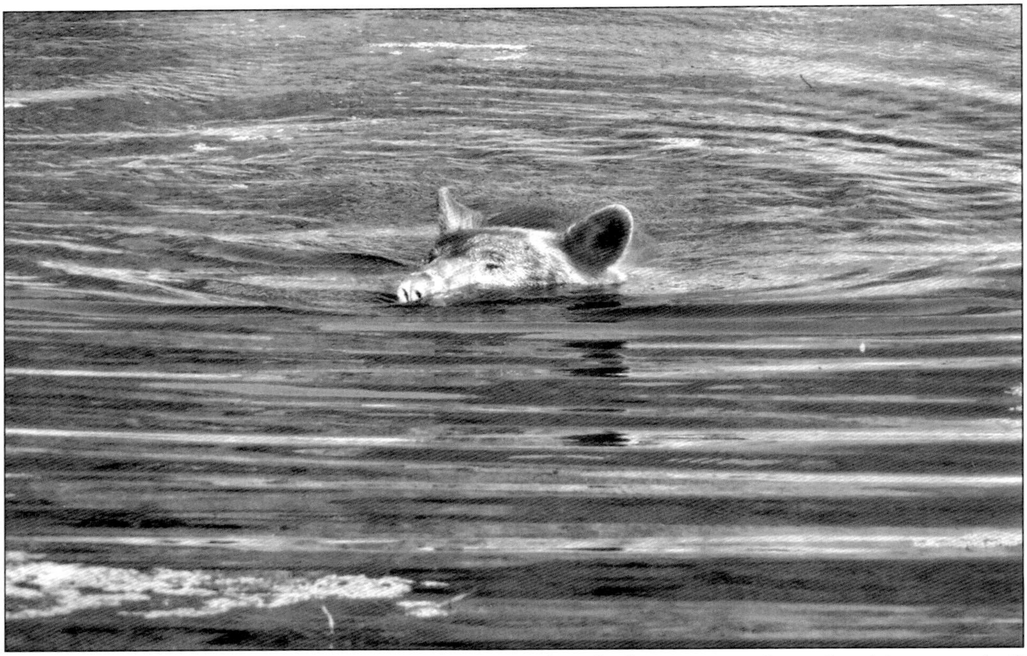

The bears that visit Bogart Park are quite furry, and in the hot summer days, they like to cool off in the pond at Bogart Park. This one enjoys a cool swim in the pool, completely unaware of any intrusion upon its private swimming pool. (Courtesy of Tori Beck.)

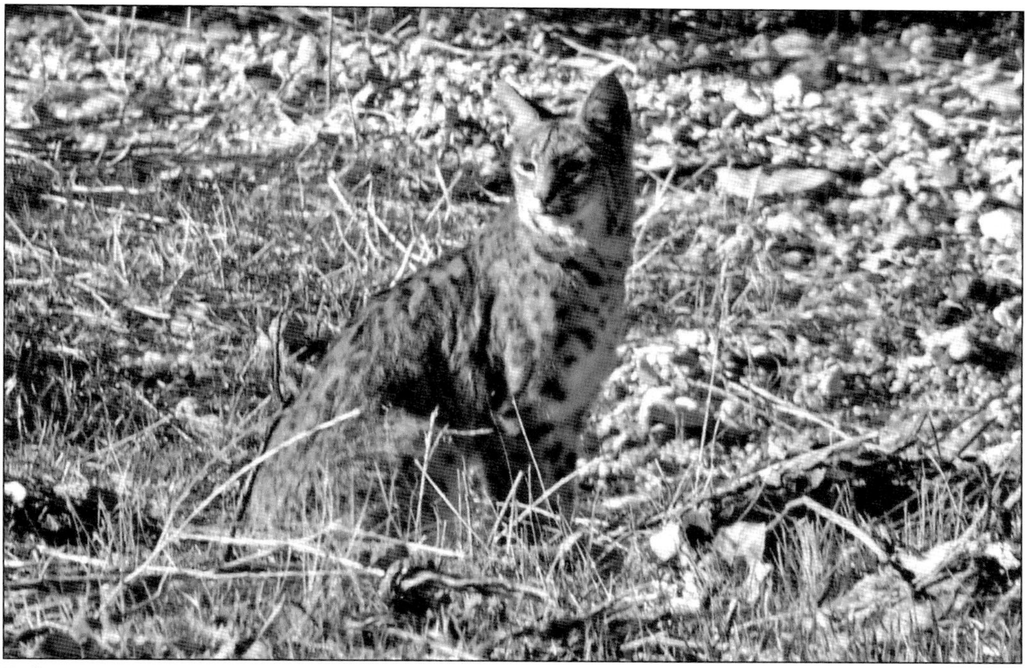

Bobcats are sometimes seen around the grounds of Bogart Park. This recently photographed cat did not appear to be afraid of the camera. Bobcats are occasionally also known as the Bay Lynx. They are a North American mammal in the cat family. Their habitat ranges from southern Canada to northern Mexico. (Courtesy of Tori Beck.)

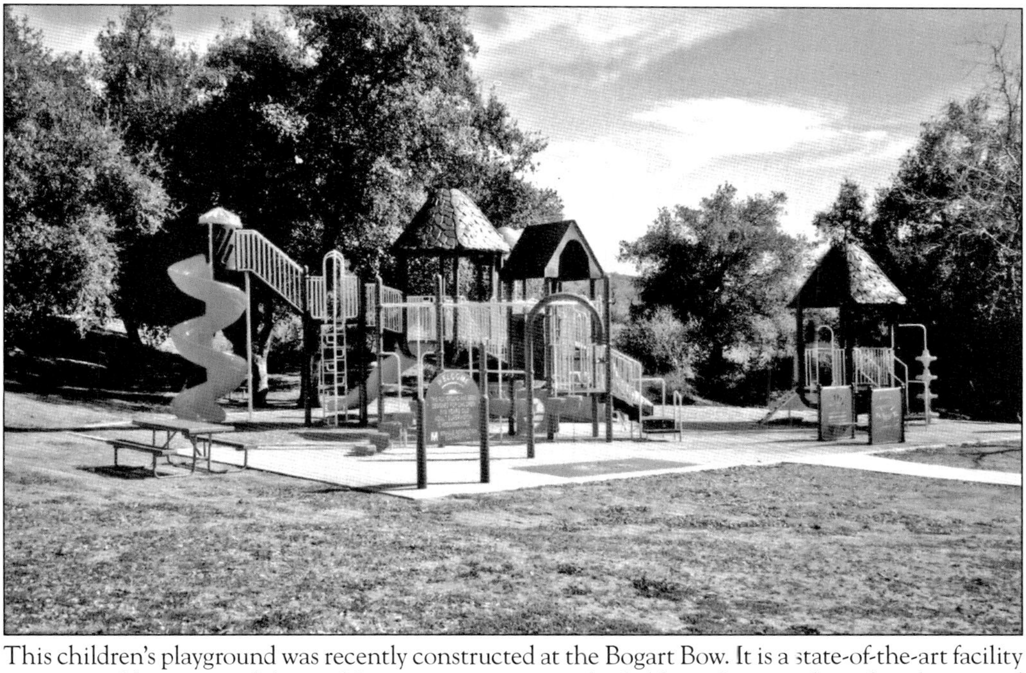

This children's playground was recently constructed at the Bogart Bow. It is a state-of-the-art facility appreciated by many of the park's visitors arriving with children. Surrounding the playground are several picnic tables and bathroom facilities for campers to use.

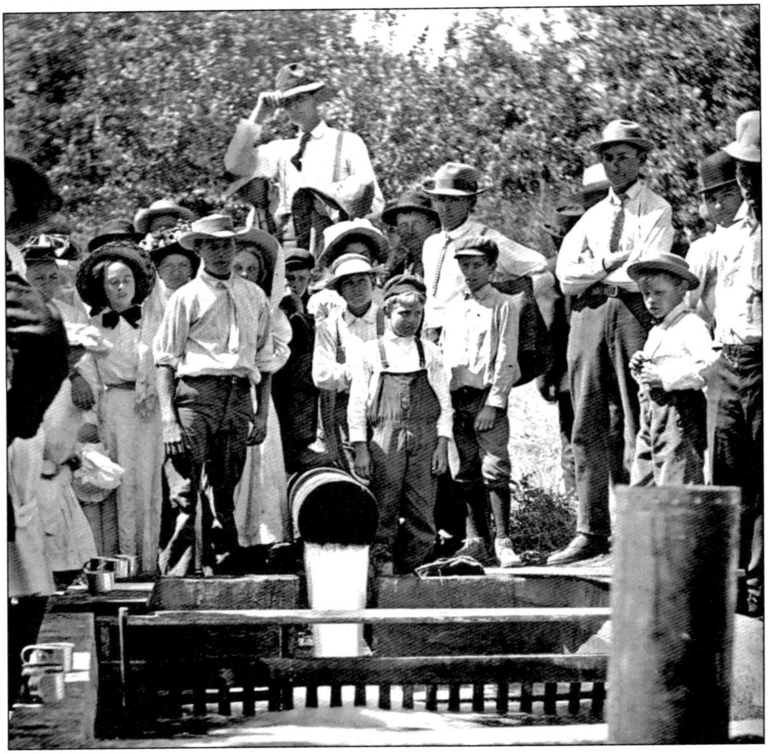

This scene near Bogart Park was climaxed after a successful well-drilling venture in Edgar Canyon in 1908. The people gathered had reason to celebrate because the event guaranteed more water for their town, which flowed from the well pipe and was fed directly into a flume that brought water down the canyon into a reservoir. (Courtesy of SGPHS.)

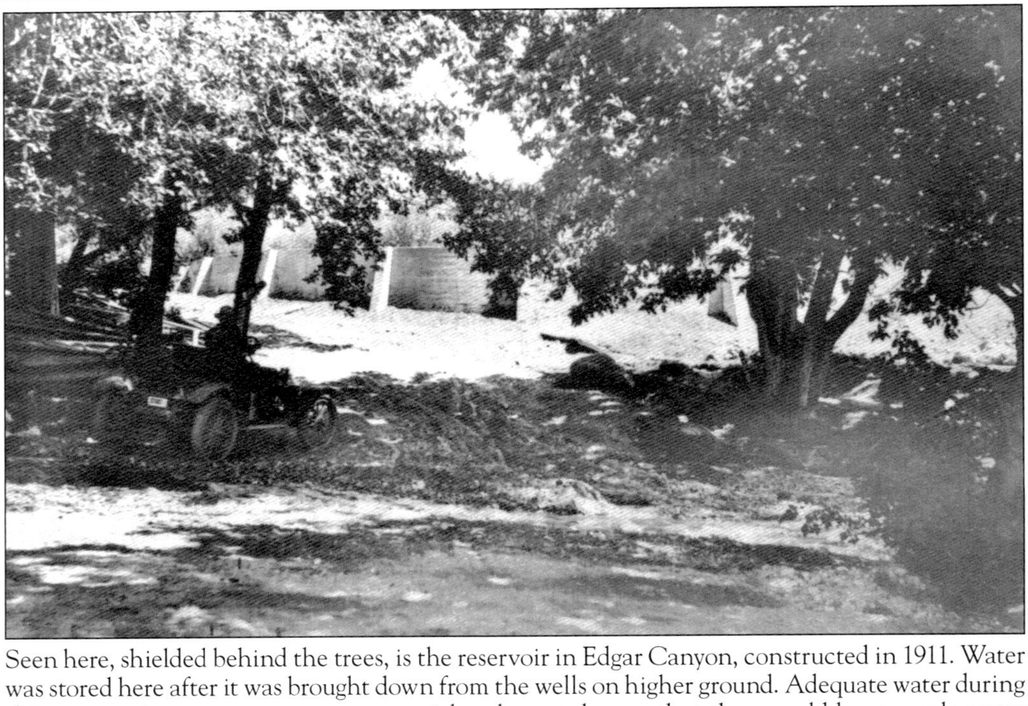

Seen here, shielded behind the trees, is the reservoir in Edgar Canyon, constructed in 1911. Water was stored here after it was brought down from the wells on higher ground. Adequate water during this era was important to assure potential real estate buyers that they would have ample water for their farming needs. (Courtesy of SGPHS.)

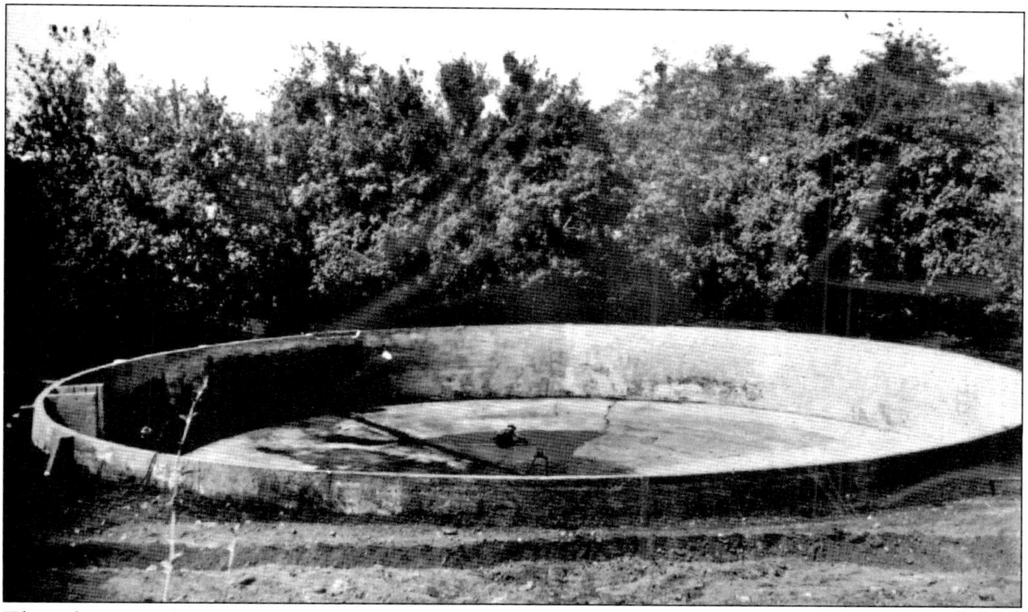

This photograph was taken looking down on the Edgar Canyon reservoir in 1911. The size of the reservoir is exemplified by viewing the image of the man sitting in the center of the circular structure. Communities during this time relied on reservoirs like this, but now use large tanks. Today Edgar Canyon is another source of water for the Beaumont/Cherry Valley Water District. (Courtesy of SGPHS.)

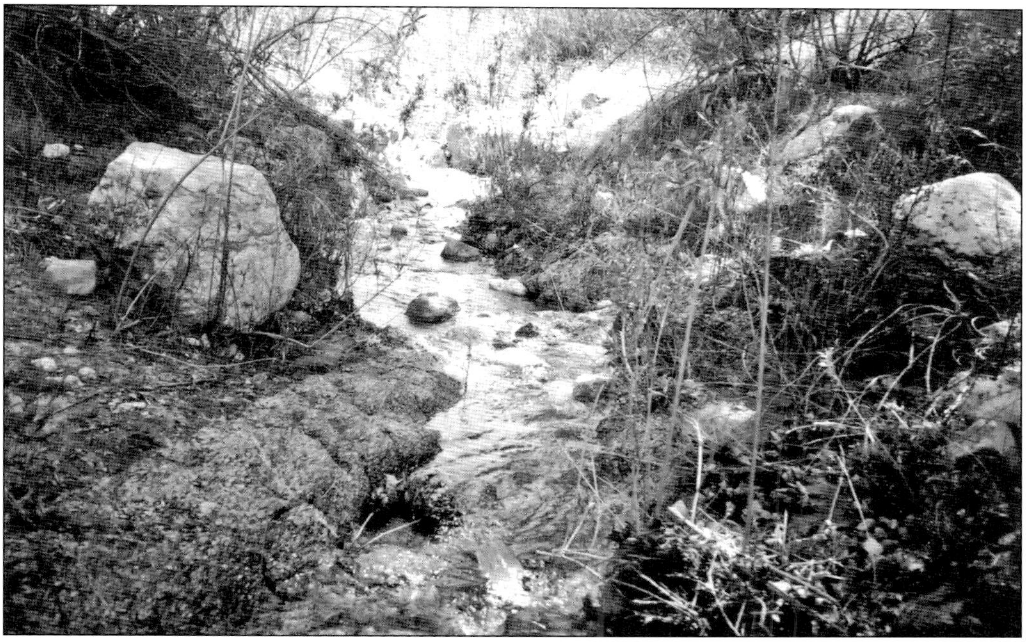

Water can be seen flowing down Noble Creek through Bogart Park above the ground's surface during the winter months when snow on the mountains is melting. When the snow finally dissipates, the flow lessens and moves underground through an aquifer. Today water is still derived from Noble Creek for Cherry Valley. (Courtesy of SGPHS.)

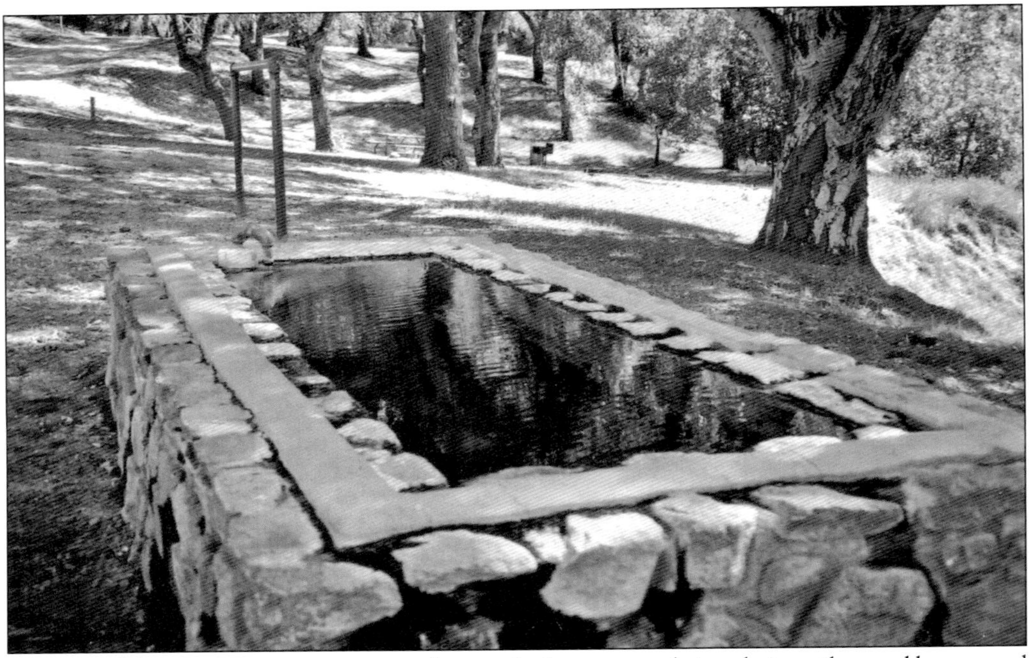

Bogart Park has an equestrian campsite for people that want to bring their trailers and horses and ride the available trails in the park. Shown here is an alluring watering trough that is available at the campsite, allowing horses to be watered before heading out on the trail. People arrive here from near and far to ride these trails.

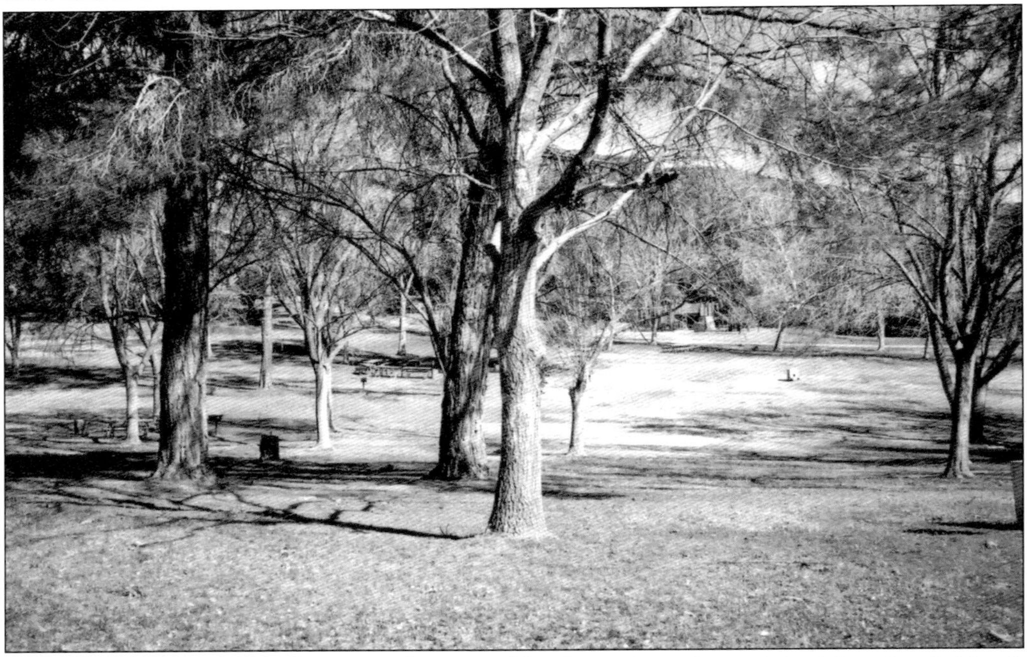

Bogart Bowl is pictured with scattered picnic tables throughout the vicinity. Note the children's playground that can be seen at the right center of the picture. This area is an alluring part of the park where many campers come to have picnics or just enjoy the serenity of the area.

Three

AGRICULTURE

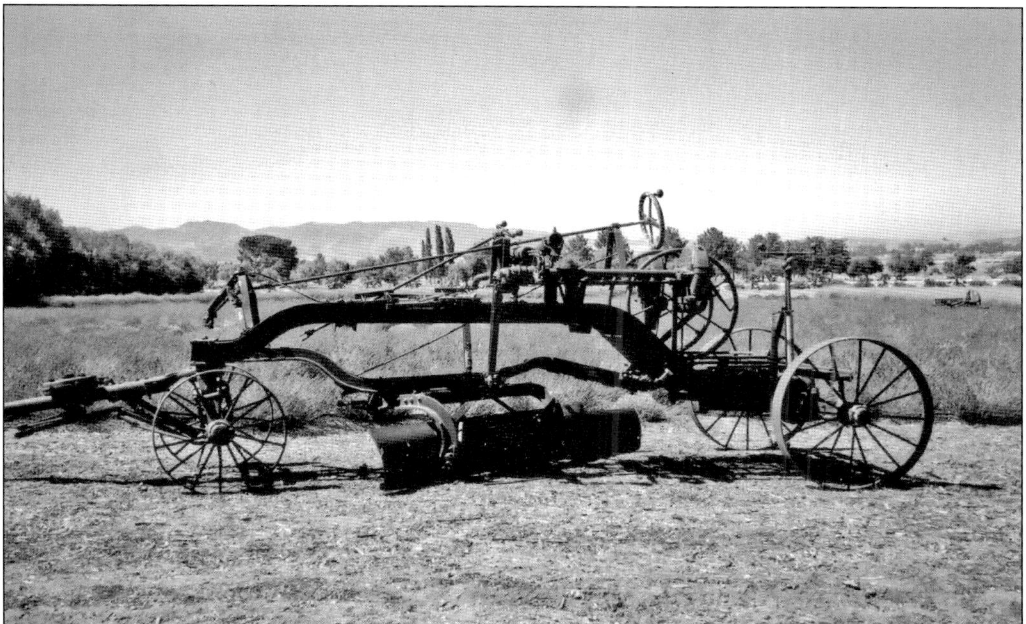

Most of the early fruit orchards and seed crops planted in Cherry Valley were often planted on small farms where the terrain was not level. However, in some cases the ground was leveled so that plowing, planting, and irrigation were made easier. The early grader pictured here did land leveling as well as road grading.

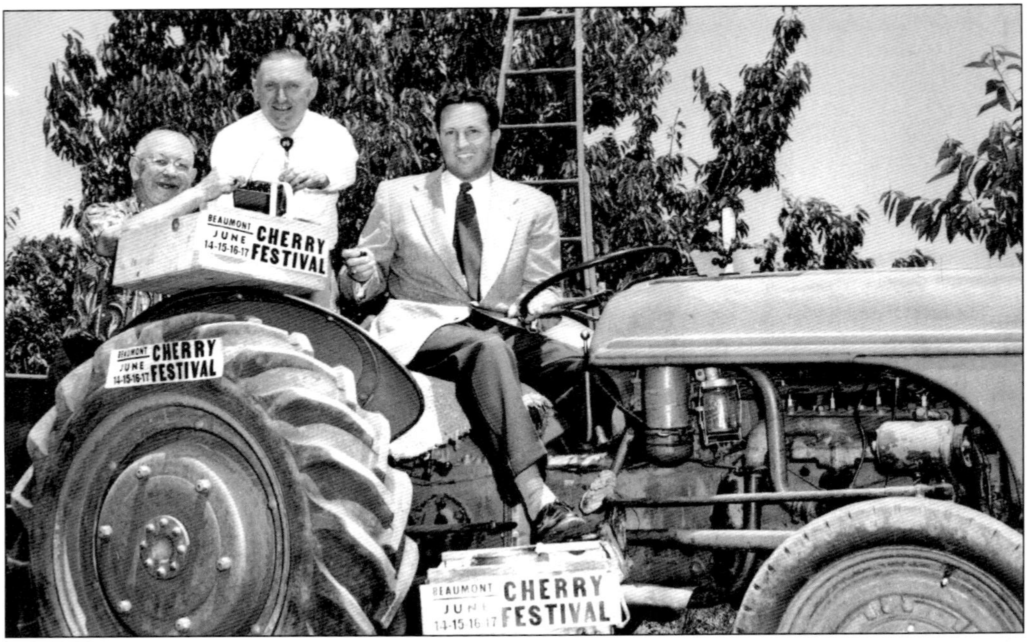

Standing behind this Ford tractor are, from left to right, Guy Bogart and Emil O. Wohlgemuth, with Norman Davis sitting in the tractor seat. They are at Emil's Cherry Orchard in Cherry Valley in 1957, where cherries were being harvested for the festival. Note the height of the tree in the background where a high ladder is required to pick cherries. (Courtesy of SGPHS.)

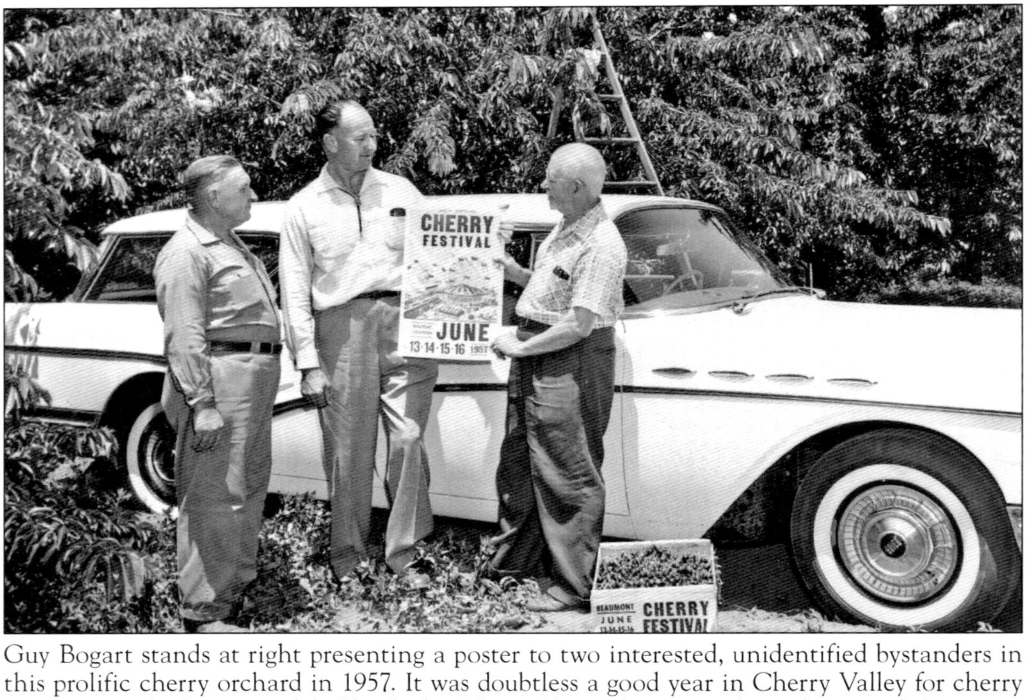

Guy Bogart stands at right presenting a poster to two interested, unidentified bystanders in this prolific cherry orchard in 1957. It was doubtless a good year in Cherry Valley for cherry production, which is exemplified by the backdrop of large cherry trees being harvested. (Courtesy of SGPHS.)

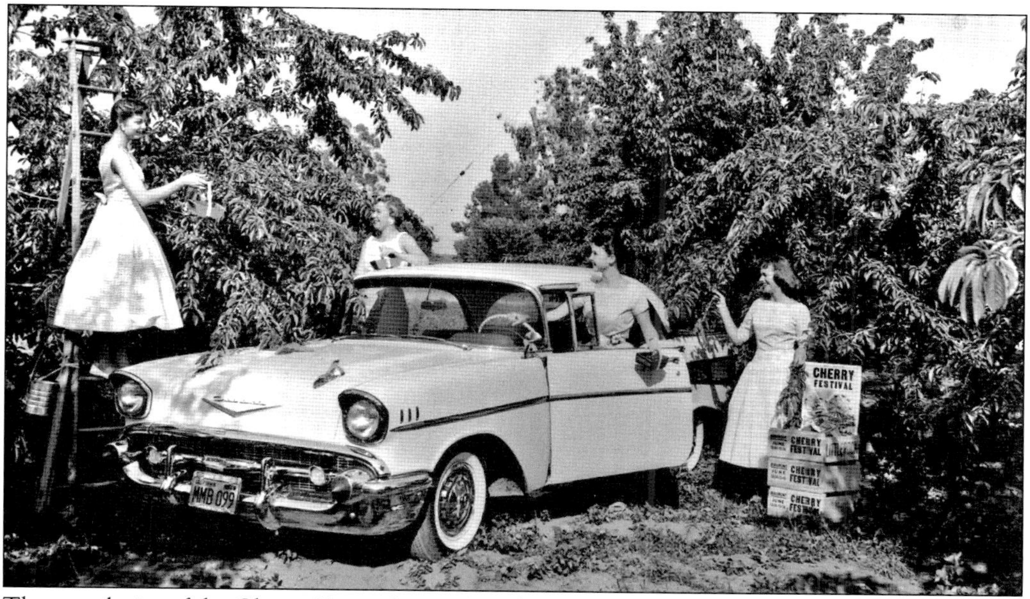

The popularity of the Cherry Festival in 1957 is illustrated in this scene, bringing to the forefront the popular new Chevrolet surrounded with pretty girls representing the Cherry Festival. Note the vigorous cherry trees in the orchard that are loaded with red-ripe cherries and the Cherry Festival boxes at right advertising the cherries picked for the festival. (Courtesy of SGPHS.)

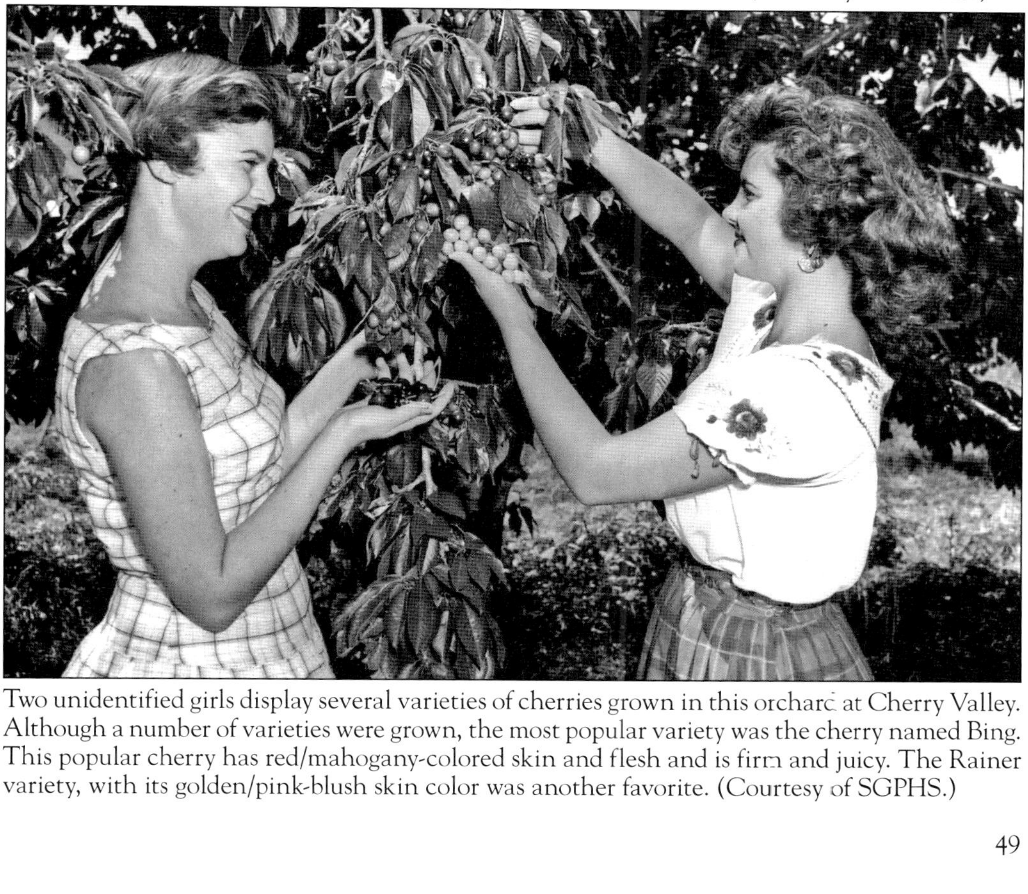

Two unidentified girls display several varieties of cherries grown in this orchard at Cherry Valley. Although a number of varieties were grown, the most popular variety was the cherry named Bing. This popular cherry has red/mahogany-colored skin and flesh and is firm and juicy. The Rainer variety, with its golden/pink-blush skin color was another favorite. (Courtesy of SGPHS.)

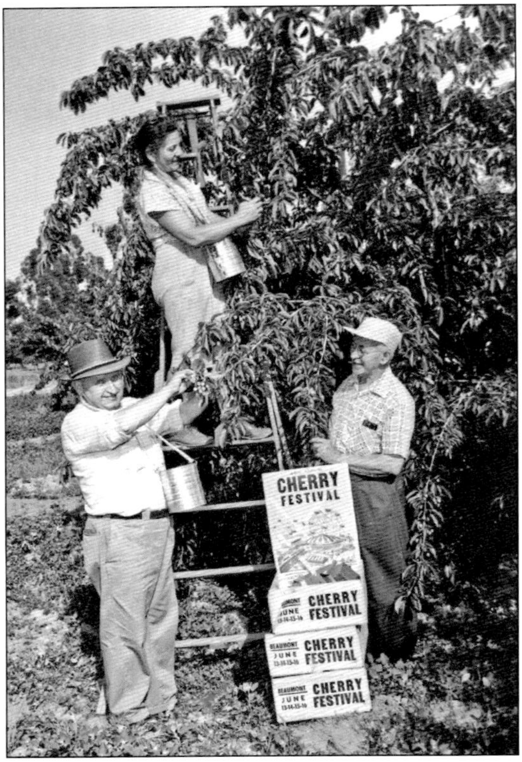

Although this is probably a promotional photograph for the Cherry Festival, Guy Bogart at the right seems to be enjoying watching the unidentified man and woman on the ladder picking cherries. "Upick" was advertised at many of the cherry orchards in Cherry Valley and the craze to pick one's own fruit was highly cherished. (Courtesy of SGPHS.)

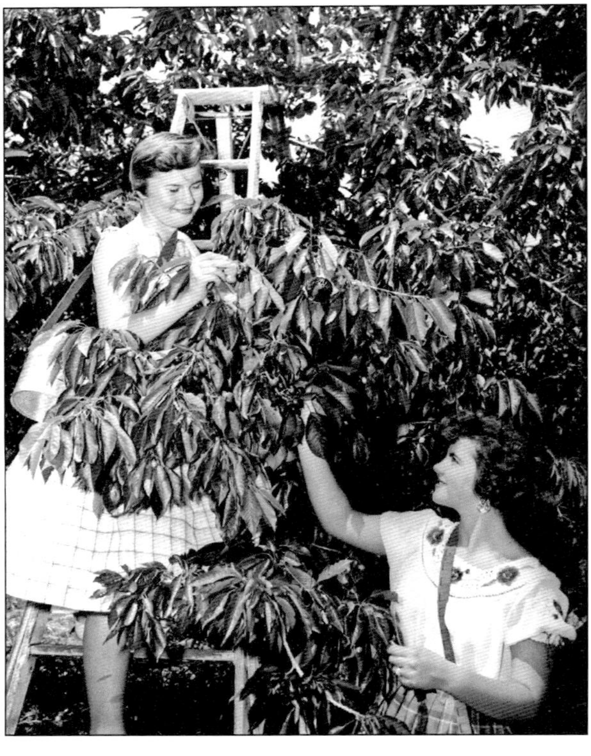

An abundance of fruit hangs from this cherry tree, and two girls place the picked fruit into a tin can strapped to their shoulders. Both girls appear to be enjoying the process while posing for the picture. (Courtesy of SGPHS.)

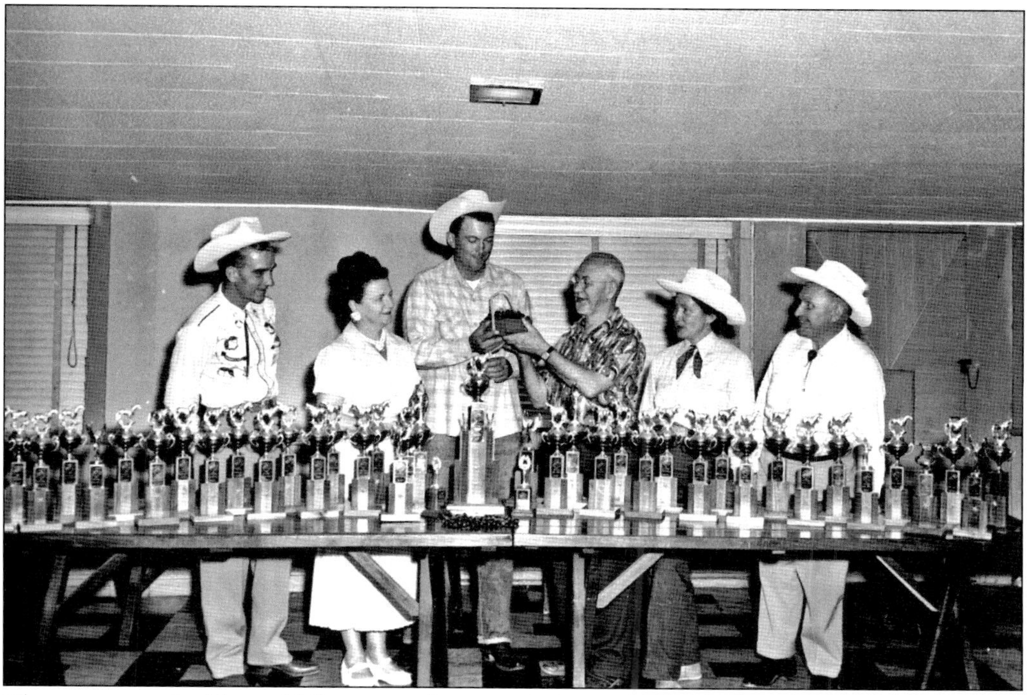

Cherry growers in Cherry Valley were often awarded a trophy for the best fruit grown during the Cherry Festival. Standing from left to right behind this large table of trophies are Jack Wolfington, Ruby Birch, Louis Robertson (receiving trophy), Guy Bogart (awarding the trophy), Martha Urton, and Emil O. Wohlgemuth. (Courtesy of SGPHS.)

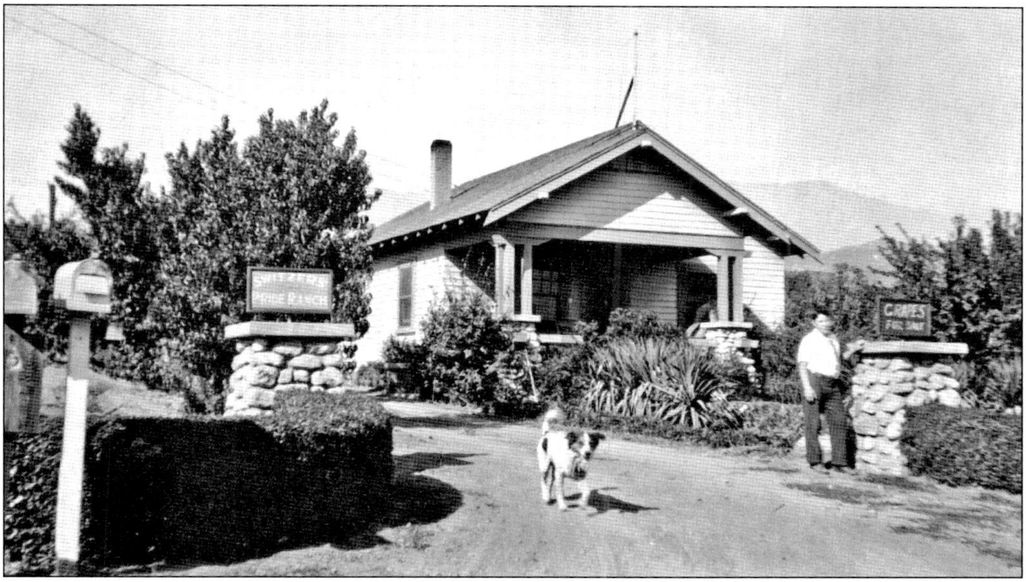

A. L. Switzer stands at right next to a rock column supporting a sign reading "grapes for sale." The rock column on the left has a sign that reads Switzer's Pride Ranch. Many small ranches like this were established in Cherry Valley during this time with many of them growing cherries. (Courtesy of SGPHS.)

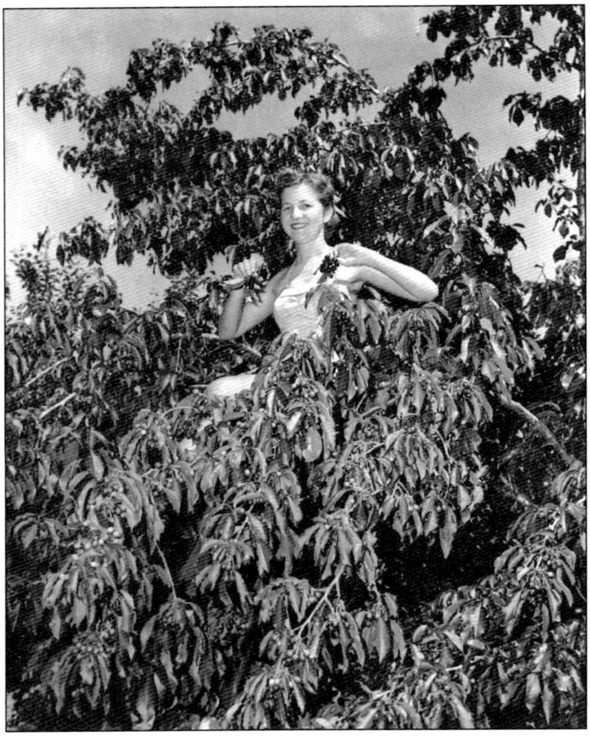

The Cherry Festival was an excellent time to advertise the cherry industry. Pictures like this were often popular during this time, and they appeared in the press and elsewhere. The tree in this case was extremely loaded with cherries, as can be noted by the abundance of fruit. (Photograph by Leonard McCulloh; courtesy of SGPHS.)

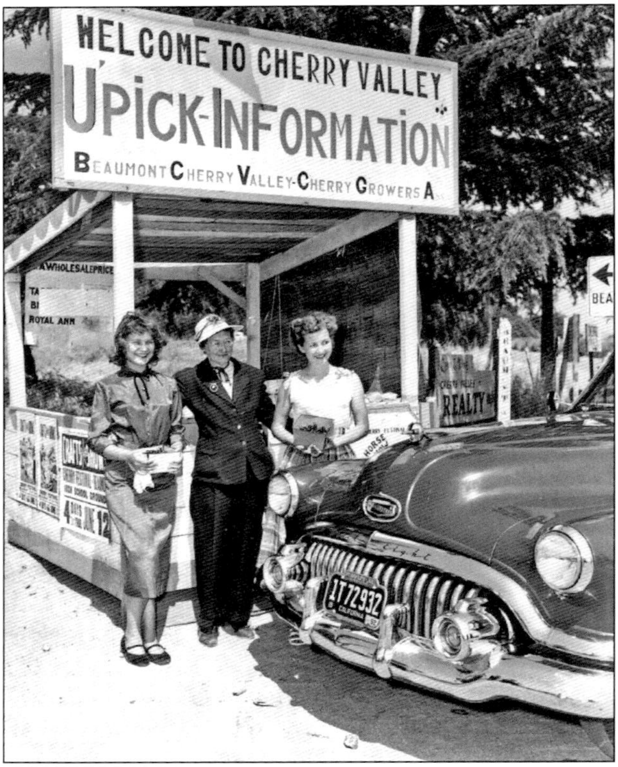

Sandra Lee Carter, 1952 Cherry Festival queen, stands at left beside Minnie Burton, information director, and Iva Hall, Cherry Festival princess. Upick was very popular during this time in Cherry Valley and whole families often came out to the orchards to pick their own cherries. It was a fun project for the children. (Courtesy of SGPHS.)

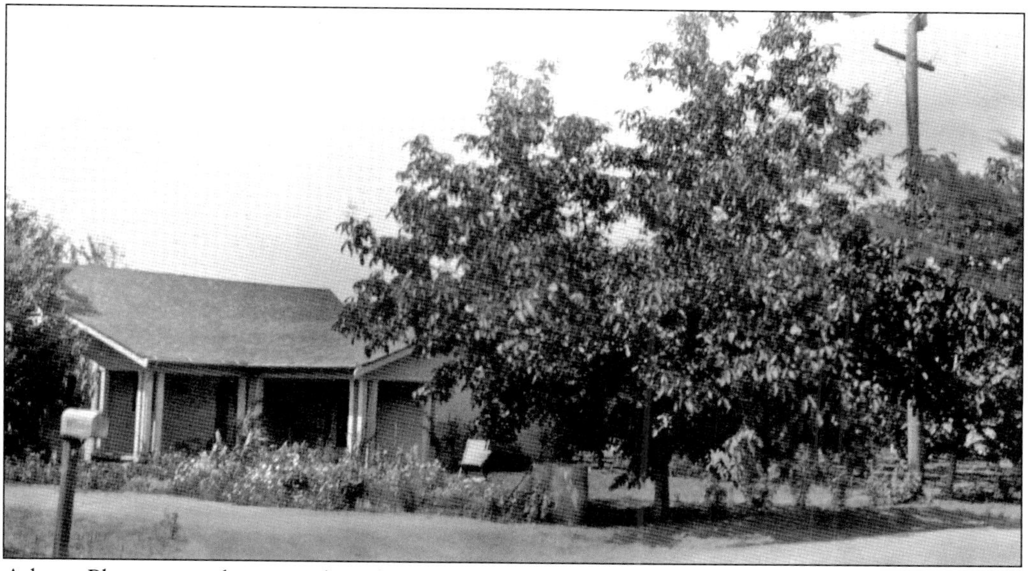

A large Placentia walnut stands in front of this Cherry Valley ranch, owned by Claude J. Pinson, in 1927. He was a grower of the Royal Ann cherry variety. This variety produces a large sweet cherry that is yellow in color with a red blush. It bears well and is an excellent canning variety. (Courtesy of SGPHS.)

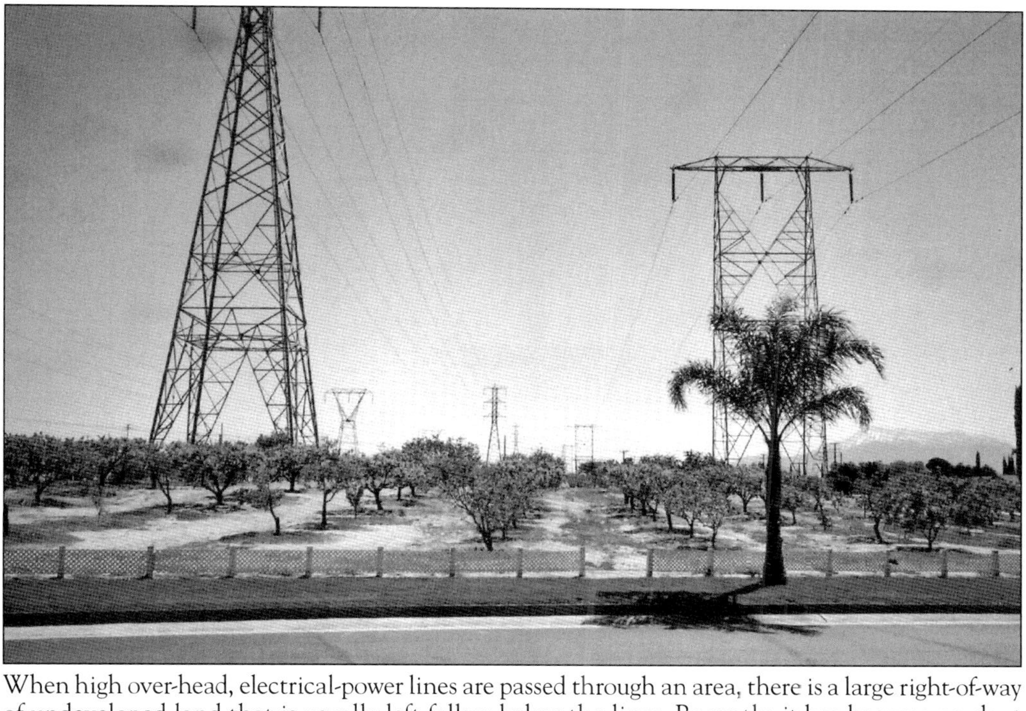

When high over-head, electrical-power lines are passed through an area, there is a large right-of-way of undeveloped land that is usually left fallow below the lines. Recently, it has become prudent to use some of this land under the lines for agriculture. The Edison Company has cooperated in this respect. Pictured here is an example of one use for the land.

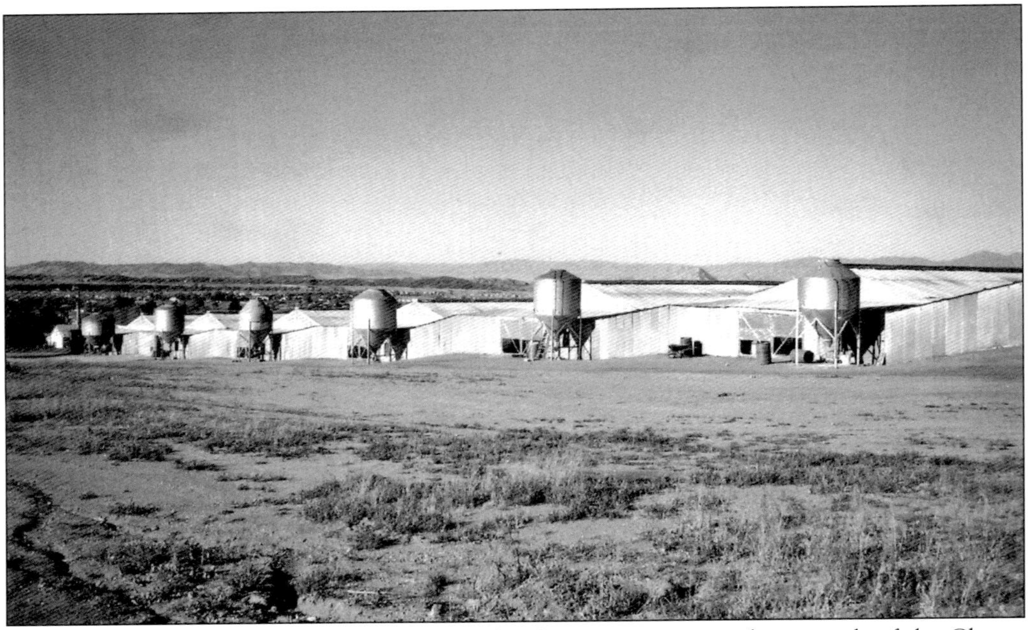

This chicken farm stands today north of Orchard Street, very near the grounds of the Cherry Valley Naval Hospital that once inhabited these grounds. It is minute when compared to the very large size of Sunny Cal Chicken Farm on Cherry Valley Boulevard, the one that was recently razed to make room for suburban development.

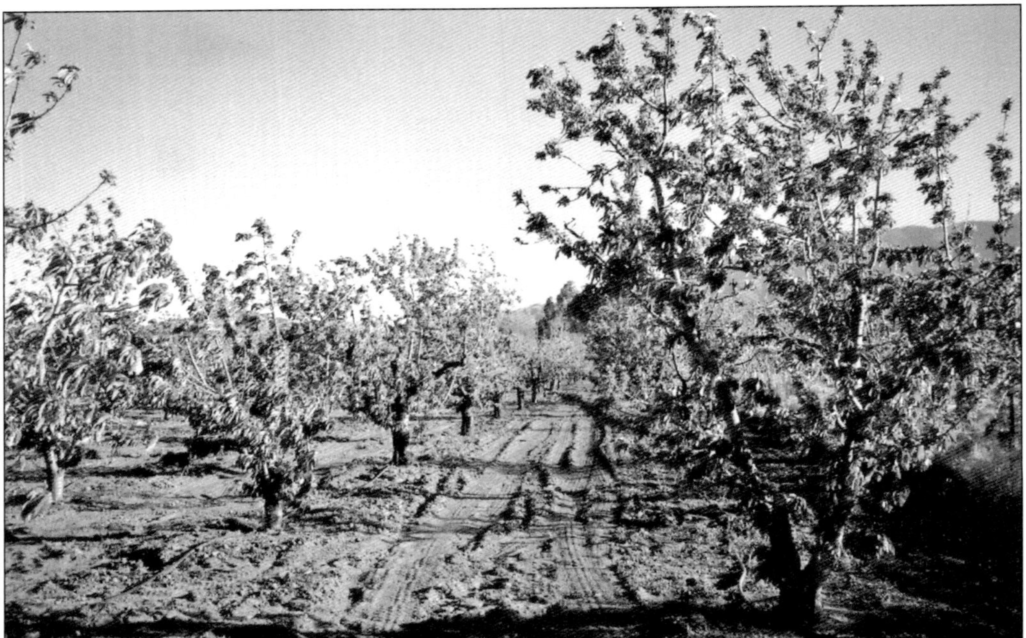

Many of the old cherry orchards that once existed in Cherry Valley have died off or been demolished to make room for housing development. However, some farmers have planted new trees like the young orchard pictured here, which is greatly helping to maintain some of the lost production.

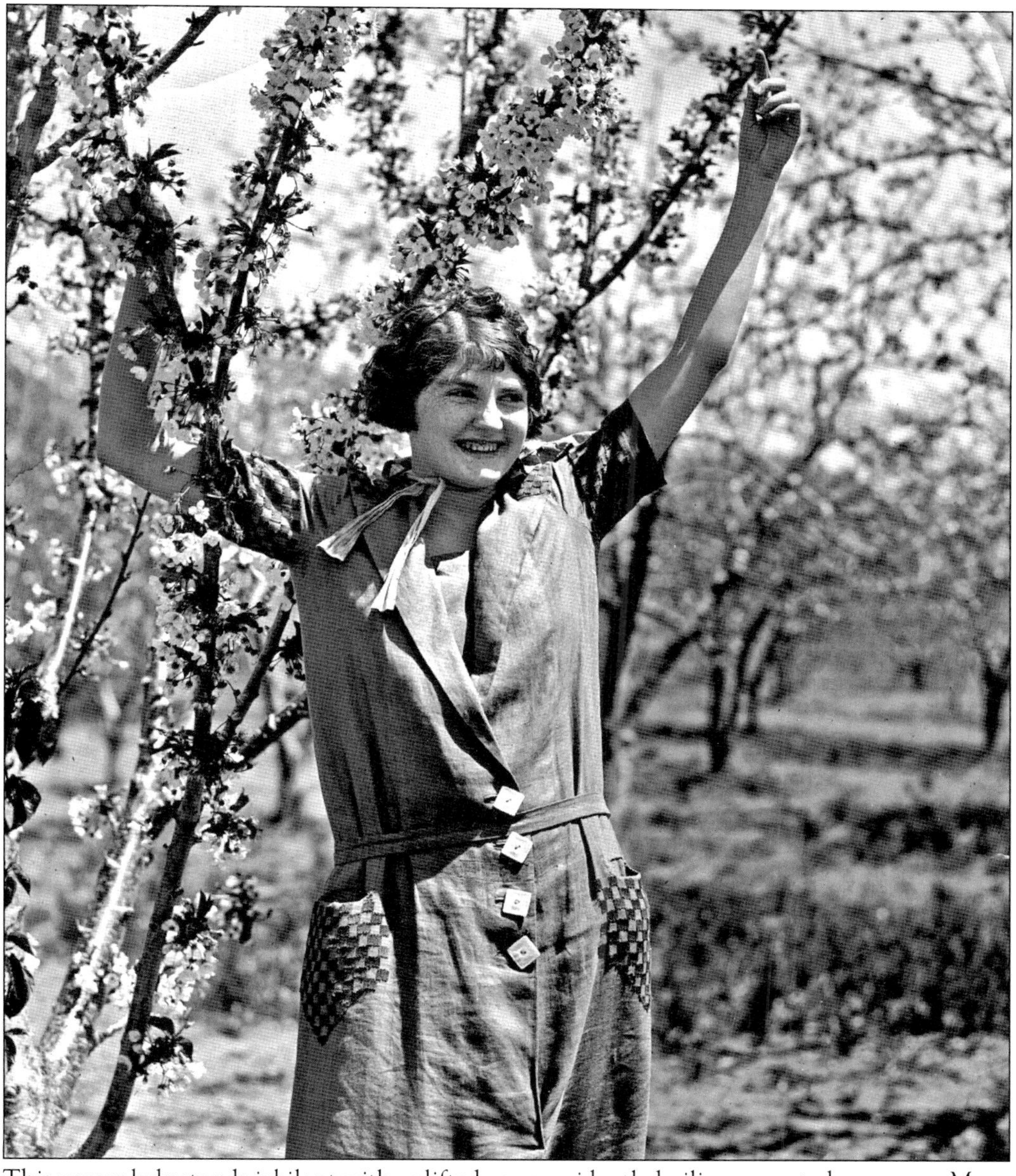

This young lady stands jubilant with uplifted arms, evidently hailing a great cherry crop. Many people came to the Cherry Festival during this time, as it was a gala event that all looked forward to each year. Originally, apples were the major fruit grown in Cherry Valley, and at one time, the community was known as Apple Valley. When cherries were introduced to the area they became the major crop, spurring the growing of apples into Oak Glen to the north. (Courtesy of SGPHS.)

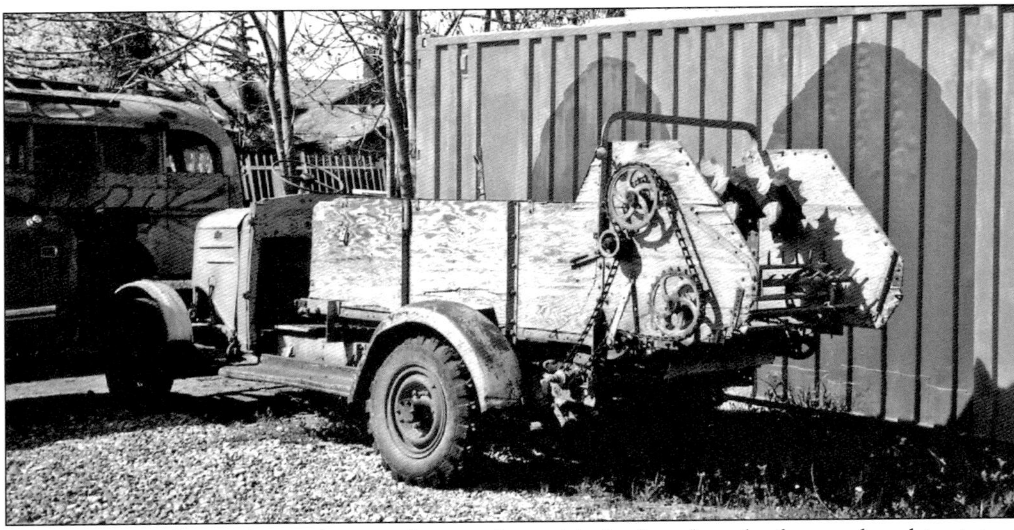

Though certainly not the modern machinery that might be found on the farm today, this vintage manure spreader once got the job done. It is still operative today, but has been retired and is used chiefly for display at a local antique store on Beaumont Avenue in the heart of Cherry Valley.

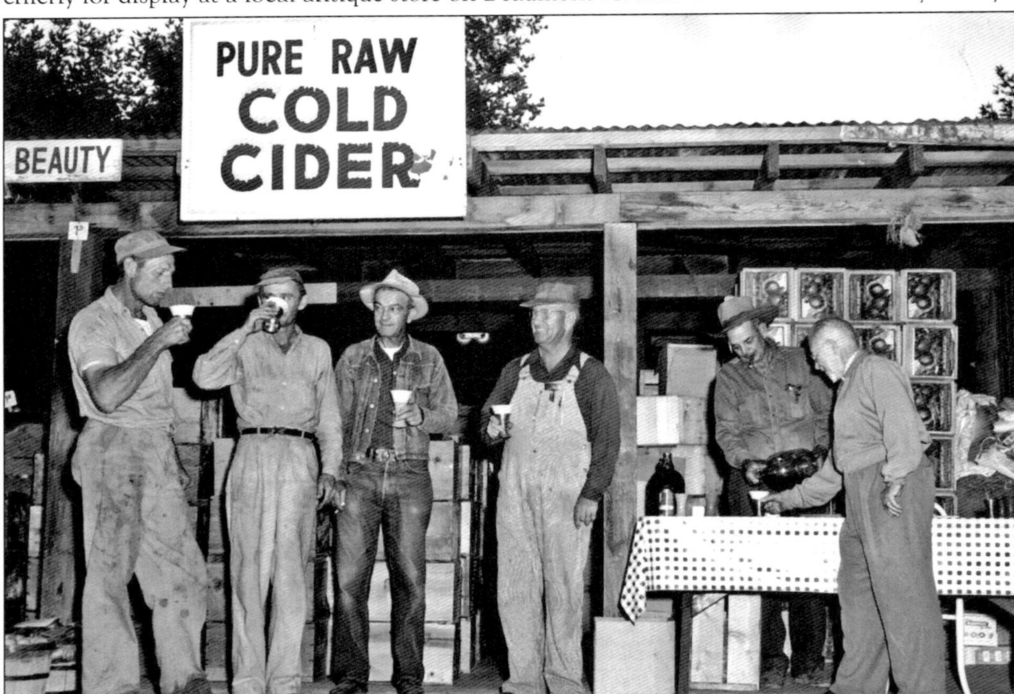

Guy Bogart stands at right receiving a glass of pure, raw, cold cider by Oak Glen apple grower Blackie Wiltshire. Although Bogart was a cherry grower in Beaumont, he was active in promoting agriculture in the surrounding communities. He was interested in shifting fruit wholesaling to tourism and direct sales. He was an early proponent of the popular Upick craze and was a great promoter of Cherry Valley and Oak Glen fruit industry. (Photograph by Leonard McCulloh; courtesy of SGPHS.)

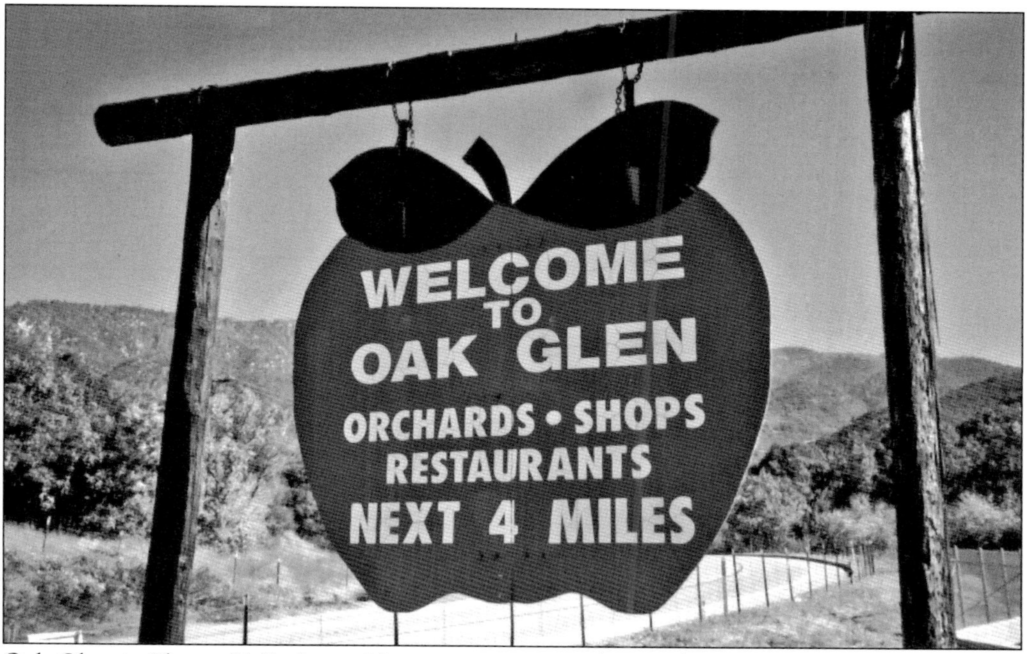

Oak Glen is Cherry Valley's neighbor community to the north. It is now looked upon as the apple-growing center of the area, as Cherry Valley was once considered. Throughout the years, it has been known for the great apples that are grown there. It attracts local residents as well as tourist from all around.

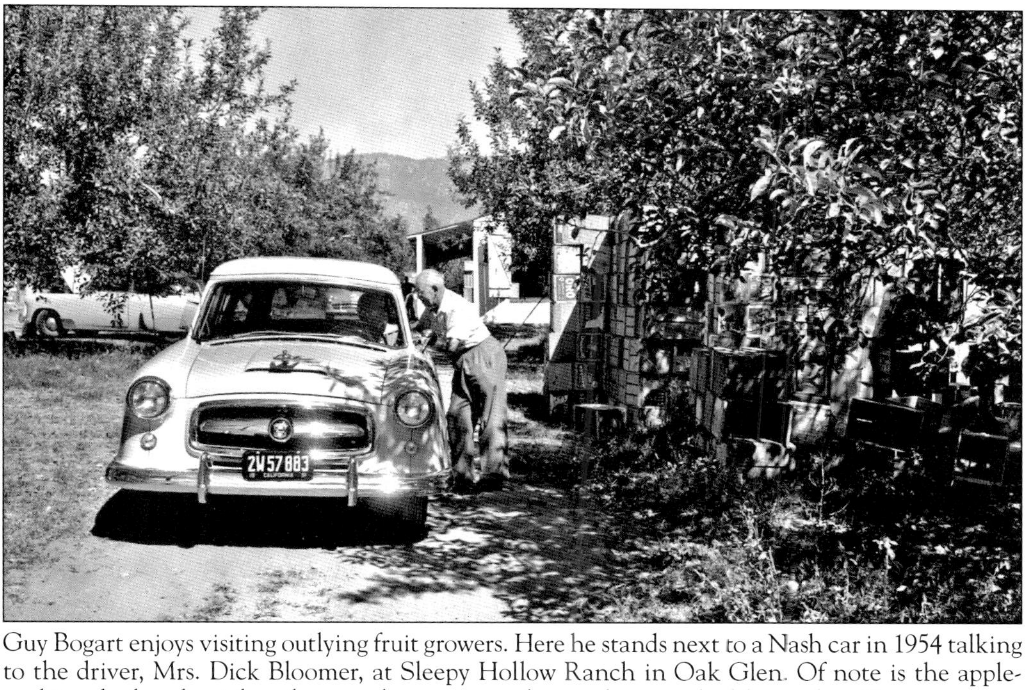

Guy Bogart enjoys visiting outlying fruit growers. Here he stands next to a Nash car in 1954 talking to the driver, Mrs. Dick Bloomer, at Sleepy Hollow Ranch in Oak Glen. Of note is the apple-packing shed to the right, where apples grown on the ranch are packed for market. However, many apples are used locally by residents for cider, fruit, and making pies. (Courtesy of SGPHS.)

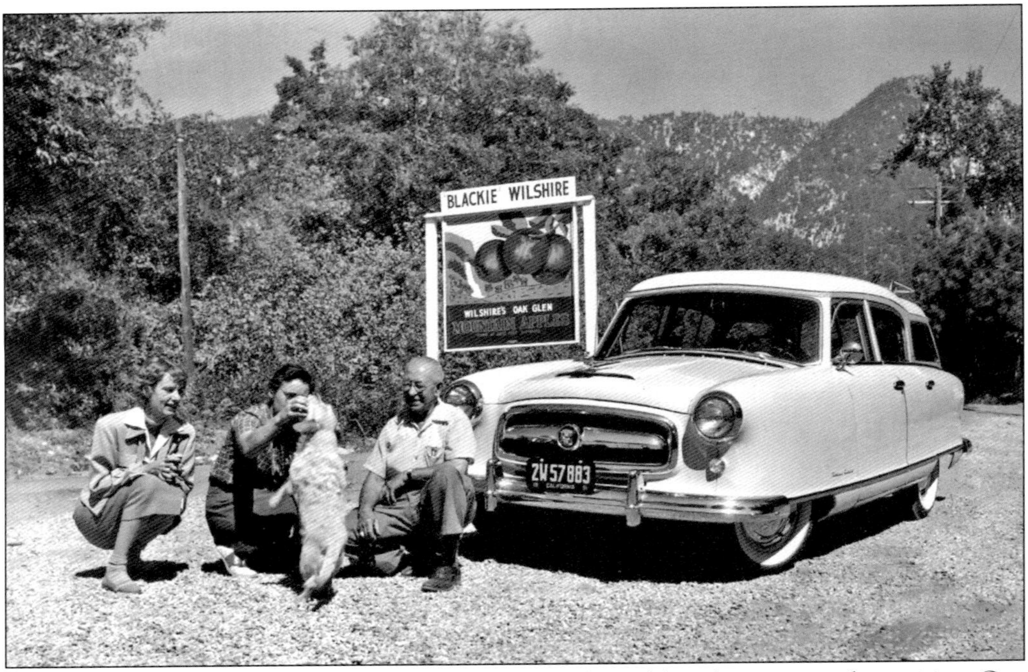

Mrs. Dick Bloomer (left) in 1954 is with Clair Sample and her dog next to their visitor Guy Bogart (right). Guy Bogart was very active in the mid-1950s, visiting apple growers in Oak Glen and Cherry Valley. He made friends with most of the growers in the agricultural community. (Courtesy of SGPHS.)

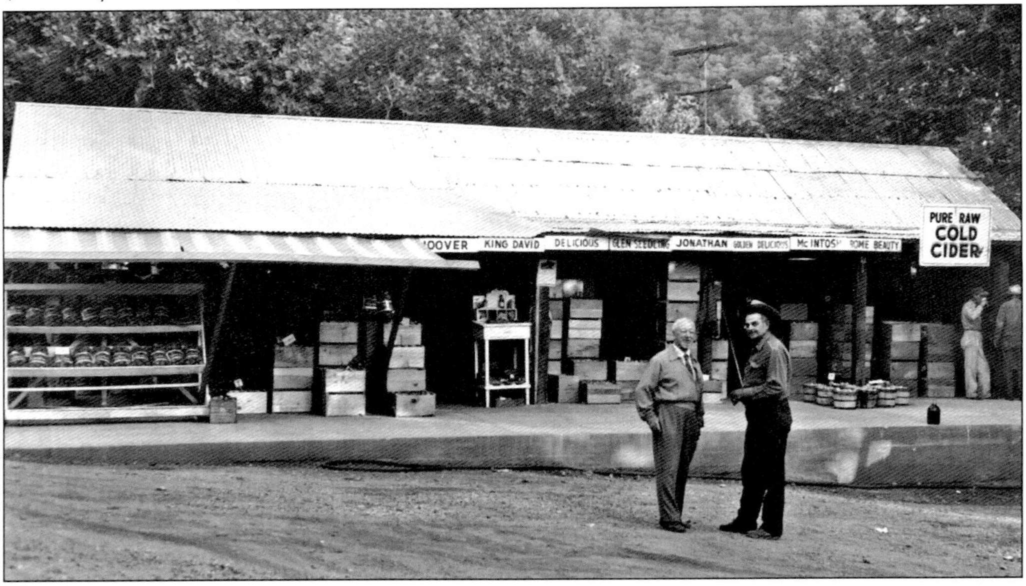

Guy Bogart stands at left talking with his friend, Blackie Wilshire, at the Wilshire Ranch packing shed. Two men stand at far right sampling the pure, raw, cold cider. Of note are the numerous varieties of apples that Blackie Wilshire grew that are listed on the fascia of the shed: Hoover, King David, Glen Seedling, Jonathan, Golden Delicious, McIntosh, and Rome Beauty. (Photograph by Leonard McCulloh; courtesy of SGPHS.)

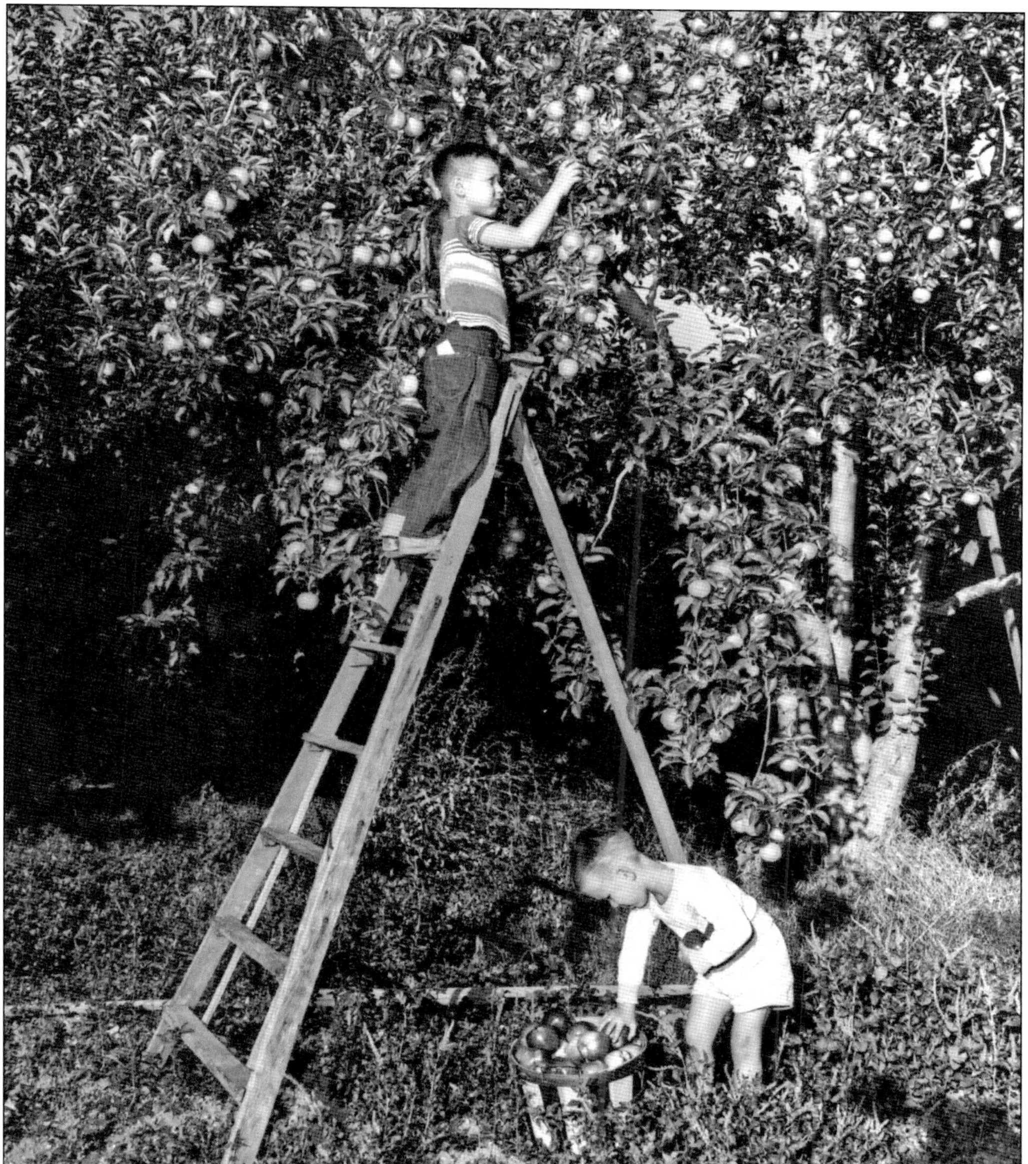

Eddie Davies (on ladder) and his brother Dick enthusiastically pick apples at the Davies's ranch in Oak Glen, north of Cherry Valley. They appear to be enjoying the reward of a bumper crop. An incentive for growing apples in this area is that the climate and soil are ideal for producing the fruit. Many farmers have also selected this site because of ample water. (Photograph by Leonard McCulloh; courtesy of SGPHS.)

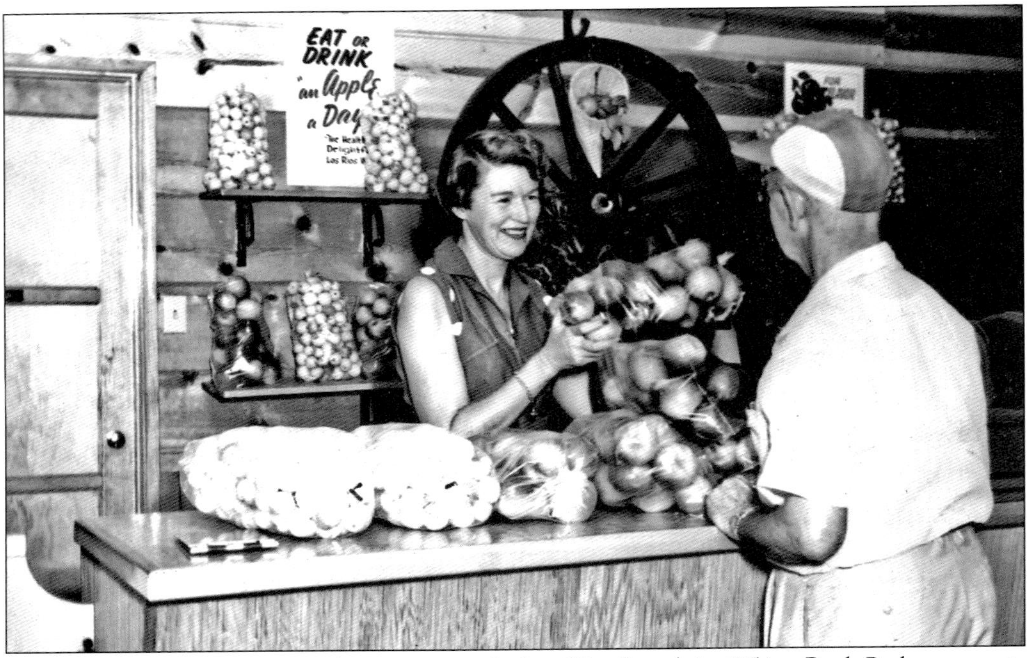

Visitor Guy Bogart steps up to the counter at the Los Rios Ranch in 1954 as Ruth Parker presents him with a sack of apples grown on the ranch. Note the sign on a shelf above Ruth that recommends eating or drinking an apple a day. Some apple ranches in this area make raw apple cider and sell it along with their apples. (Courtesy of SGPHS.)

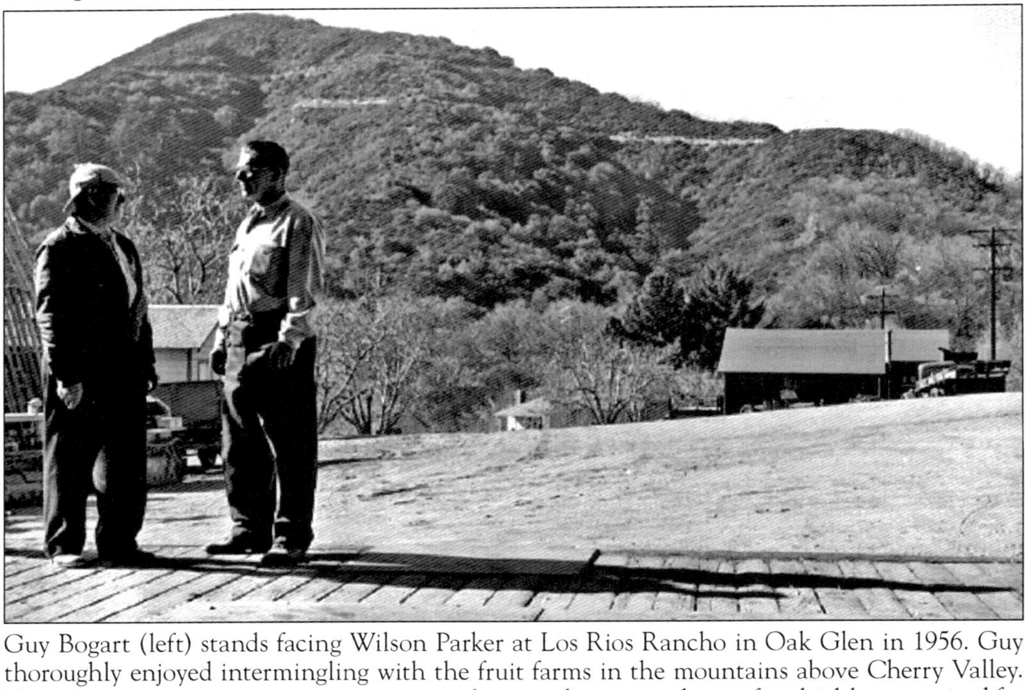

Guy Bogart (left) stands facing Wilson Parker at Los Rios Rancho in Oak Glen in 1956. Guy thoroughly enjoyed intermingling with the fruit farms in the mountains above Cherry Valley. He took a great interest in promoting agriculture in the area and was often highly recognized for his effort in this respect. (Courtesy of SGPHS.)

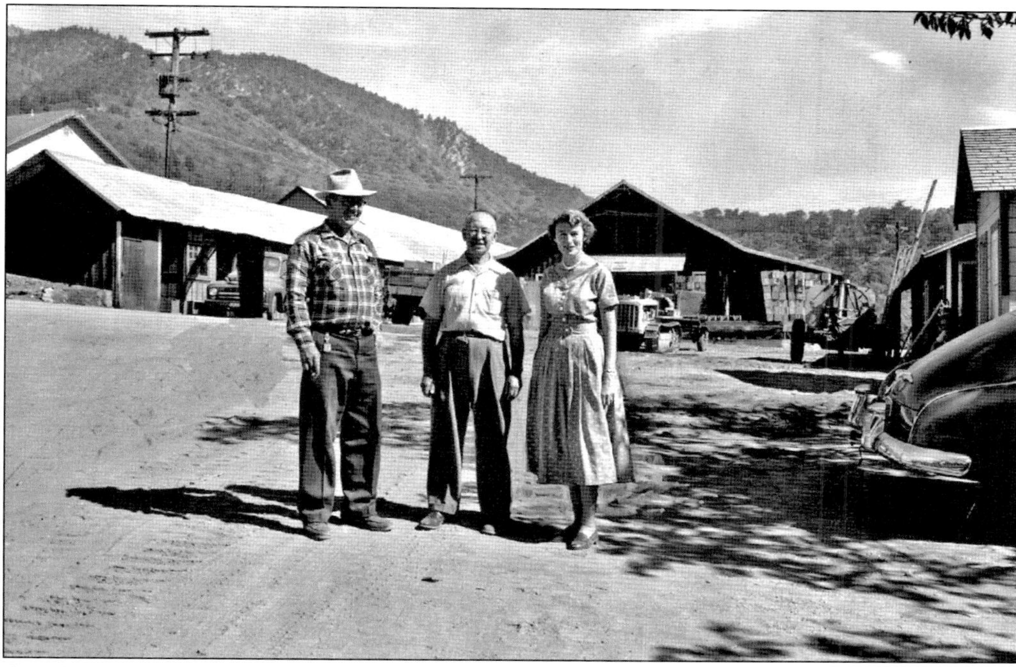

Guy Bogart spent much time at Los Rios Rancho helping owners to promote good agriculture practices. He stands here with two Los Rios Rancho members. He was always welcome at the ranch. Note the backdrop, which includes the old packing shed that still exists today; it is now over 100 years old and still used at the ranch for packing apples. (Courtesy of SGPHS.)

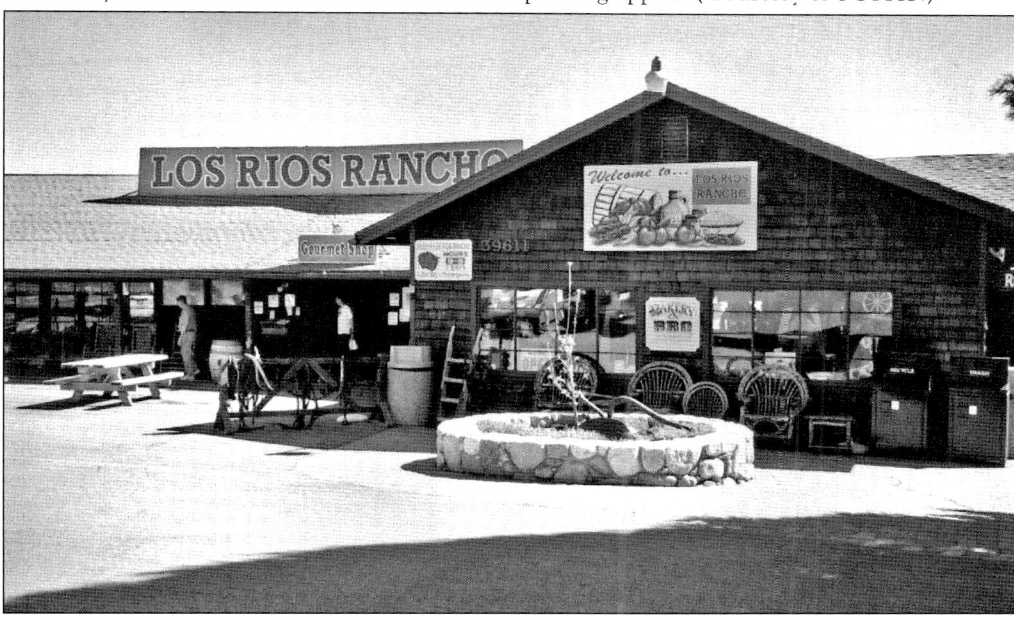

Los Rios Rancho is an alluring place to visit, and many families come here with their children to enjoy the serenity it provides. The entrance pictured beckons the visitor to the picturesque apple orchards, surrounding gardens, and leisure walks found everywhere. Horse-drawn wagon hayrides are provided on some occasions.

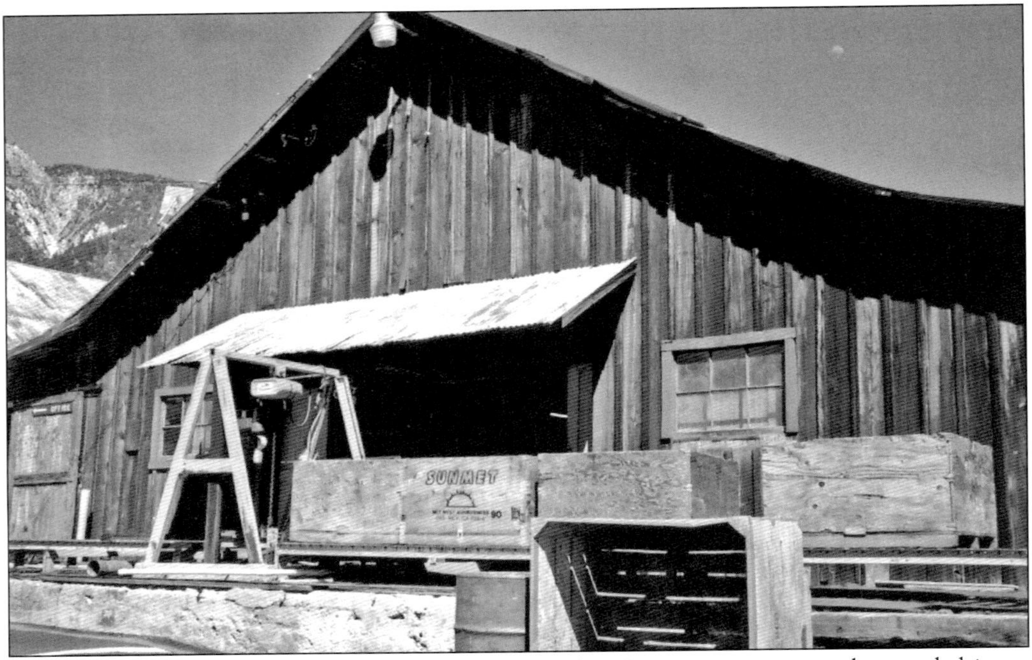

Los Rios Rancho first began in 1906 when Howard L. Rivers, a grower, packer, and shipper from the Pasadena area, purchased over 300 acres of property from the Wilshires to expand his operation to include apple growing. The apple-packing shed stands firmly here today, now over 100 years old. It is still used to process many of the apples grown on the ranch.

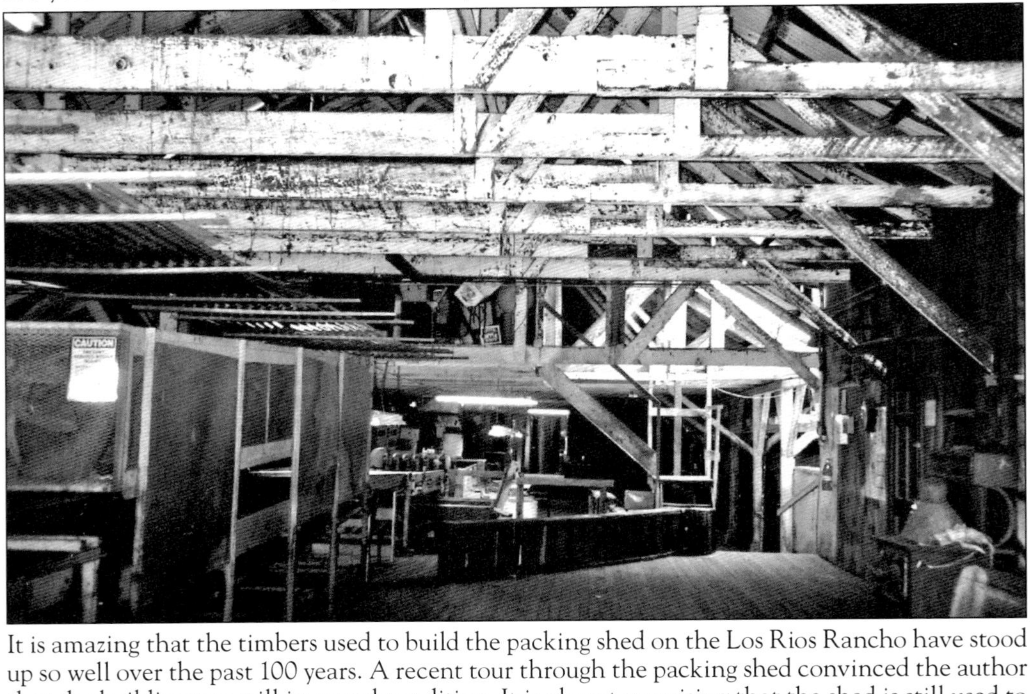

It is amazing that the timbers used to build the packing shed on the Los Rios Rancho have stood up so well over the past 100 years. A recent tour through the packing shed convinced the author that the building was still in sound condition. It is almost surprising that the shed is still used to process apples in a similar way as was done those many years ago.

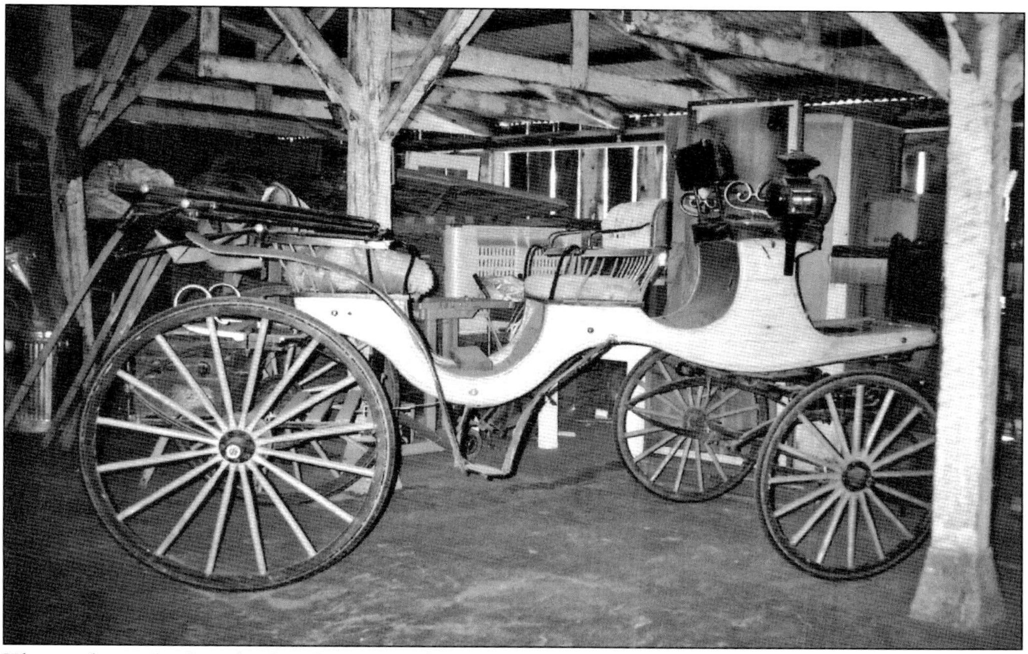

The packing shed at the Los Rios Rancho is immense and harbors a large cold-storage room for storing apples. The pictured buggy parked in the shed belongs to the Rileys and is one of their prized possessions. It is a well-known, familiar entity in the community, often entered in parades passing along the streets of Yucaipa.

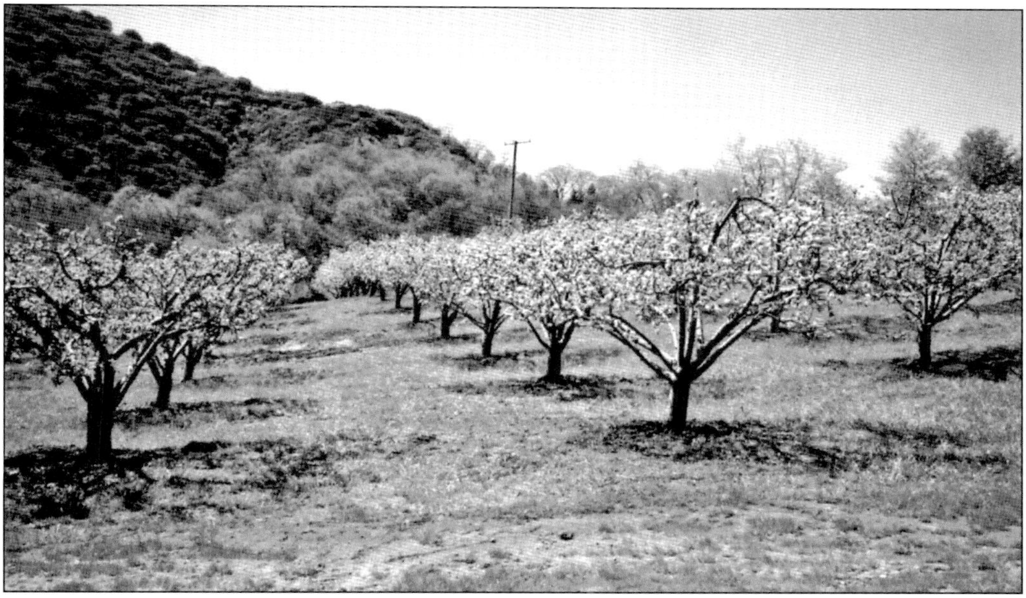

In 1995, the Wildlands Conservancy purchased the large ranch, now the Los Rios Ranch, from the descendents of the Rivers in an effort to save it from certain development. They worked diligently to return some of the land to native habitat. In 2004, the Wildlands Conservatory and Devon Riley joined forces on preservation and the Rileys were able to purchase the property and plant new trees.

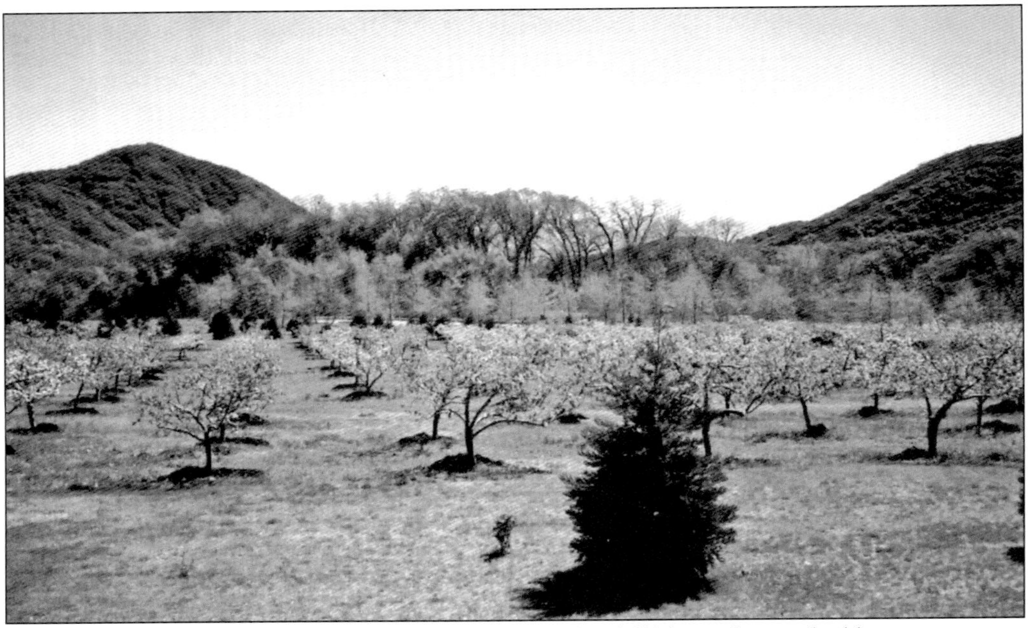

There is perhaps no greater beauty than a fruit orchard in full bloom during the blooming season. This photograph was captured during the height of the blooming season at the Los Rios Rancho, an orchard with mature apple trees. These trees produce an abundance of apples during the season. The ones shown here are organically grown with compost instead of synthetic fertilizer surrounding the tree trunk.

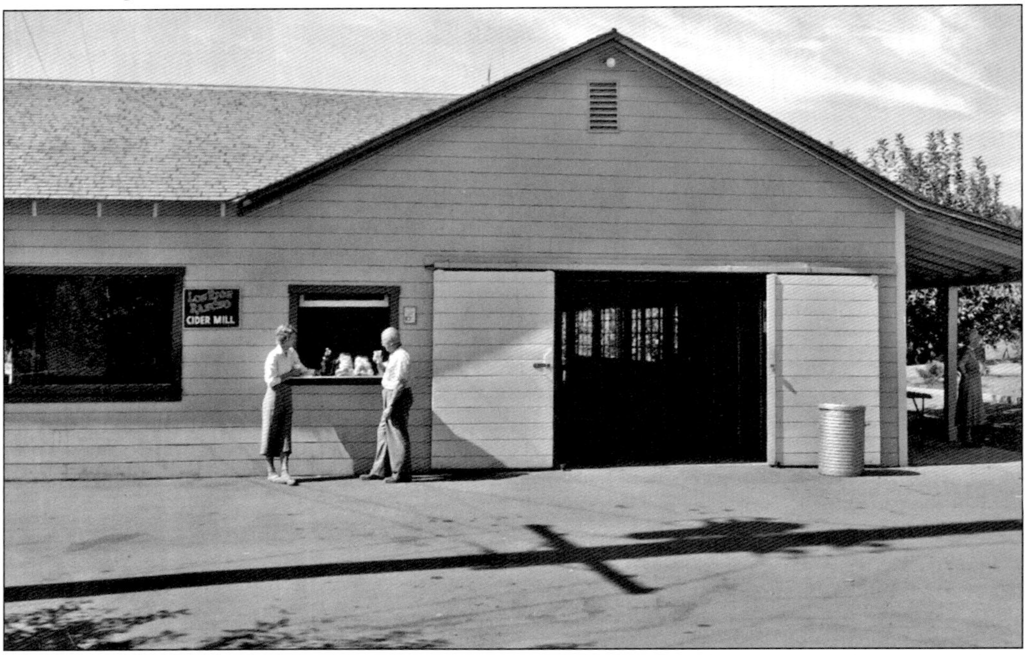

Mrs. Dick Bloomer and Guy Bogart stand enjoying a drink of apple cider outside a cider mill in 1954 at the Los Rios Ranch. Cider is one of the major by-products of the apples grown in this area and tourists often come here to buy cider, as well as apples. (Courtesy of SGPHS.)

Guy Bogart stands holding a basket of apples as Isaac Ford describes the apple variety to him. Ford, who is 94 years old in this 1956 photograph, owns the Ford Ranch and sells the popular Snow-line apple brand and cider. Note the many baskets of apples that have been picked and will be marketed. (Photograph by Leonard McCulloh; courtesy of SGPHS.)

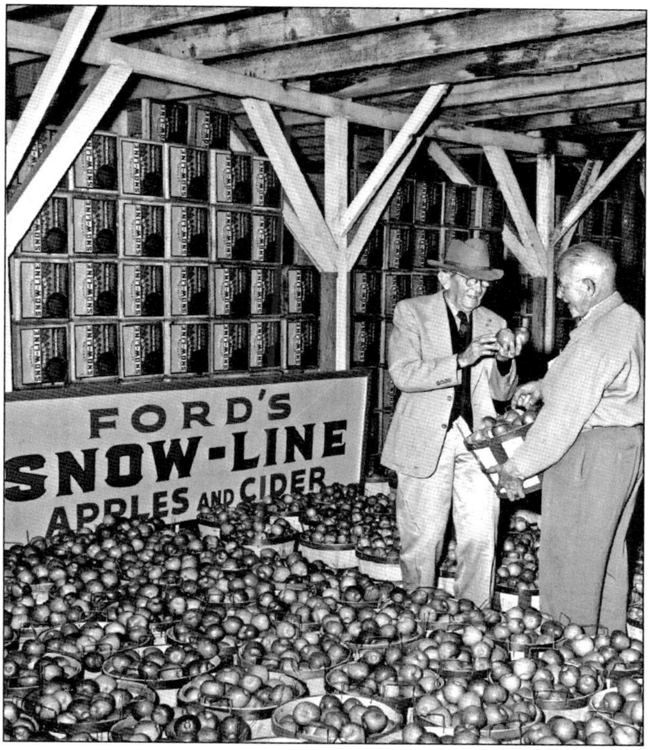

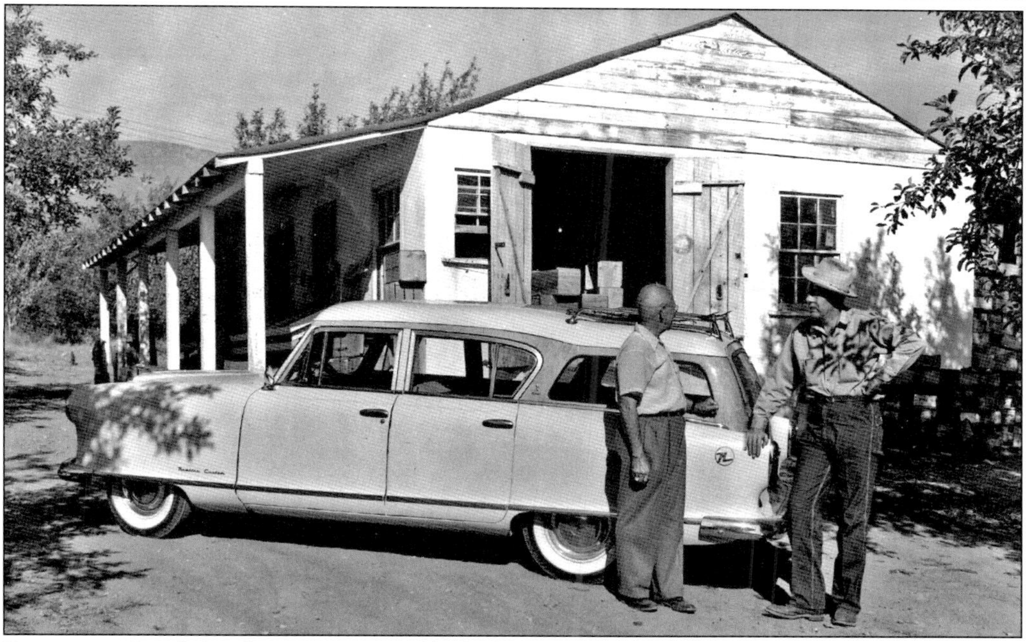

Bogart stands at left talking to Stan Bedford of Sleepy Hollow Ranch in 1954. Bogart made many friends in the agricultural community and he often visited them and gave them his support. It was apple ranches such as this, north of Cherry Valley, that grew apples rivaling places nearby. People came long distances to buy apples here. (Courtesy of SGPHS.)

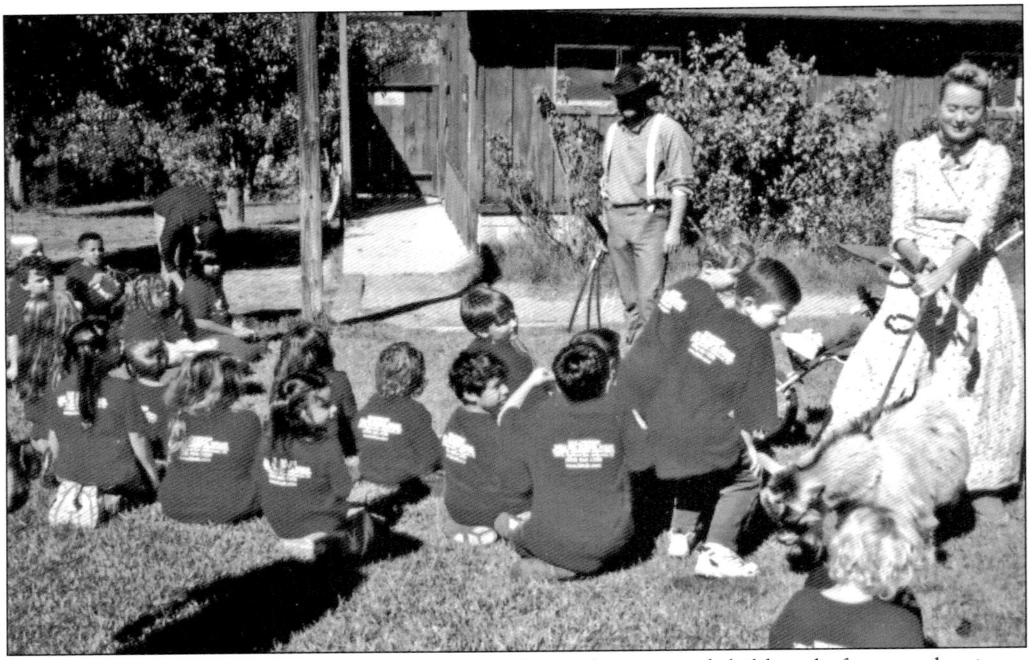

Jessie Riley, one of 36 Riley relatives, stands in front of a group of children before conducting a tour of one of the Serrano and Yucaipa Indian trails around the Riley Ranch grounds. Field trips, hayrides, dances, and barbecues are frequent at the ranch. Although a farming venture, the Riley farm has become a great tourist site. (Courtesy of Jessie Riley.)

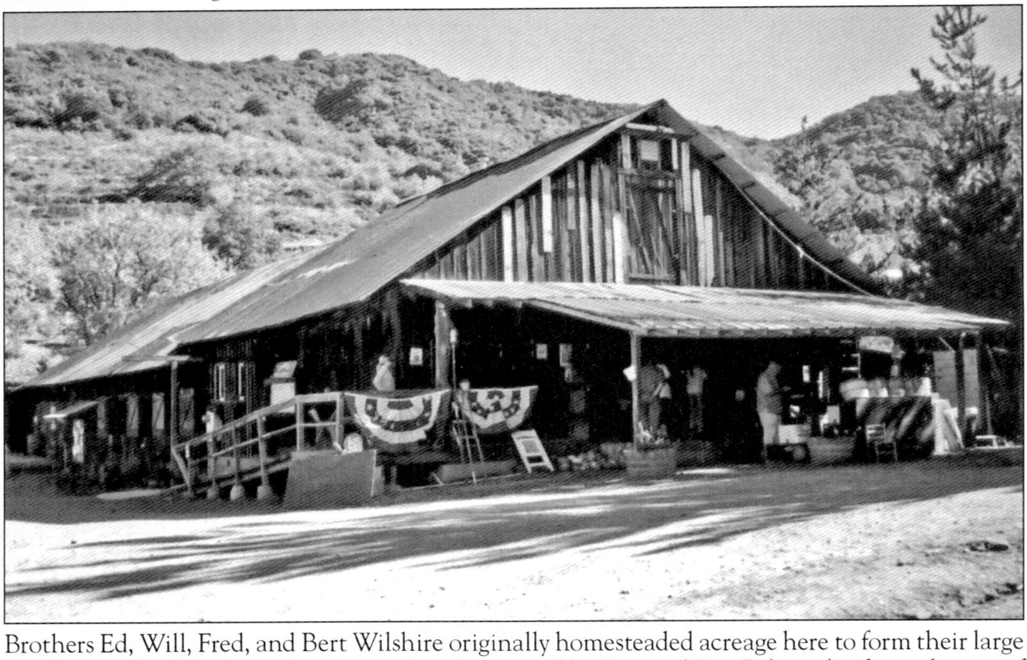

Brothers Ed, Will, Fred, and Bert Wilshire originally homesteaded acreage here to form their large ranch in Oak Glen. It was later owned and operated by Ray and Bea Riley, who farmed some of the 760 acres, growing apples and other fruits. More recently, it has been adapted to a tourist site as well. The old Wilshire packing shed pictured still stands.

Four

Edward Dean Museum and Gardens

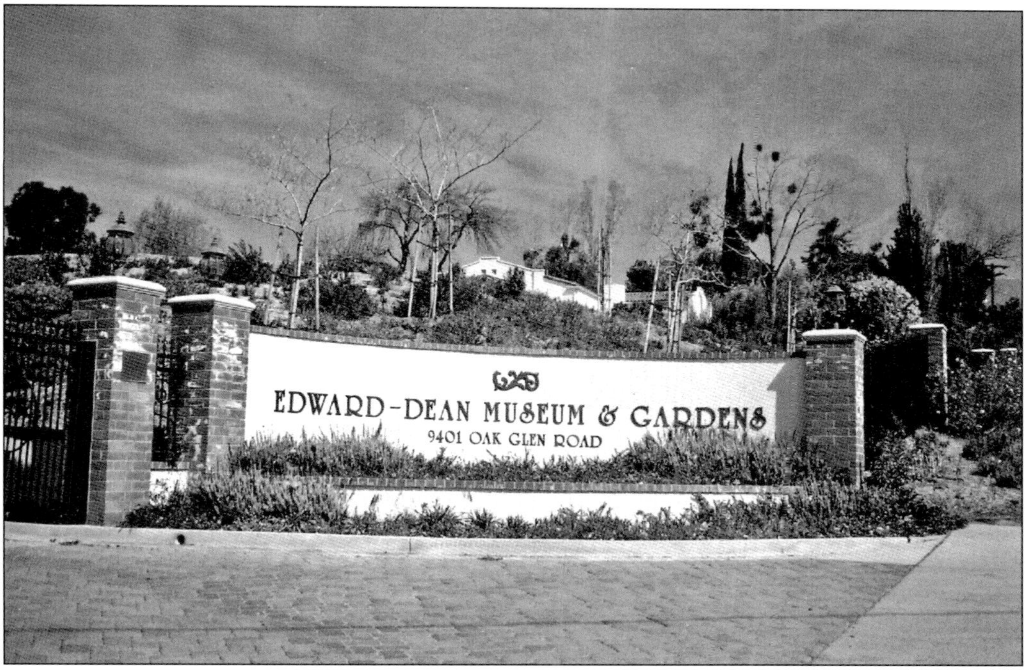

This is the entrance to the Edward Dean Museum and Gardens, located at Cherry Valley in the foothills leading to Oak Glen. The museum has a prized collection of 16th–19th century decorative arts. Temporary exhibits are shown routinely each year, featuring local, national, and international displays of decorative arts from past and present artists and collectors.

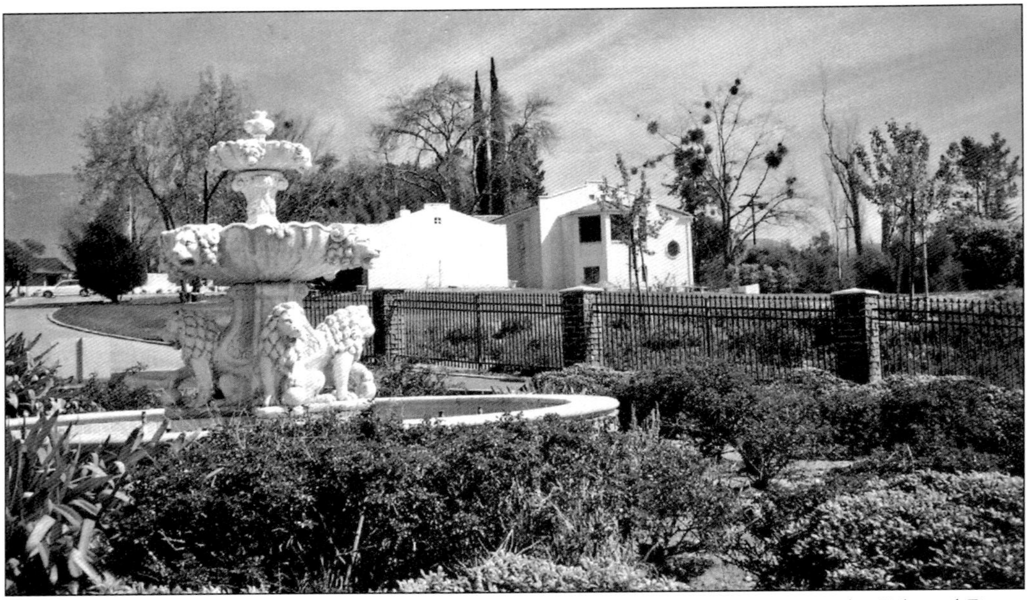

A large fountain, decorated with lions, stands just inside the entrance gate to the Edward Dean Museum and Gardens. A circular drive circumvents the fountain giving convenient ingress and egress to the museum. The backdrop of the museum is highlighted behind the fence along the entrance drive.

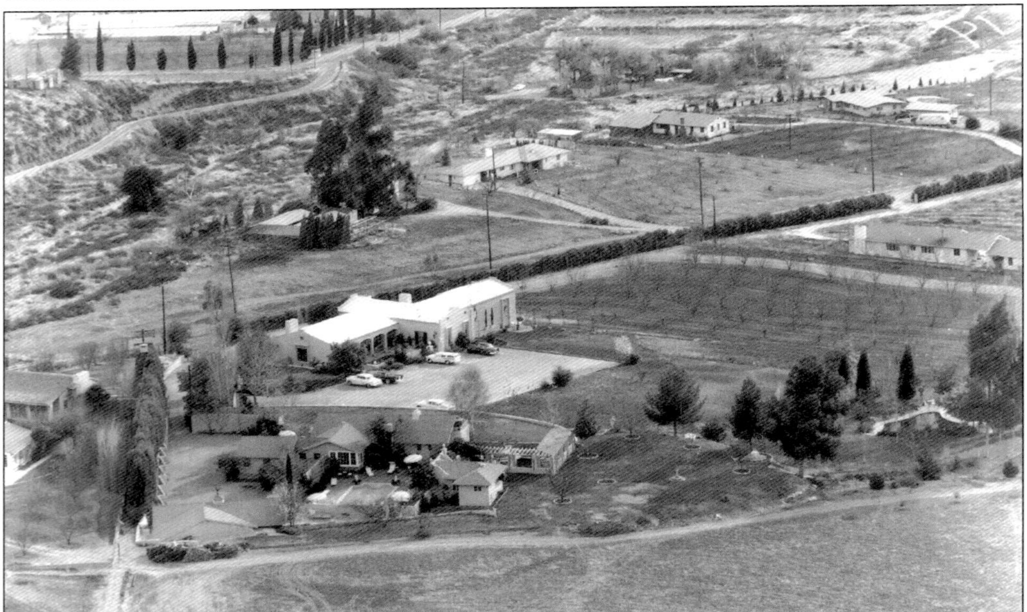

This 1957 aerial photograph shows the Edward Dean Museum surrounded by a group of sparse houses, contrasting what is seen today. The old house in the foreground of the picture was on the grounds before the acreage for the museum site was purchased, when in the 1950s Edward Eberle and Dean W. Stout decided to purchase a cluster of buildings on beautifully landscaped grounds in Cherry Valley. (Courtesy of EDM&G.)

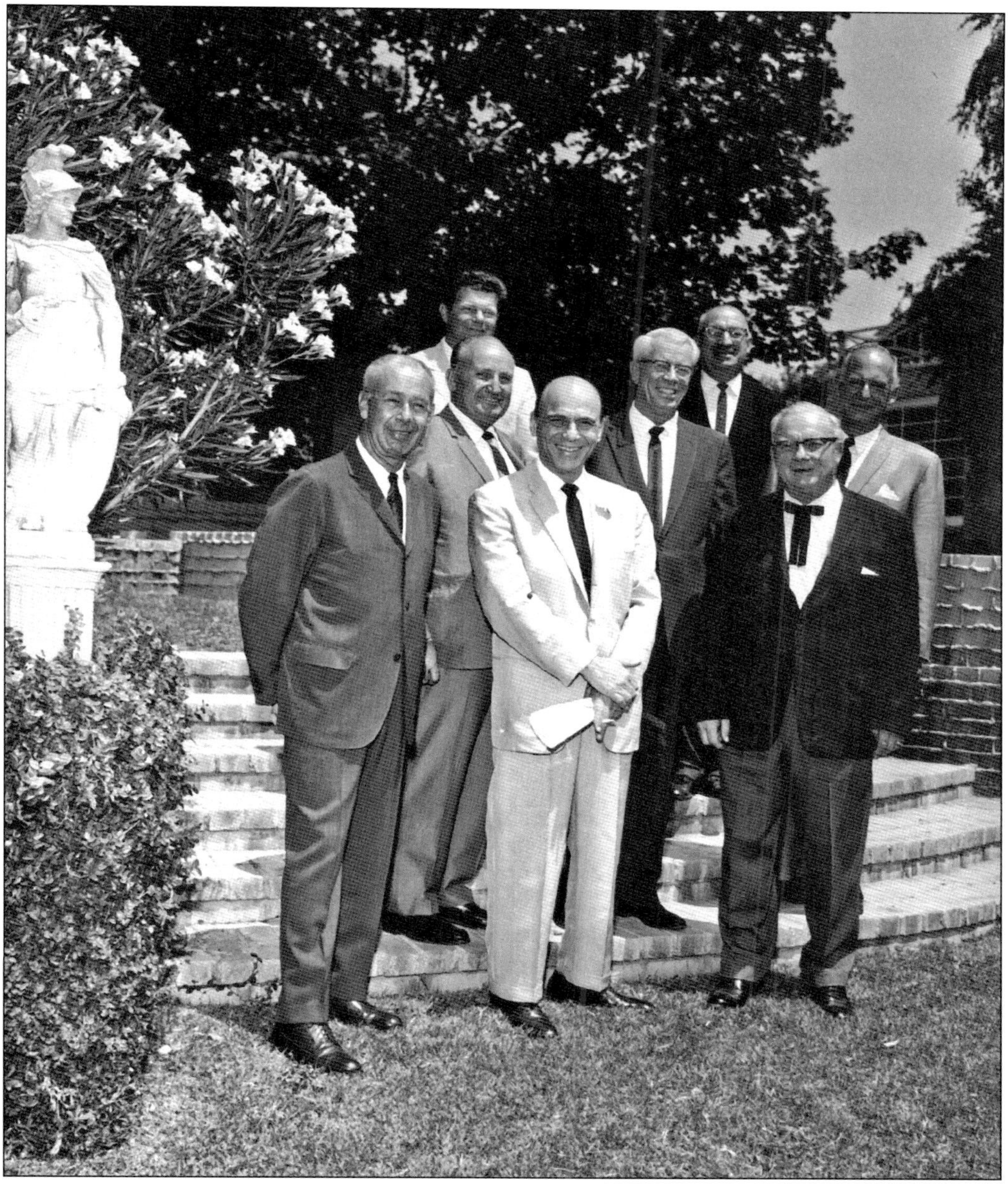

On the steps of the Formal Garden area is a group of owners and supporters from the early era of the museum. Shown from left to right are (first row) Dean Stout, John Green, and supervisor Paul Anderson; (second row) Edward H. Walker, supervisor William Cook, and Edward Eberle; (third row) Arthur Littleworth and Harry Creasy. (Courtesy of EDM&G)

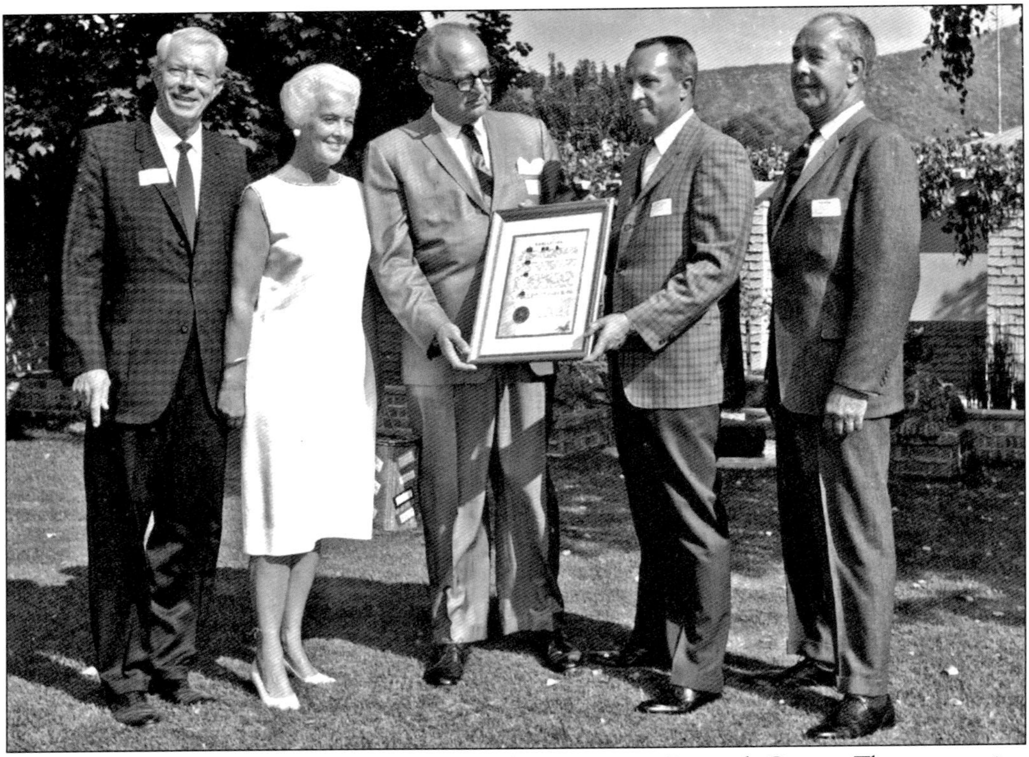

In 1964, Edward Eberle and Dean W. Stout gifted their museum to Riverside County. The presentation of this gift is captured in this photograph. Standing from left to right are county supervisor W. Cook, Mrs. Cook, Edward Eberle, Dean Stout, and supervisor N. Davis. Edward and Dean are accepting the award presented in appreciation by the county. (Courtesy of EDM&G.)

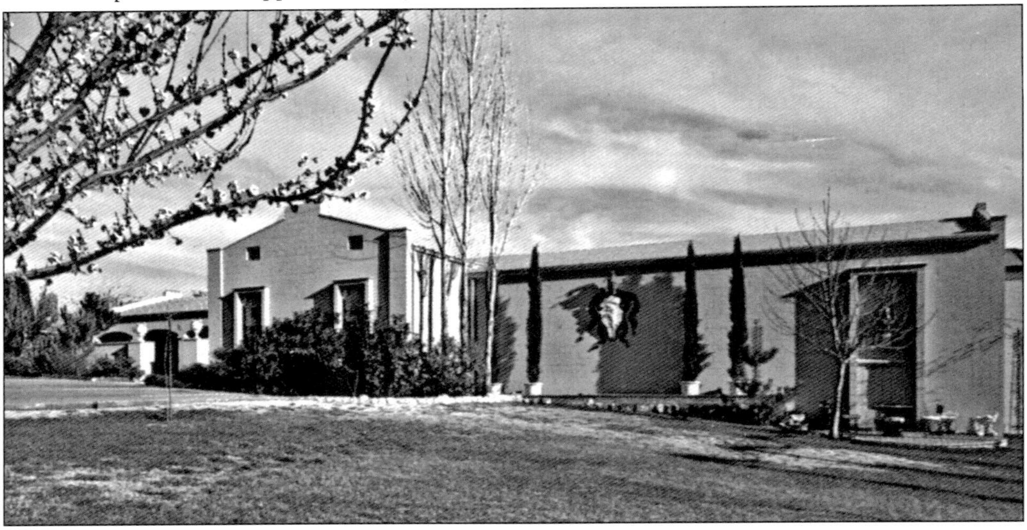

An early scene of the museum structure is shown in this photograph. The 14th-century crest seen on the wall of the right wing of the museum building was later moved to the west wall, in the upper portion of the building to the left. Of note is the small chestnut tree that was planted at the right of the picture. (Courtesy of EDM&G.)

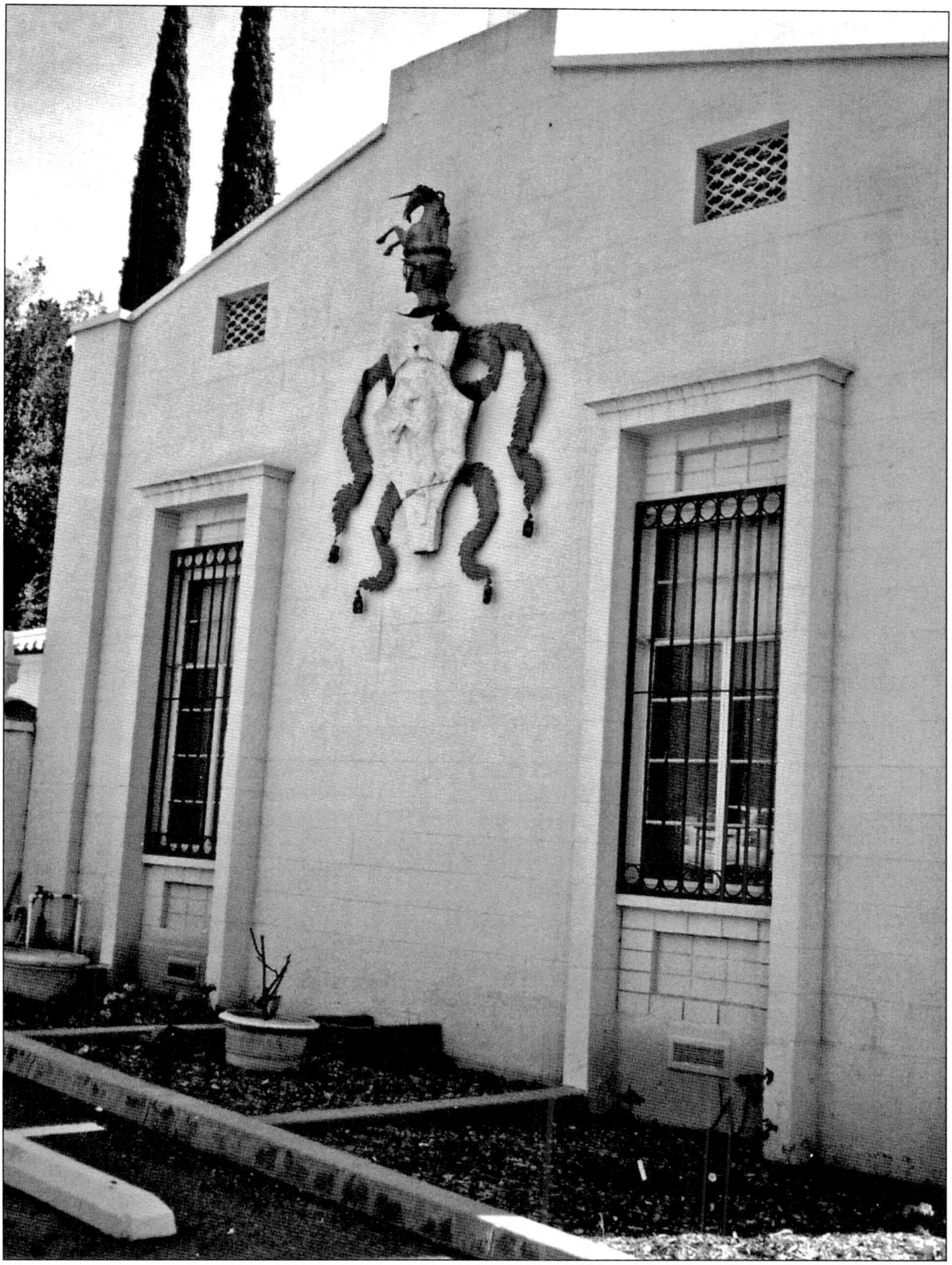

The 14th-century crest of the Piccinardi family in Italy is mounted on the west wall of the museum. It measures 8 feet high and 5.5 feet across. Originally, it was mounted on the villa of the Marchese Sommi-Piccinardi in Brescia, Italy, near Verona. After the villa was ruined during World War II bombing, the crest was found, restored, and later purchased by Edward Eberle.

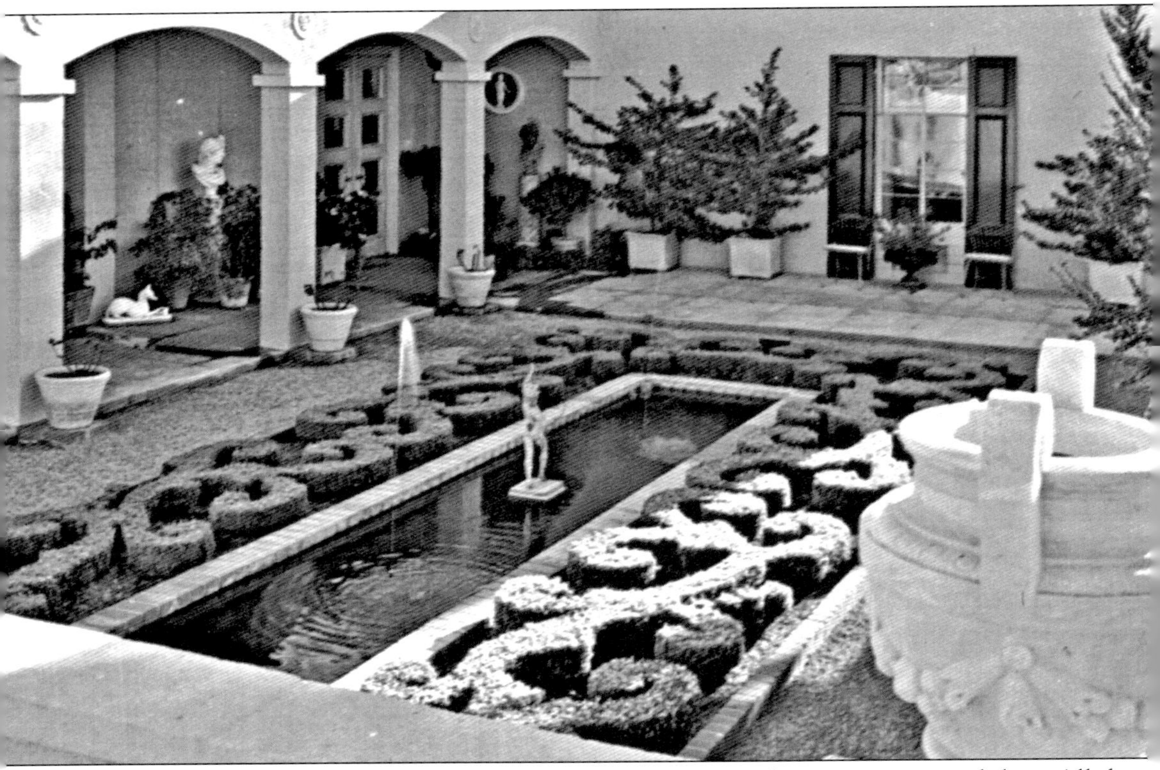

The reflecting-pool, garden entry to the museum in 1964 is shown as it appeared then. All the decorative boxwood was removed sometime in the 1990s. However, the attractive entry to the museum still remains and is an important entity of the museum; it is used as a reception gathering place for opening of special events. (Courtesy of EDM&G.)

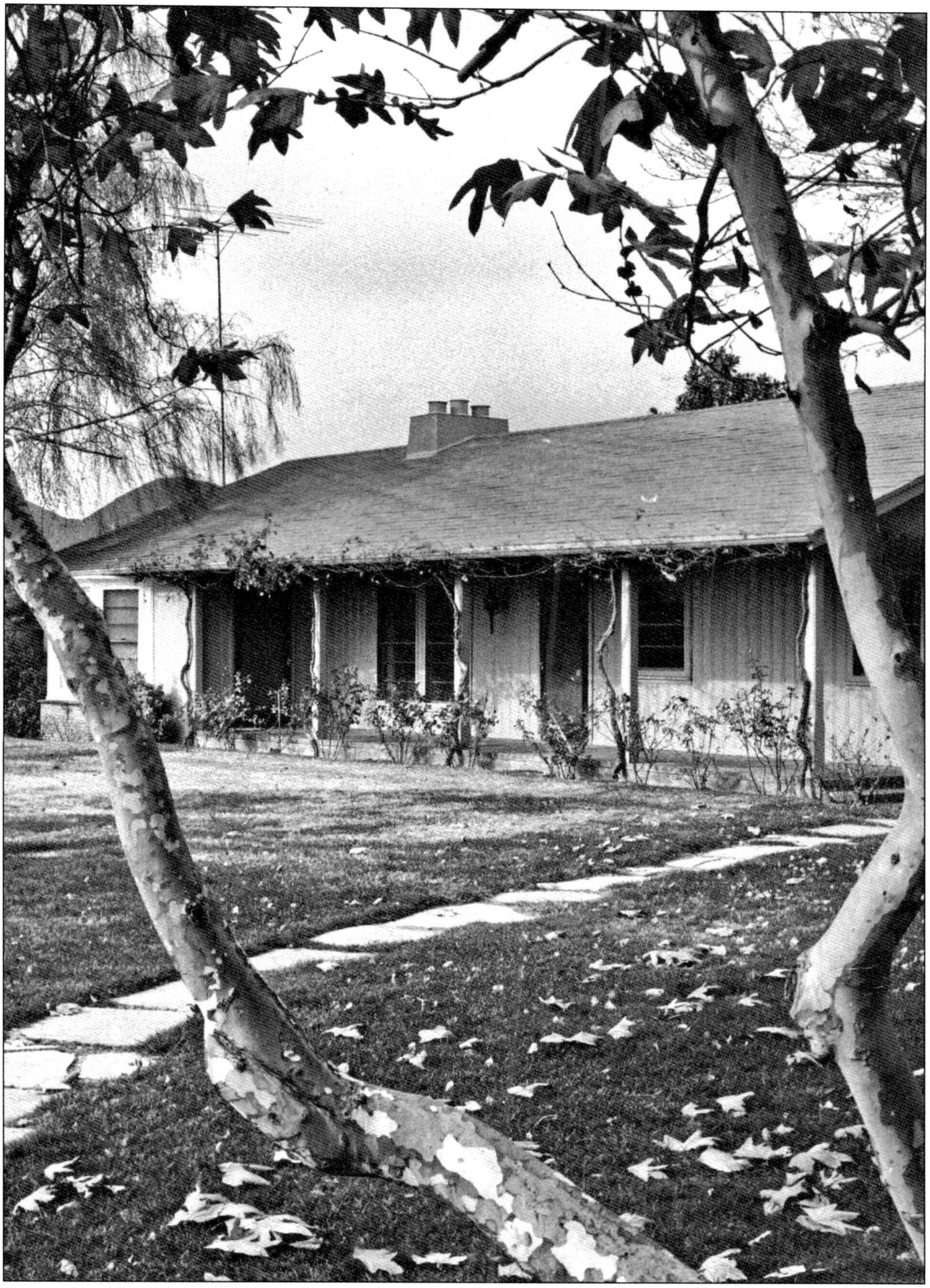

Framed between the limbs of this tree, the museum office and conference room can be seen as it appeared in 1972. Later in the 1970s, the building was renovated, the pool covered, and a pavilion was built to accommodate weddings. Other functions are held in the pavilion as well.

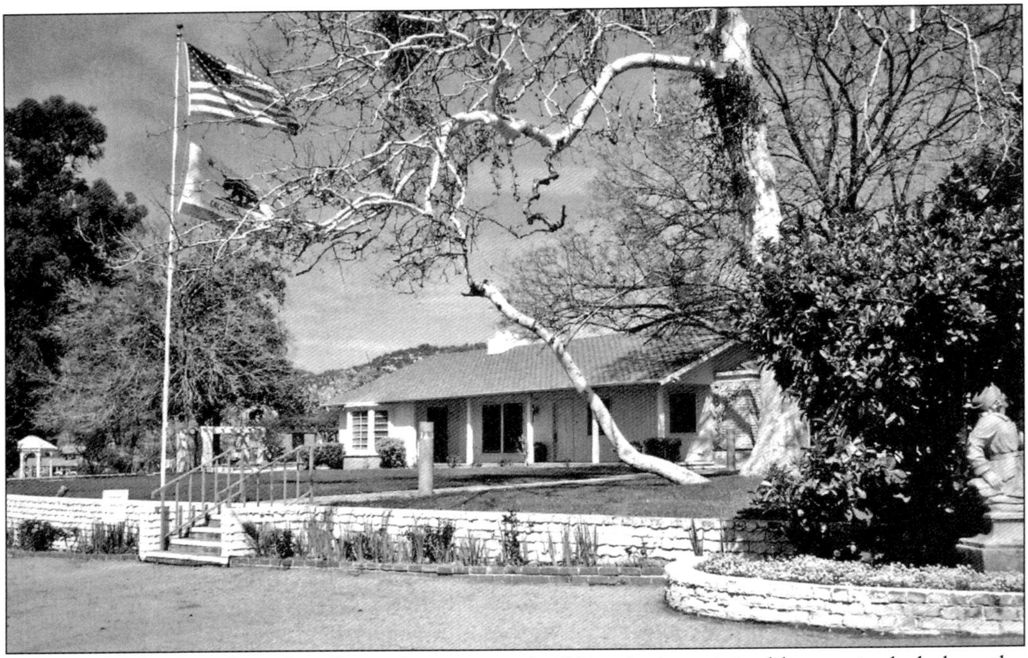

Shown standing on the ridge above the museum building is the original house, included on the acreage purchased for the museum site, which today is called the Upper House; it is the home of the museum office and conference room where board meetings are routinely held each month. Note the landscape that has been added since it was acquired. (Courtesy of EDM&G.)

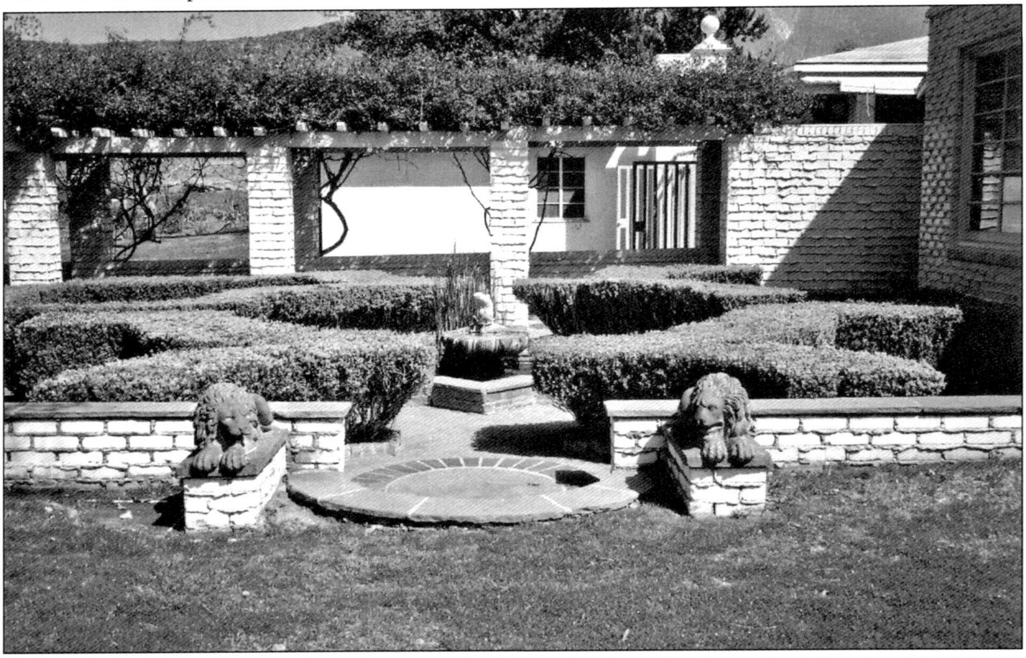

Two lions lie crouched, guarding the Lion's Garden, which was built on the left side of the Upper House. The maze of hedges that wraps through the garden surrounds a water fountain in the center. A walkway leads to the rear of the house, to a pavilion, and another small outer building.

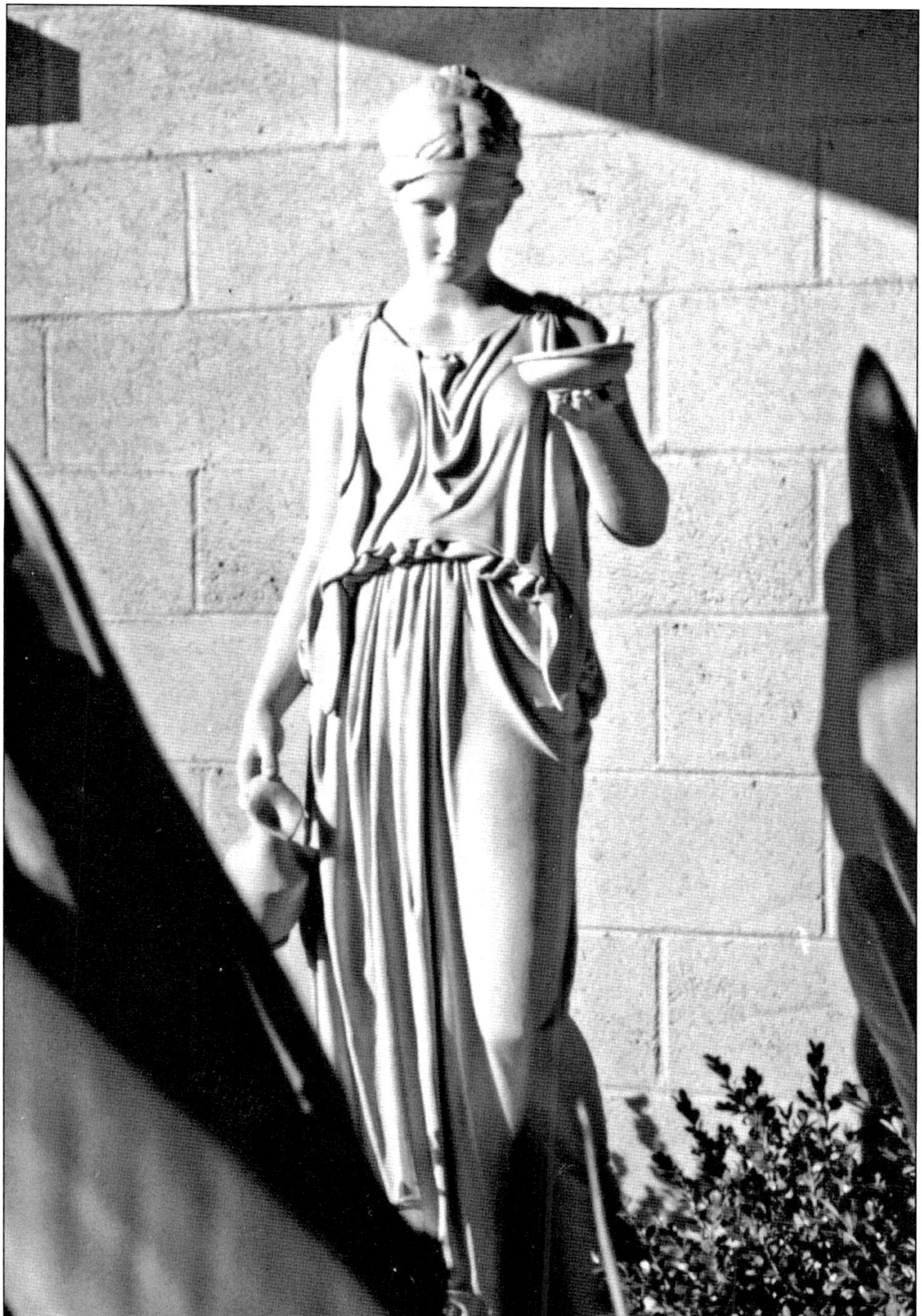

A Hebe goddess statue stands near to the entrance of the museum. The statue represents the daughter of Zeus and Hera. Hebe was the goddess of youth, and according to one myth, she became the wife of Hercules after she was defied. Hebe is a minor Greek goddess that later was replaced by Ganymedes.

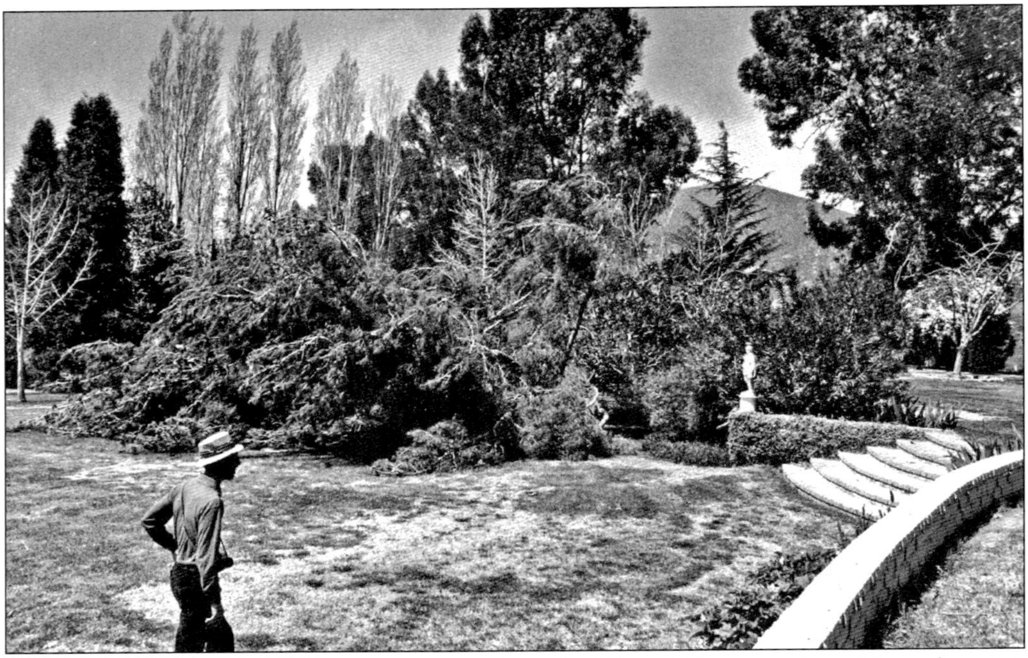

An unidentified man walks across the grounds of the Edward Dean Gardens. Many that visit these gardens find the stroll on these grounds pleasant. This man has a camera strapped over his shoulder and, likewise, is equipped to take photographs of some of the beautiful sights throughout his walk.

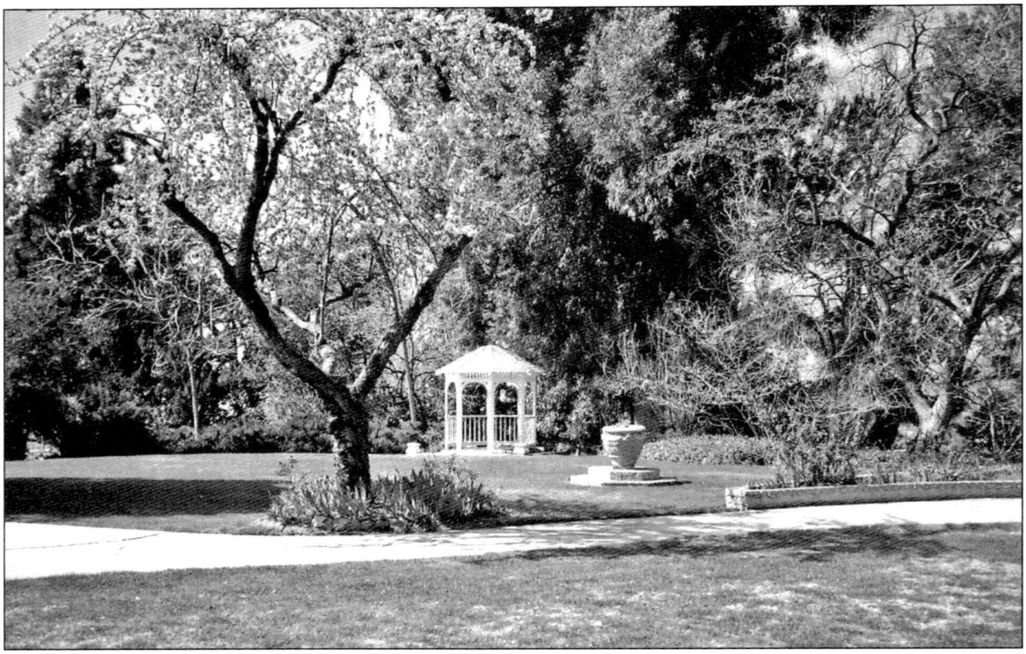

A gazebo highlights an area under the blush, green foliage in the parklike garden section of the Edward Dean Gardens. Many find this an enjoyable place to stop and visit during their walk through the park. Some relish it as a place to come back for future activities.

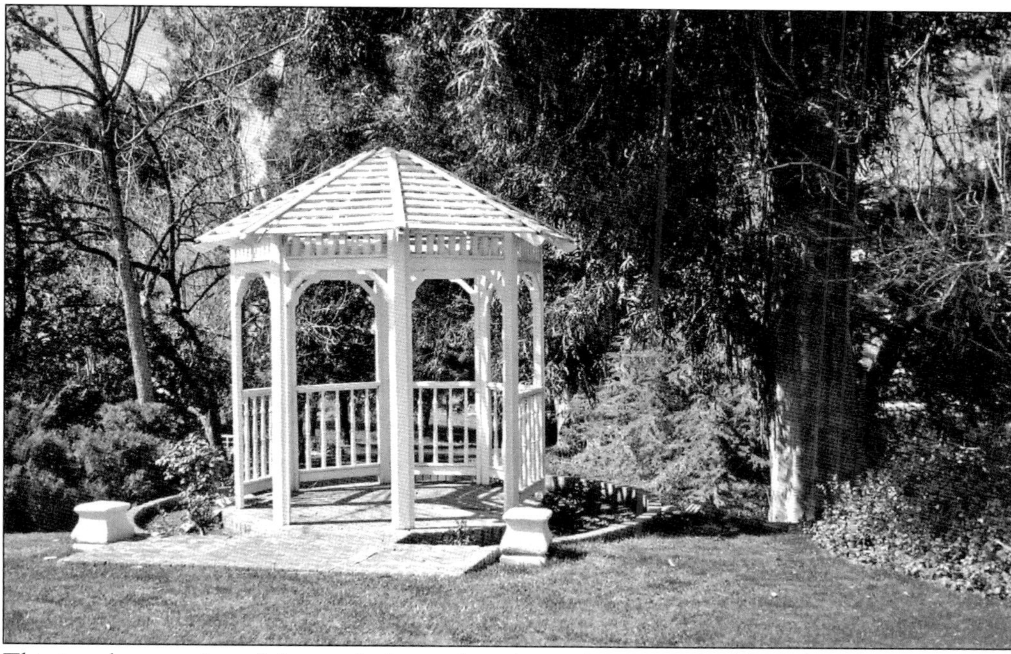

This is a close-up view of the gazebo located on the garden grounds of the Edward Dean Museum and Gardens. It allures many who come here to use the site as a center for small group functions or events.

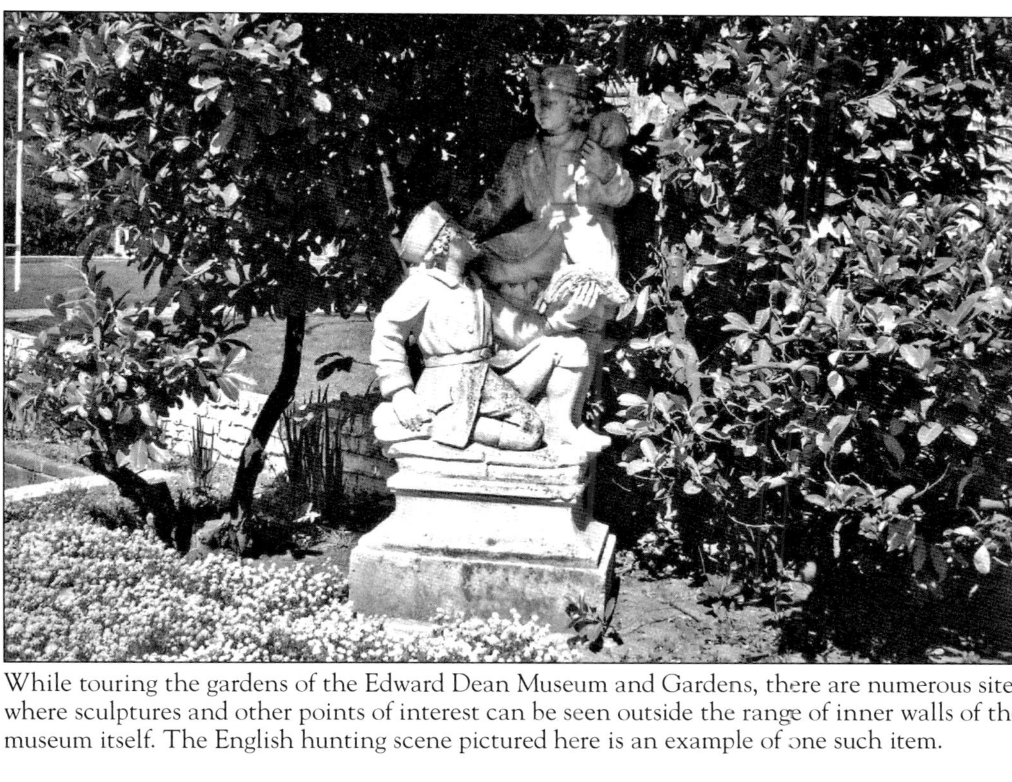

While touring the gardens of the Edward Dean Museum and Gardens, there are numerous sites where sculptures and other points of interest can be seen outside the range of inner walls of the museum itself. The English hunting scene pictured here is an example of one such item.

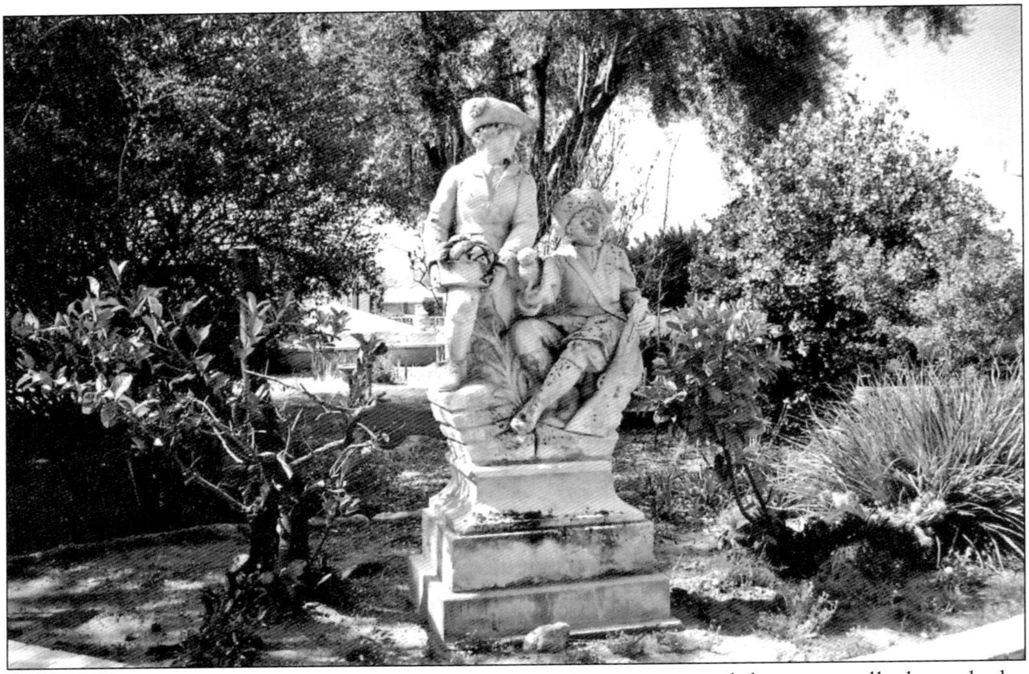

This sculpture is an English hunting scene that can be encountered during a walk through the museum's park gardens. It is adapted from the era when hunting was often exemplified. Note the small gun held by the boy sitting at right. Sculptures of this type were popular during this era.

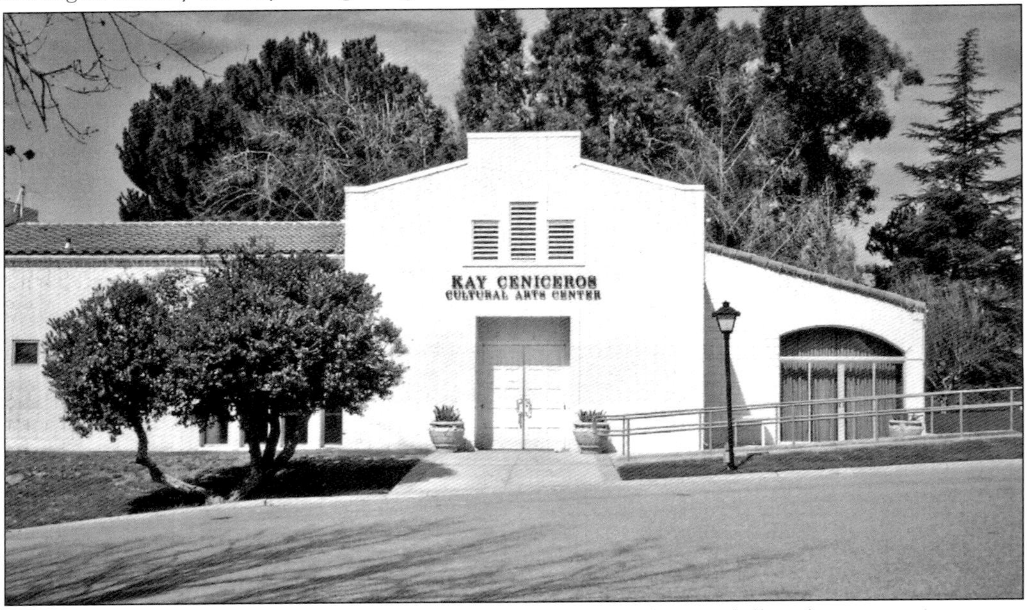

The Kay Ceniceros Cultural Arts Center came into existence during a lull in the museum's activity. Supporters of the museum rallied to set up a museum foundation to help negotiate operations. Hoping to attract revenue-generating events, the county went the extra mile and built a 3,300-square-foot, special-events hall and named it in honor of a respected former supervisor. Many exciting events happen here throughout the year, including a free fall concert series.

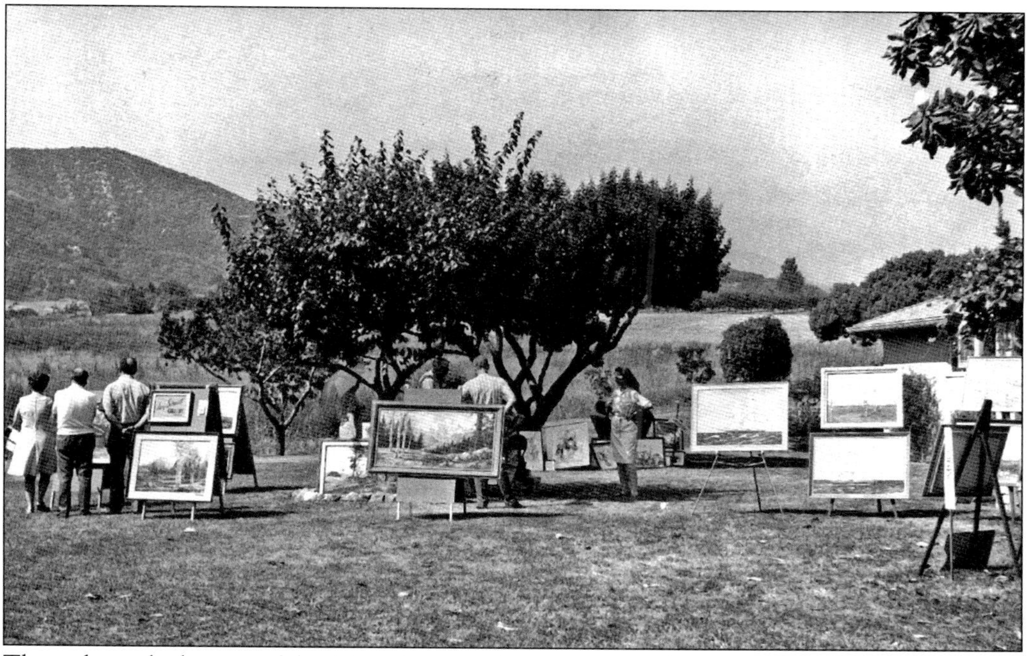

Throughout the history of the Edward Dean Museum and Gardens, art shows have been popular events. Pictured at this particular show are the paintings of some artists participating in the event. The art shows are not limited to locals, as people from far distances also come to present their artwork. (Courtesy of EDM&G.)

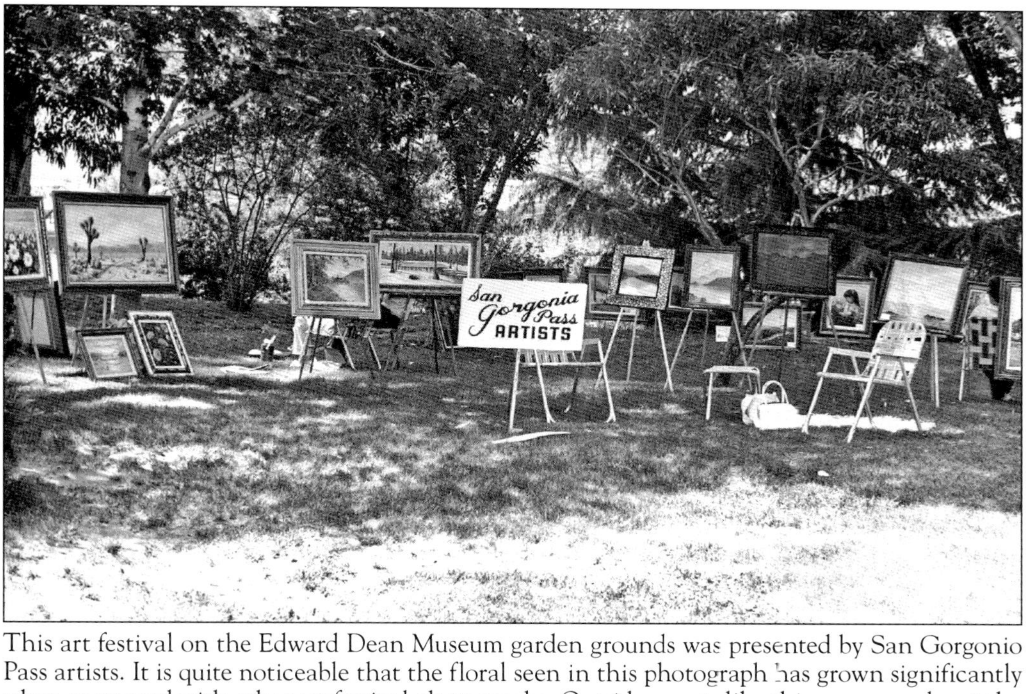

This art festival on the Edward Dean Museum garden grounds was presented by San Gorgonio Pass artists. It is quite noticeable that the floral seen in this photograph has grown significantly when compared with other art festival photographs. Outside events like this were popular at the Edward Dean Museum. (Courtesy of EDM&G.)

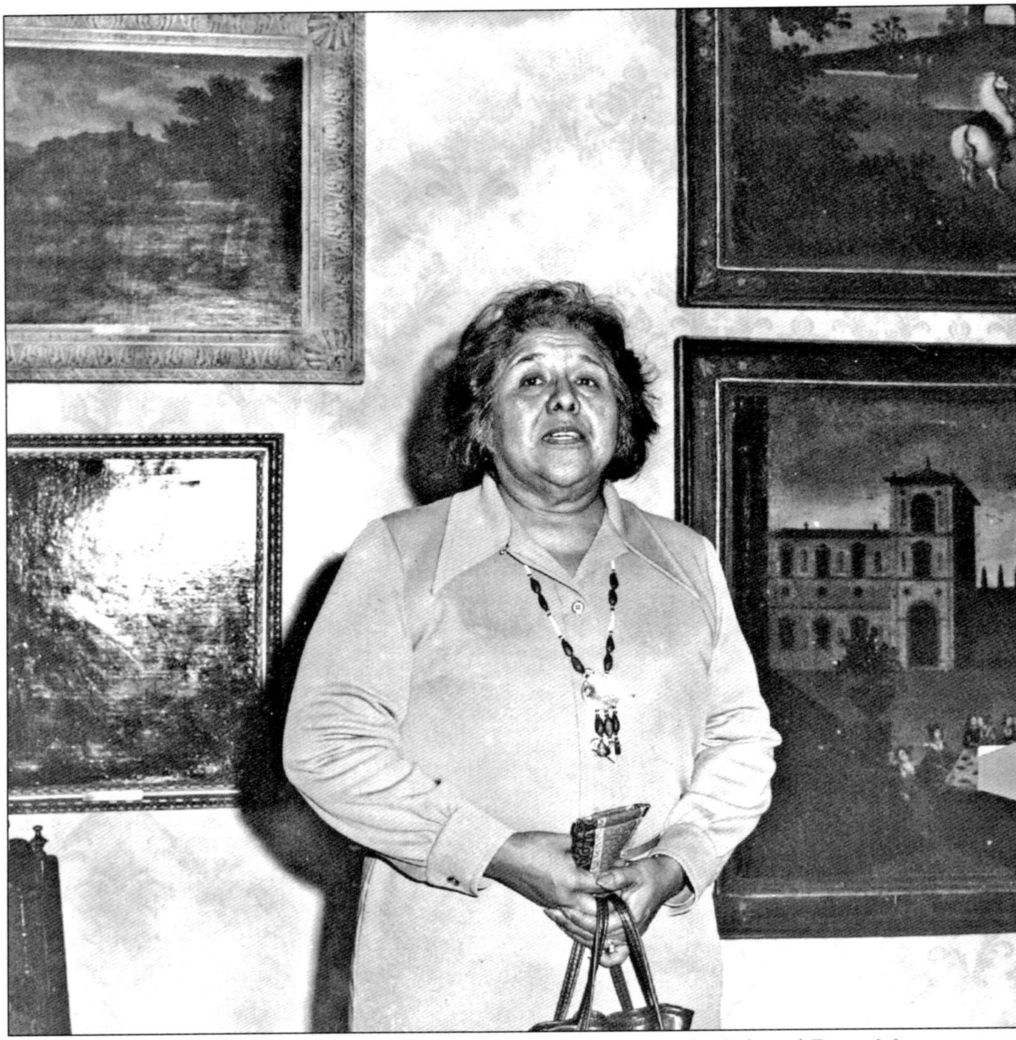

Katherine Siva Sauvel is in the South Gallery during a visit to the Edward Dean Museum in its early days. Katherine today lives on the Morongo Indian Reservation. She was cofounder of the Malki Museum, a landmark on the reservation, with Jane Penn and still manages the museum today. (Courtesy of EDM&G.)

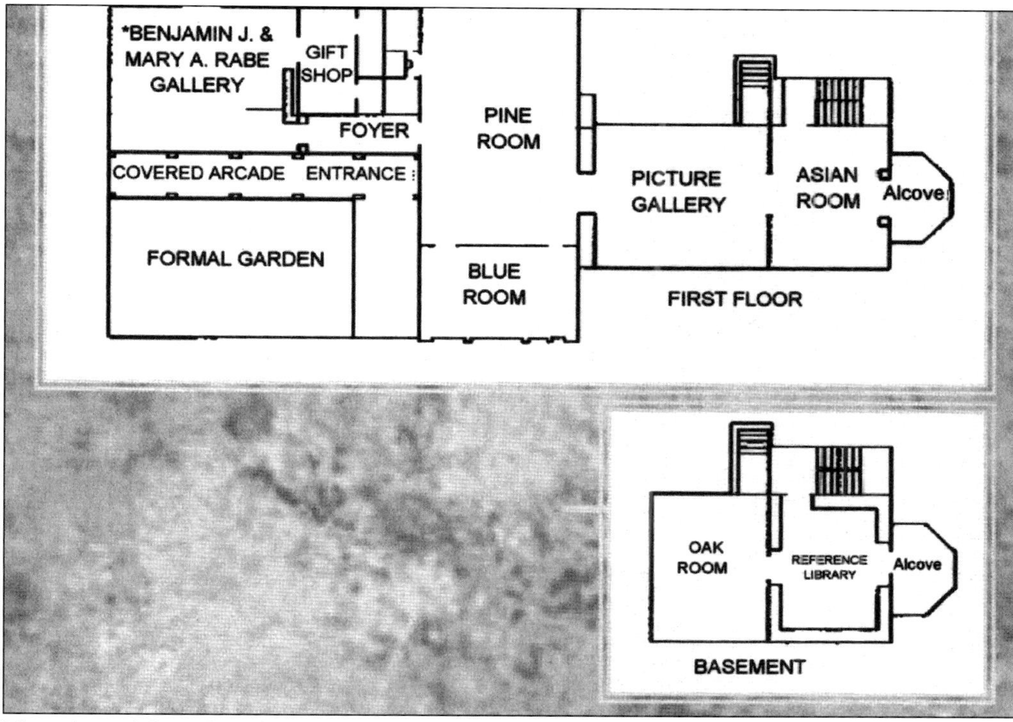

This plan of the Edward Dean Museum outlines the location of all the rooms, both upstairs on the first floor and in the basement. The Oriental Room (Asian Room) leads with a stairway to the bottom floor. (Courtesy of EDM&G.)

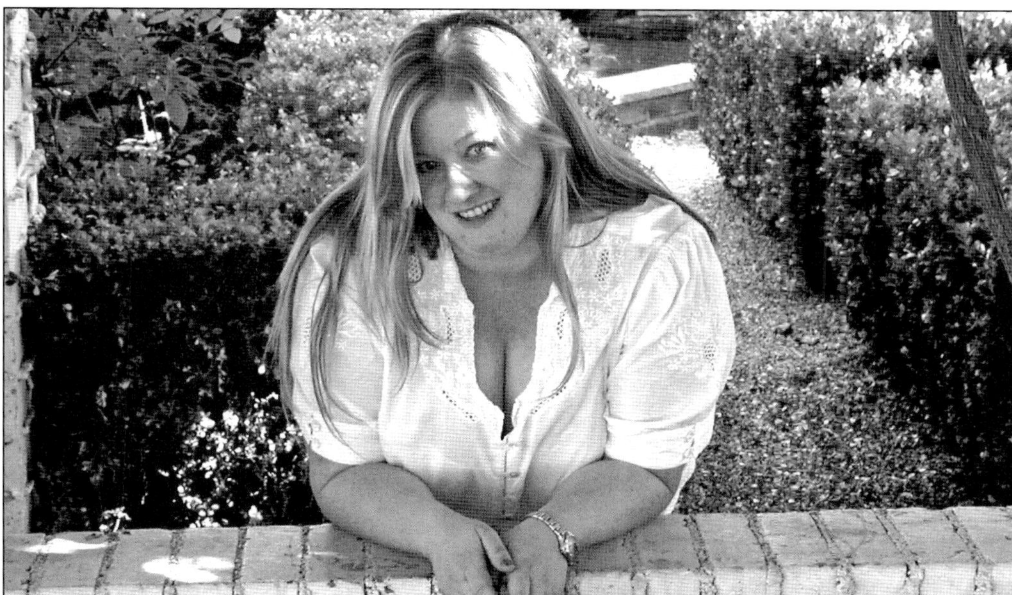

The Edward Dean Museum curator, Christine Burton, stands at a block wall next to her office in the Upper House. During the week, she is either here or at the Gilman Historical Ranch and Wagon Museum in Banning, where she is also the curator. (Courtesy of Christine Burton.)

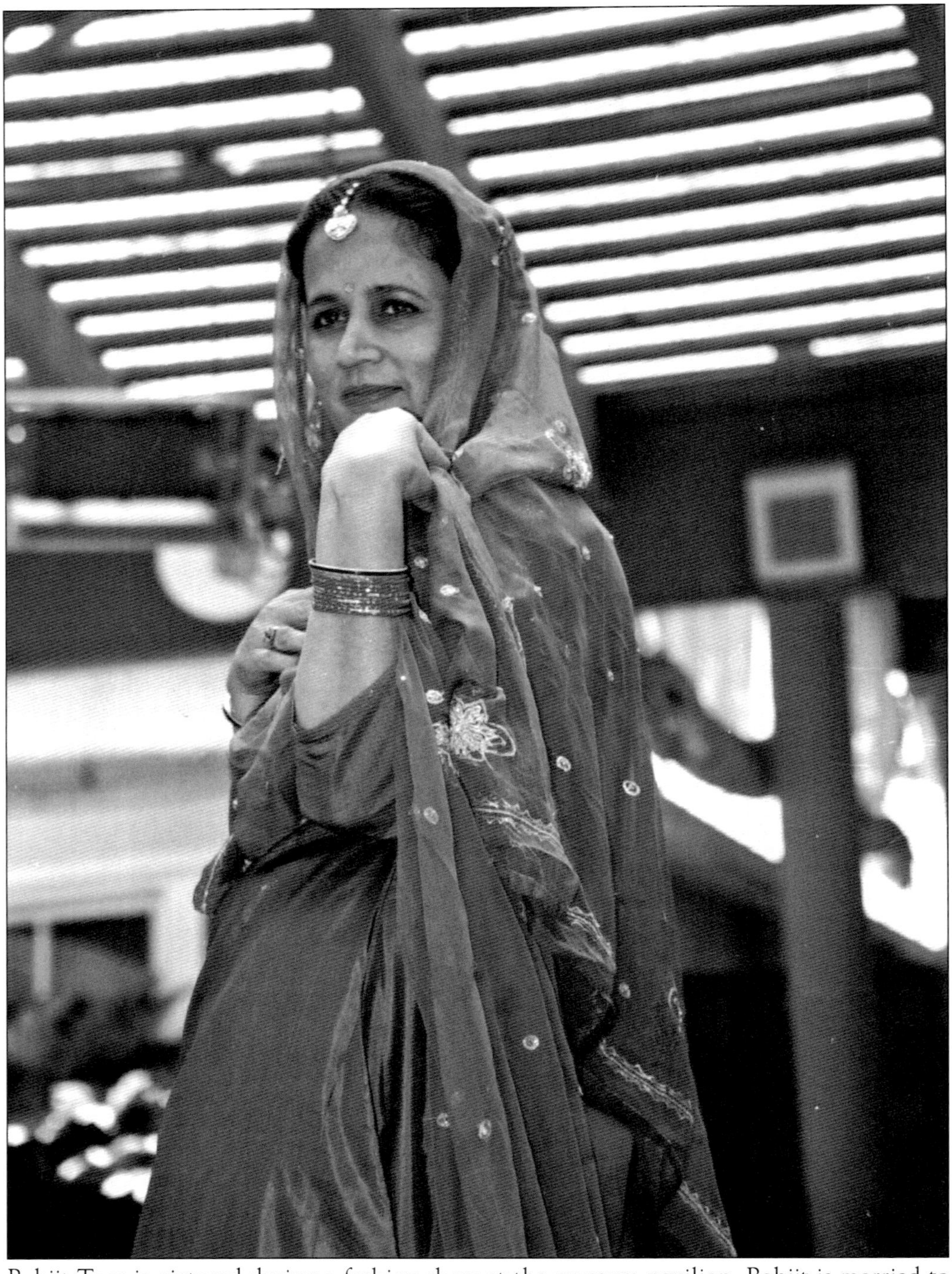

Bahjit Toor is pictured during a fashion show at the museum pavilion. Bahjit is married to Paul Toor and has worked almost 20 years for the Edward Dean Museum. She holds the title of museum assistant/education. Bahjit received a master of arts degree in modern history from Punjab University, Chandigarh, India. She remembers being interested in history since she was six years old. (Courtesy of EDM&G.)

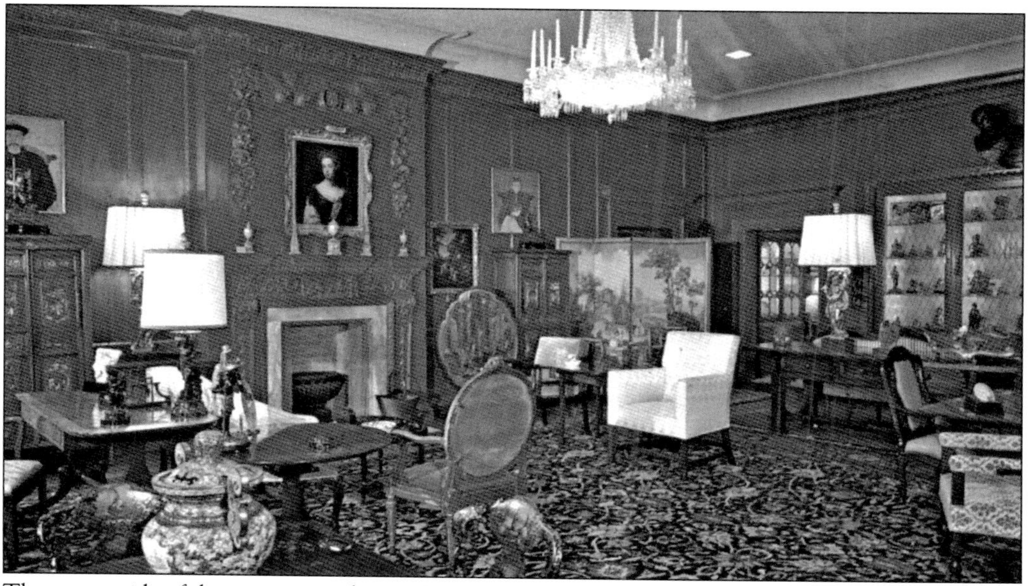

The great pride of the museum is the c. 1680 Pine Room. The room was originally the state bedroom of Cassiobury Park, the home of the Earl of Essex. William Randolph Hearst originally bought this home to incorporate its features into Hearst Castle, which was being built in California. The central stairway went to the Metropolitan Museum for their English display. The paneling, mantel, and cabinets were later incorporated in a house, and when it was demolished, Edward Eberle and Dean W. Stout purchased these items to build the Pine Room, as seen today. (Courtesy of EDM&G.)

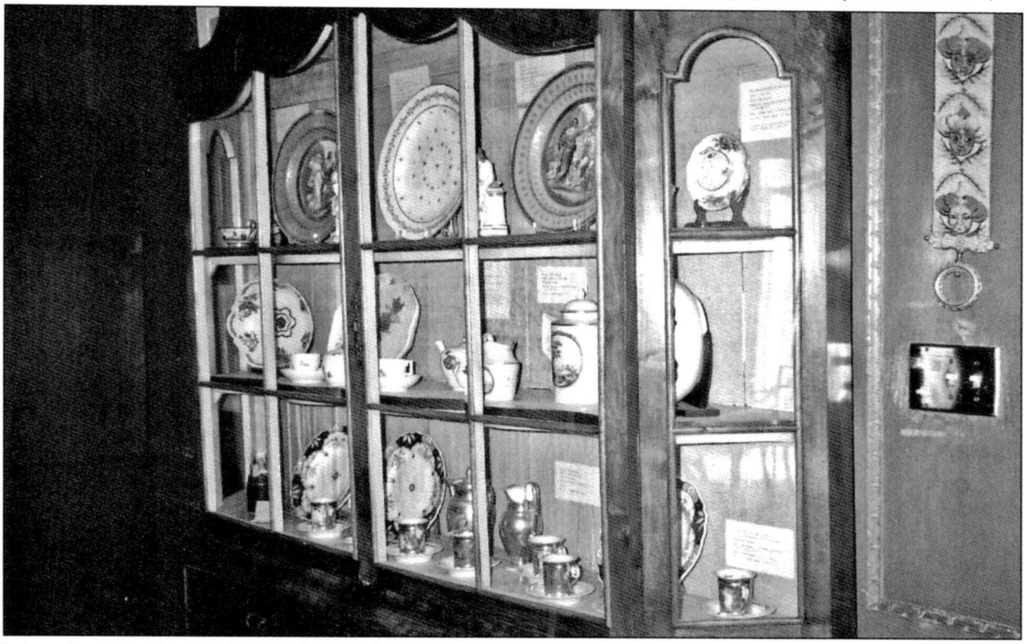

This display of porcelain is located in the Pine Room and can be seen at the beginning of the museum. The production of porcelain has a long history. While a type of soft-paste porcelain was made in Florence, Italy, at the Medici workshops in the 16th century, it was not until 1720 that porcelain was again produced in Italy on a significant scale. (Courtesy of EDM&G.)

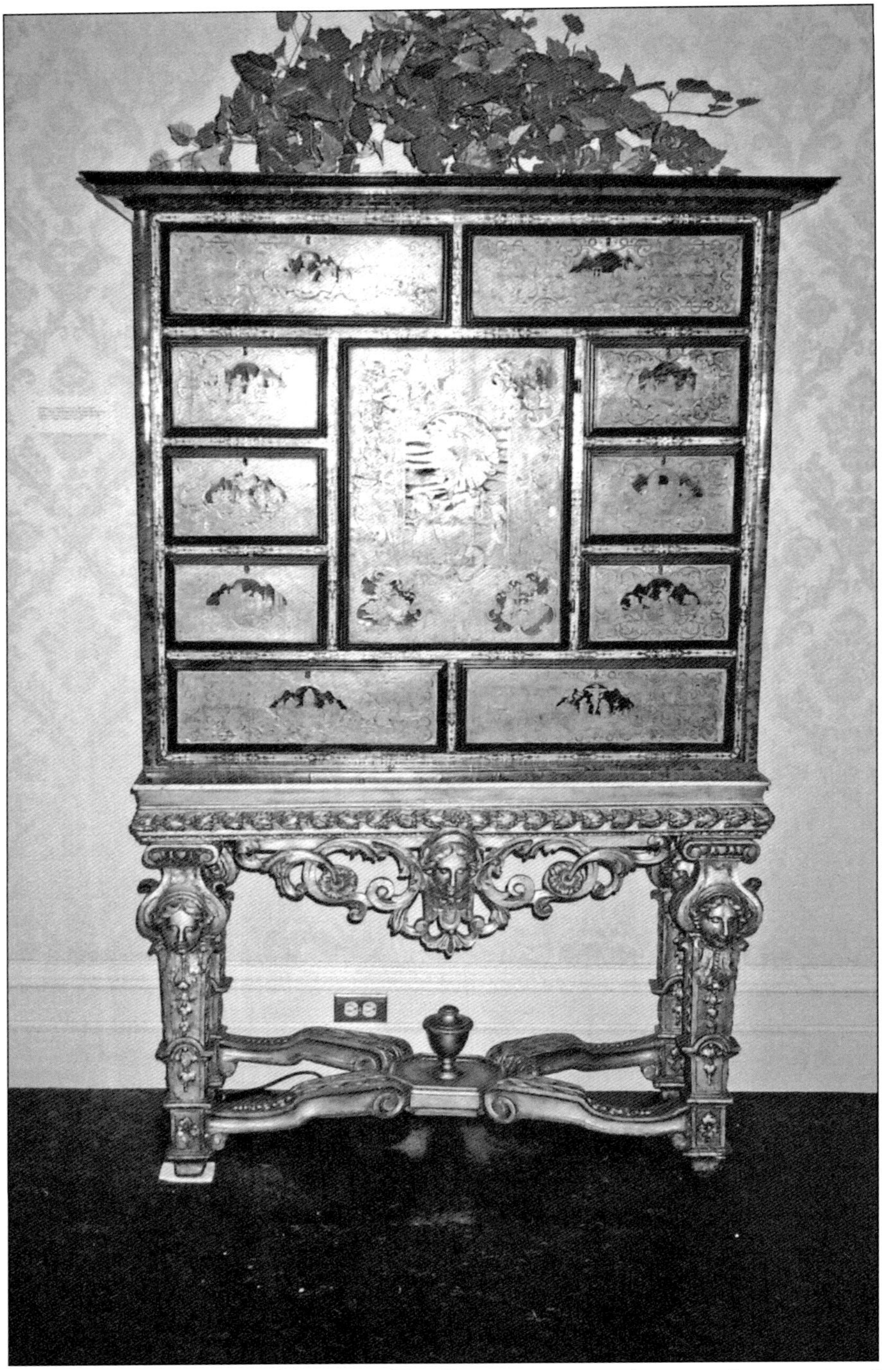

An 18th-century French chest of drawers of Boulle marquetry can be seen after entering the Pine Room. It was called Boulle marquetry because of the impressive and extensive use made of it by the French cabinetmaker, Andre-Charles Boulle (1642–1732). It is the art of applying decorative surface veneer onto solid wood. Thin sheets of veneer can be made from various types of exotic woods, horn, metals, turtle shell, bone ivory, and mother-of-pearl. (Courtesy of EDM&G.)

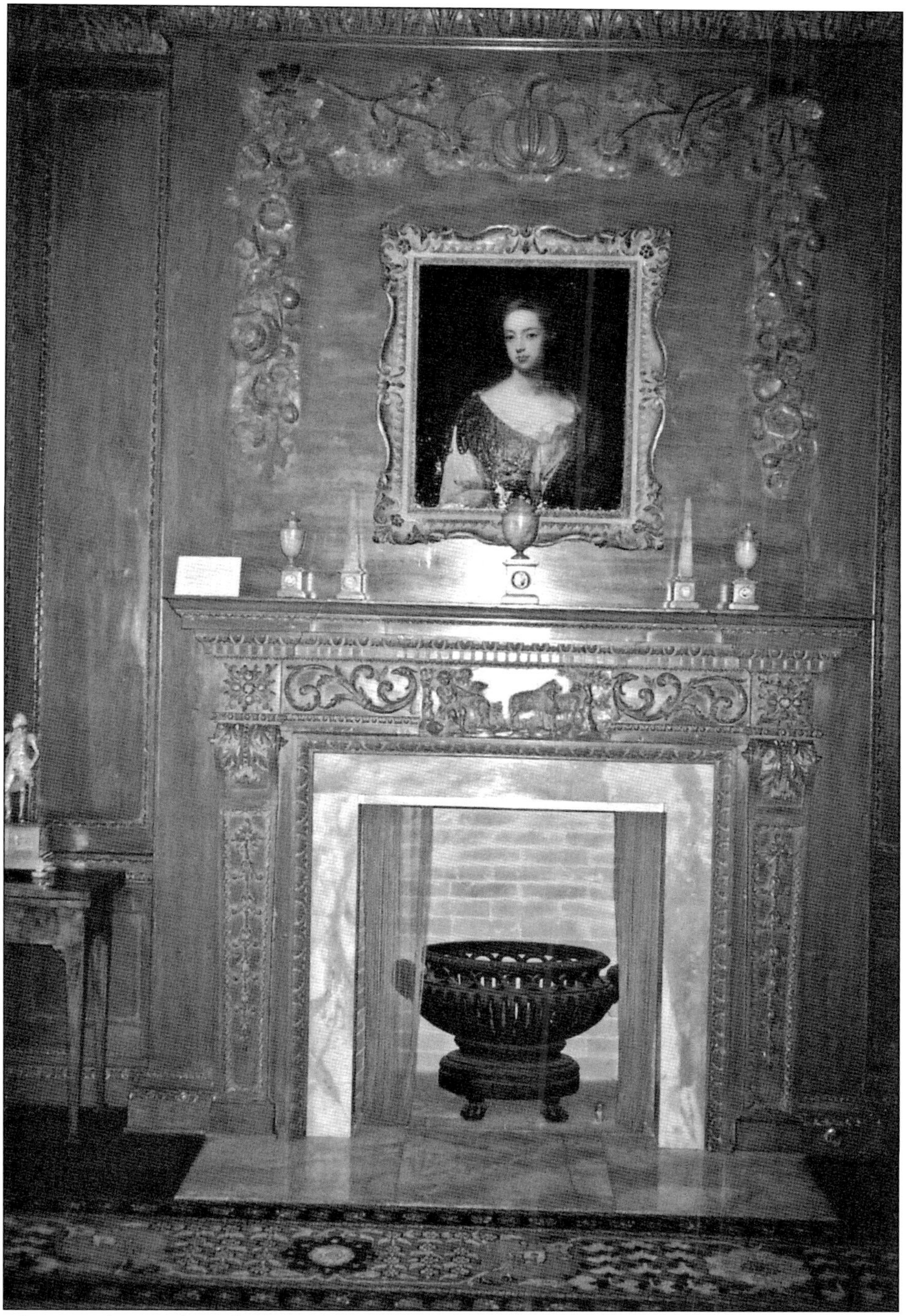

One feature that makes the Pine Room so impressive is the carvings by Grinling Gibbons, highlighted in this photograph, which surround Sir Peter Lely's painting over the mantel and the carvings around the mantel. Master wood-carver Gibbons was born in Rotterdam in the Netherlands and moved to England around 1667. He was an extremely talented wood-carver; some have said he was the finest of all time. (Courtesy of EDM&G.)

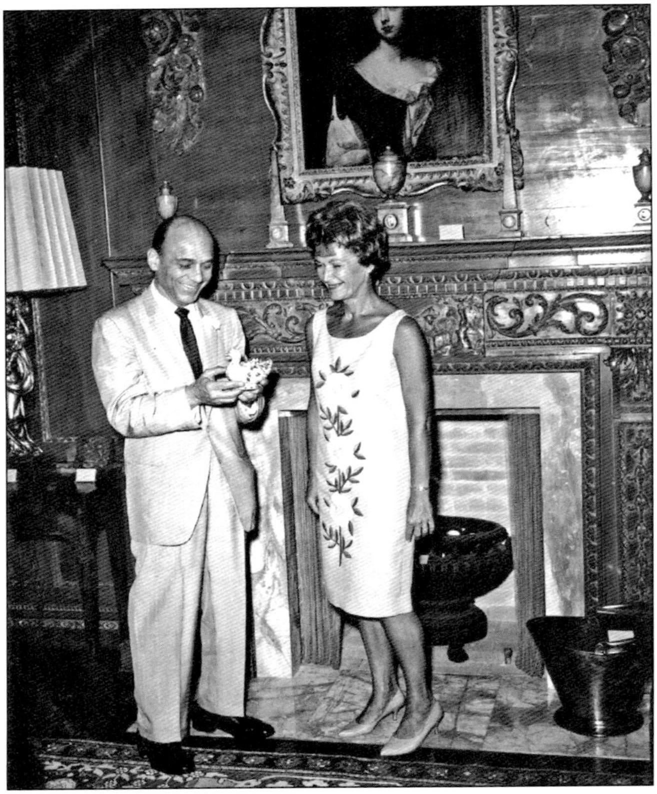

John Green and Virginia Barker stand in front of the hearth outlined by Grinling Gibbon's carvings. They appear to be examining a museum artifact that Green is holding. The hearth pictured here in the Pine Room presents a popular backdrop for photography because of the popularity of Gibbon's exceptional carvings. (Courtesy of EDM&G.)

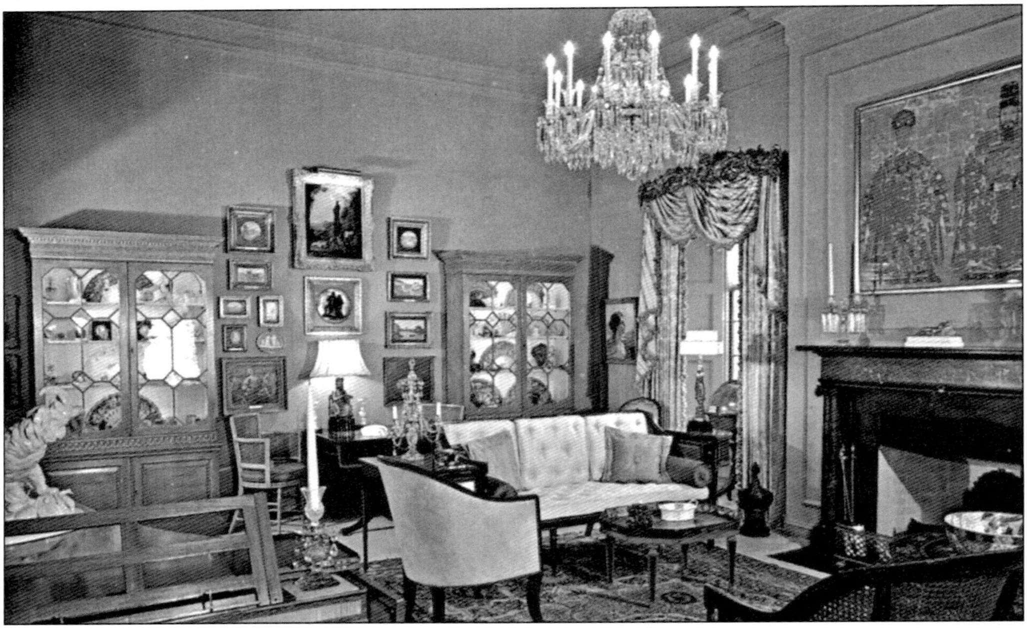

Next to the Pine Room is the Blue Room, about one-third the size of the Pine Room. Here Georgian pine cabinets display a collection of paperweights, Chinese fans, and mosaics of the Ming Dynasty, highlighted by the large imperial portrait above the mantel. (Courtesy of EDM&G.)

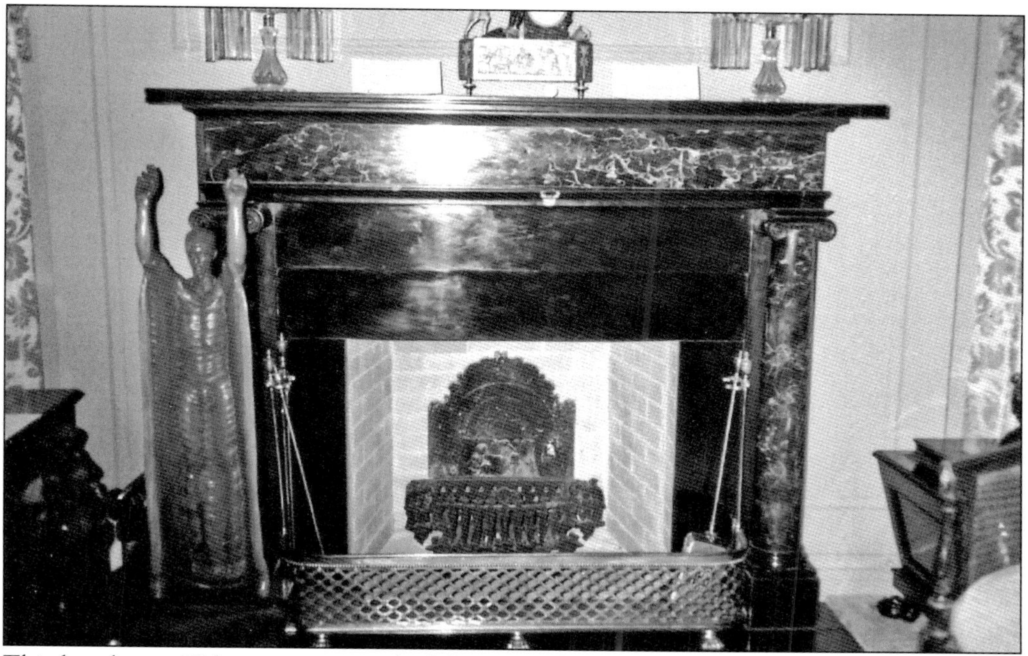

This handsome 18th-century mantel of Georgian design located in the Blue Room was made from black Belgian marble. This particular type of marble, also called noir fin, is the finest quality quarried at St. Denis, in Namur, Belgium. Note the intriguing artifact that sits in the hearth. (Courtesy of EDM&G.)

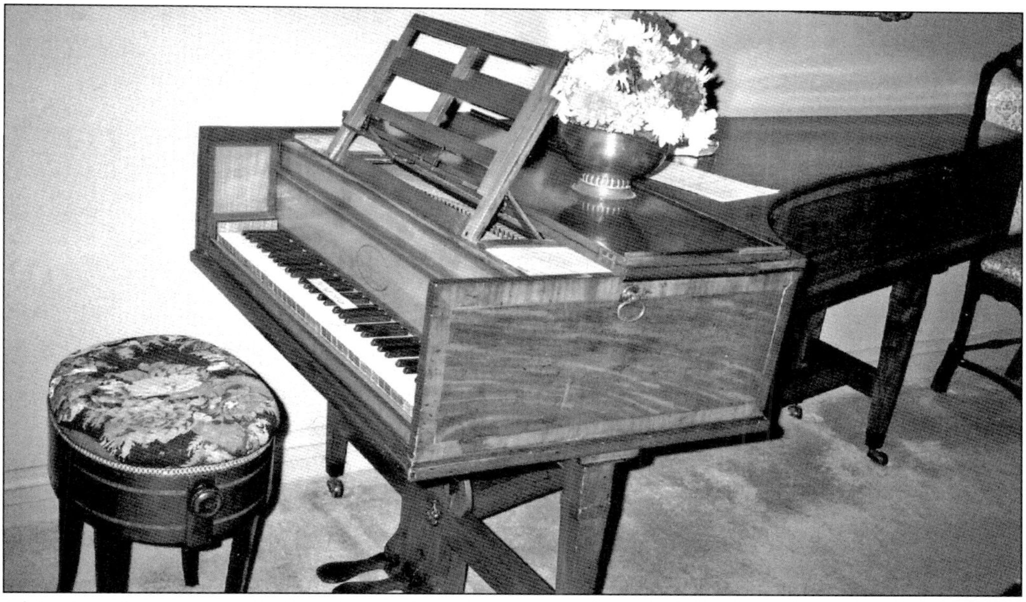

This pianoforte was made from Spanish mahogany and built by John Broadwood and Sons. John Broadwood and Sons is one of the oldest and most prestigious piano companies in the world, holding the Royal Warrant of Appointment, which designates them as a manufacturer of pianos for Queen Elizabeth. It is one of the finest acquisitions in the Blue Room, being one out of six that exists today. (Courtesy of EDM&G.)

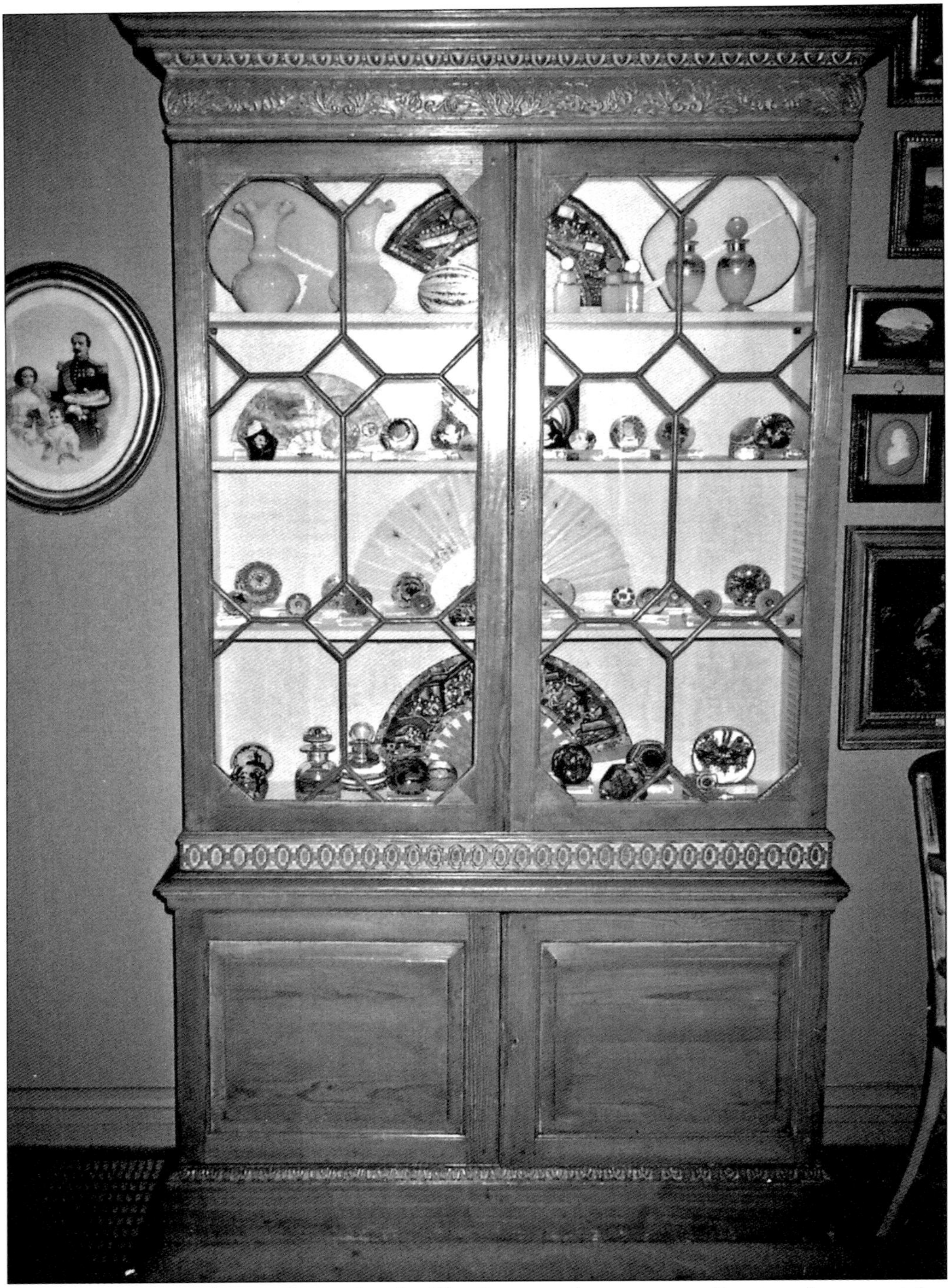

This 18th-century cabinet is located in the Blue Room and contains a collection of paperweights ranging from St. Louis, Clichy, Whitefriars, Bohemians, Baccarat, and Millefiori. Today's culture perceives a heavy object like a stone as a paperweight; but to the ancient scribe for whom the stone was his paper, the suggestion that he should need a paperweight was ludicrous.

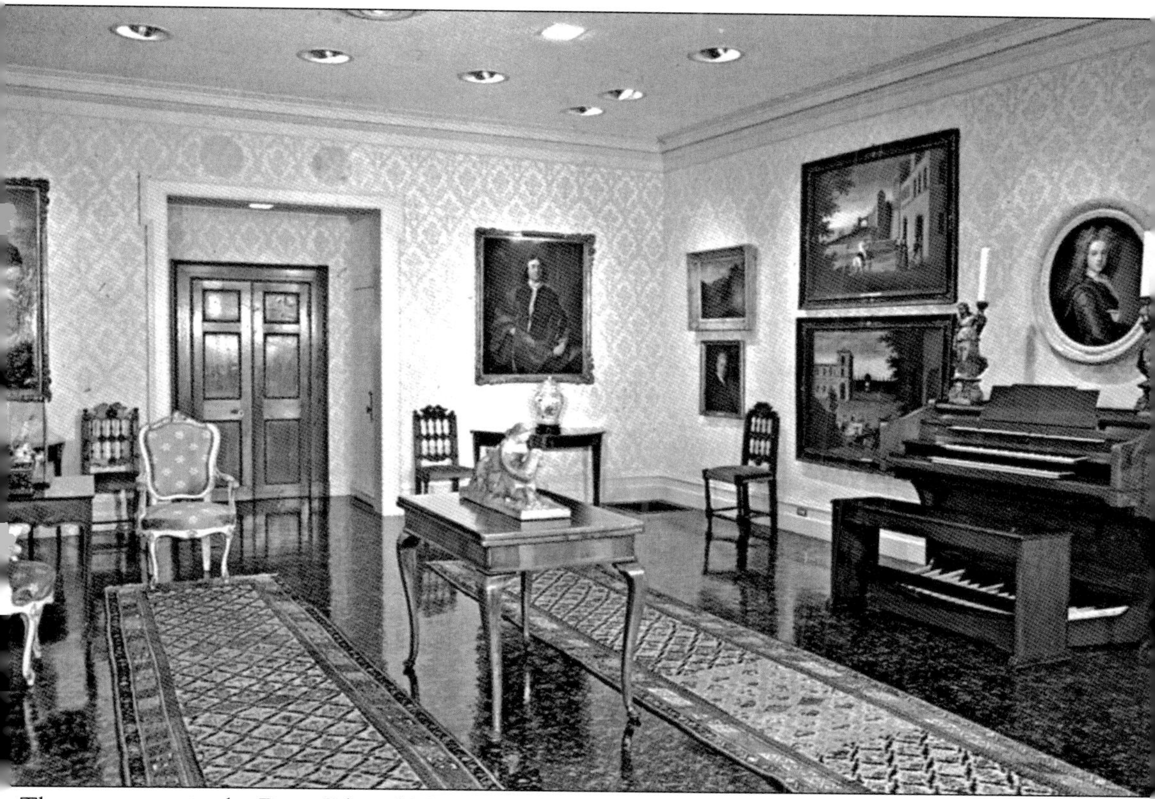

The next room in the Dean Edward Museum is the Picture Gallery, where some of the finest art can be seen. The photograph depicts an earlier arrangement of pictures in the gallery. Today the two large pictures at right are accompanied by two similar-sized pictures, completing a set of four 16th-century Italian paintings with original frames. They tell the biblical story of the prodigal son. (Courtesy of EDM&G.)

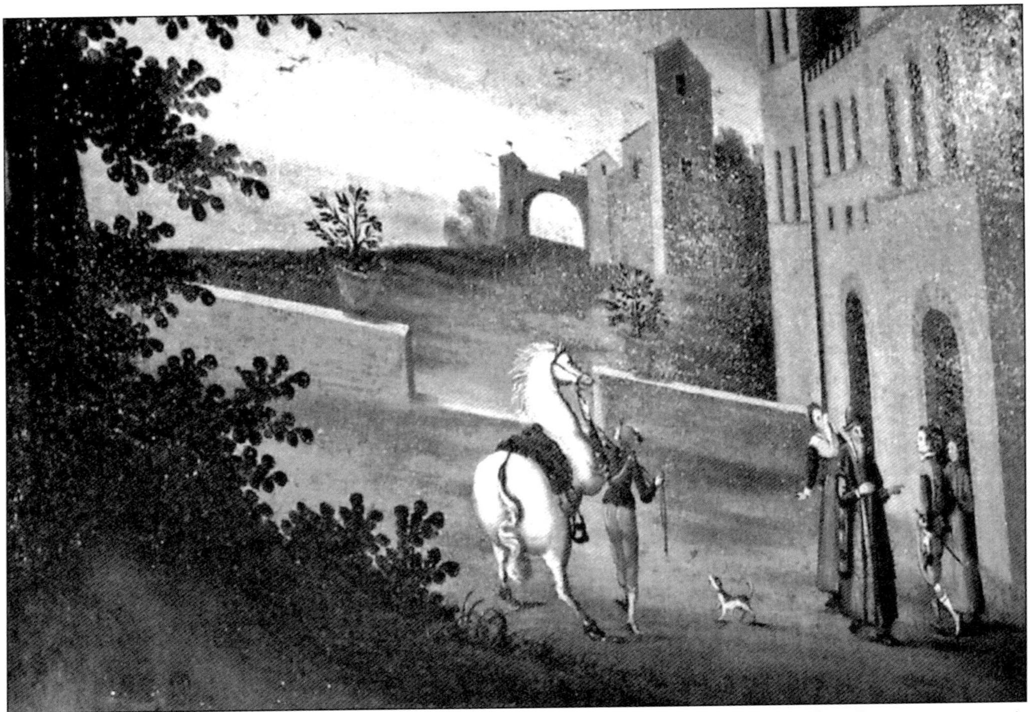

The story of the prodigal son in the Gospel of Luke in the Bible begins in this first painting. A rebellious son rejects his father's upbringing, demands his share of his inheritance while his father is still living, and heads off to a far-away land. This first painting shows him arriving and approaching a group of people in a distant place, where he is soon accepted. (Courtesy of EDM&G.)

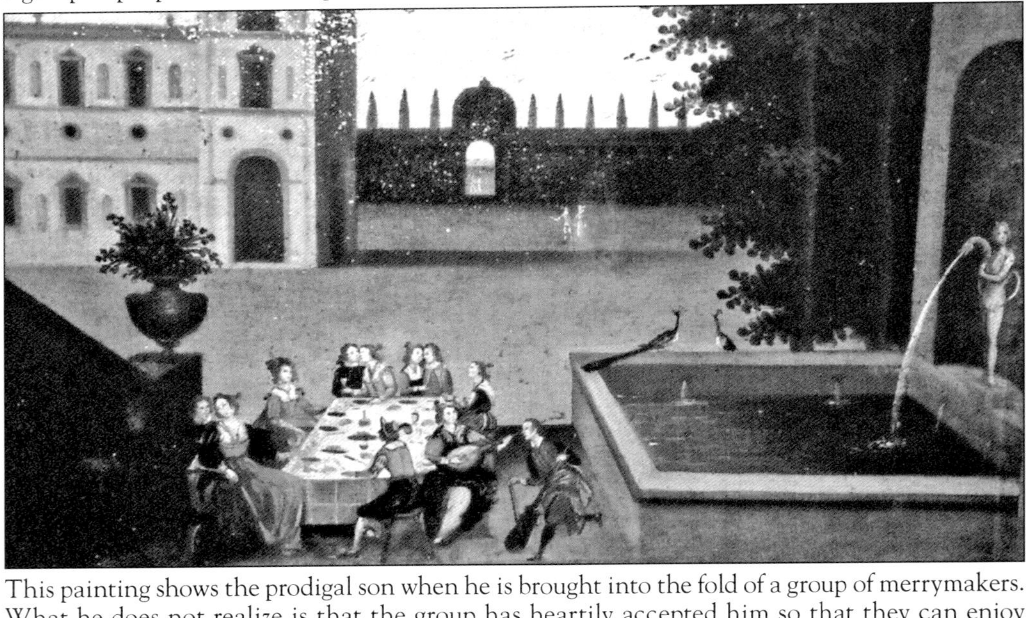

This painting shows the prodigal son when he is brought into the fold of a group of merrymakers. What he does not realize is that the group has heartily accepted him so that they can enjoy the inheritance that he has exposed to them. Here the joyous group celebrates his arrival as he wrestles his wealth with so-called friends. (Courtesy of EDM&G.)

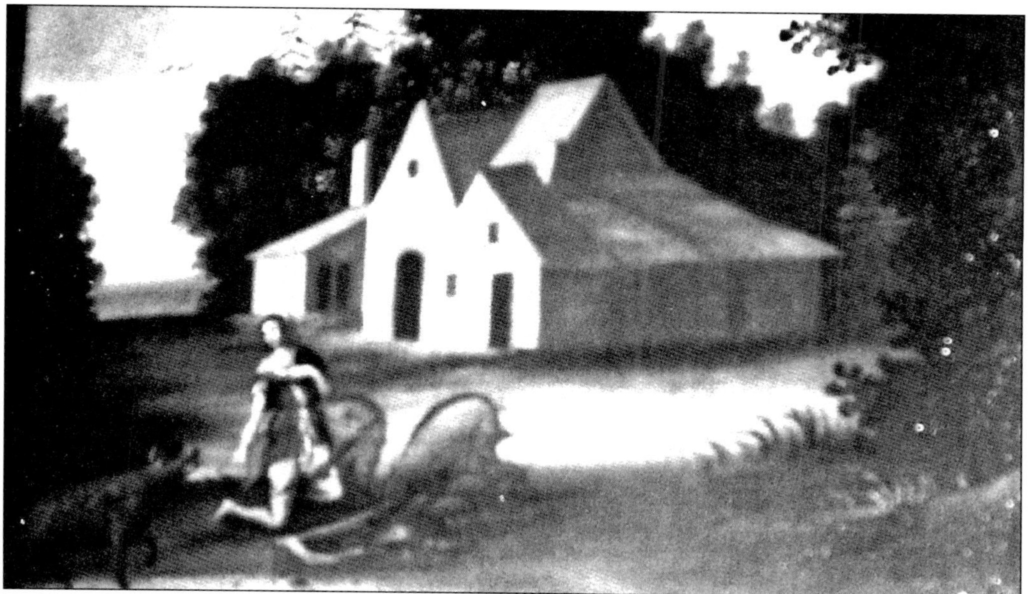

In this painting, after the prodigal son has wasted his substance with riotous living, he eventually has to take work as a swineherd, which is clearly the low point of his journey. He is destitute and has to eat with the swine. When he comes to his senses, he determines to return home and throw himself on the mercy of his father. (Courtesy of EDM&G.)

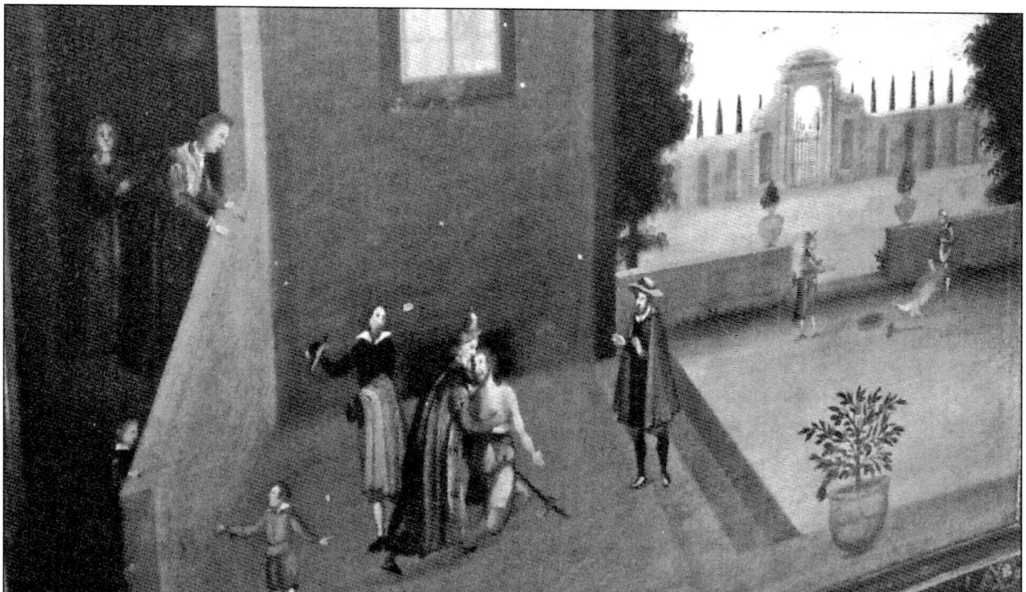

As the prodigal son returns home, to his surprise, he is greeted with open arms by his father who hardly gives him a chance to express his repentance. His father kills a fatted calf to celebrate his return. The older brother, who remained home, becomes jealous of the favored treatment of his faithless brother and upset at the lack of reward for his own faithfulness. The father decried that it was logical that "we should make merry, and be glad: for this thy brother was dead, and is alive again; and was lost, and is found." (Courtesy of EDM&G.)

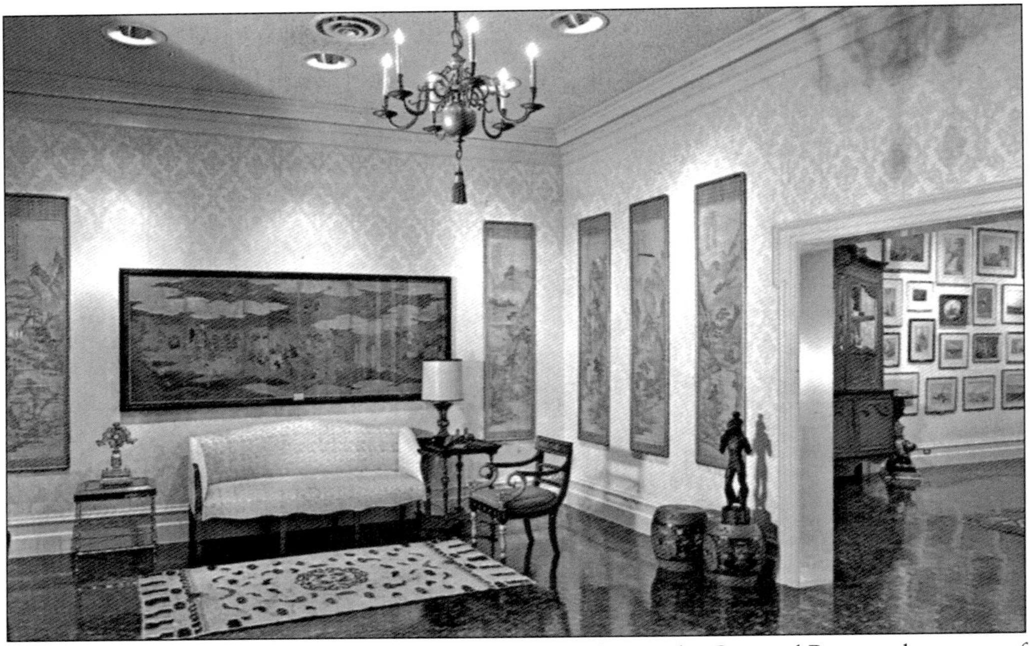

Continuing through the museum, the next room to explore is the Oriental Room, where part of the set of 12 paintings of the Diamond Mountains of Korea can be observed. The paintings were done by one of the 16th-century masters. Also, there are numerous Asian paintings to be seen throughout the room. (Courtesy of EDM&G.)

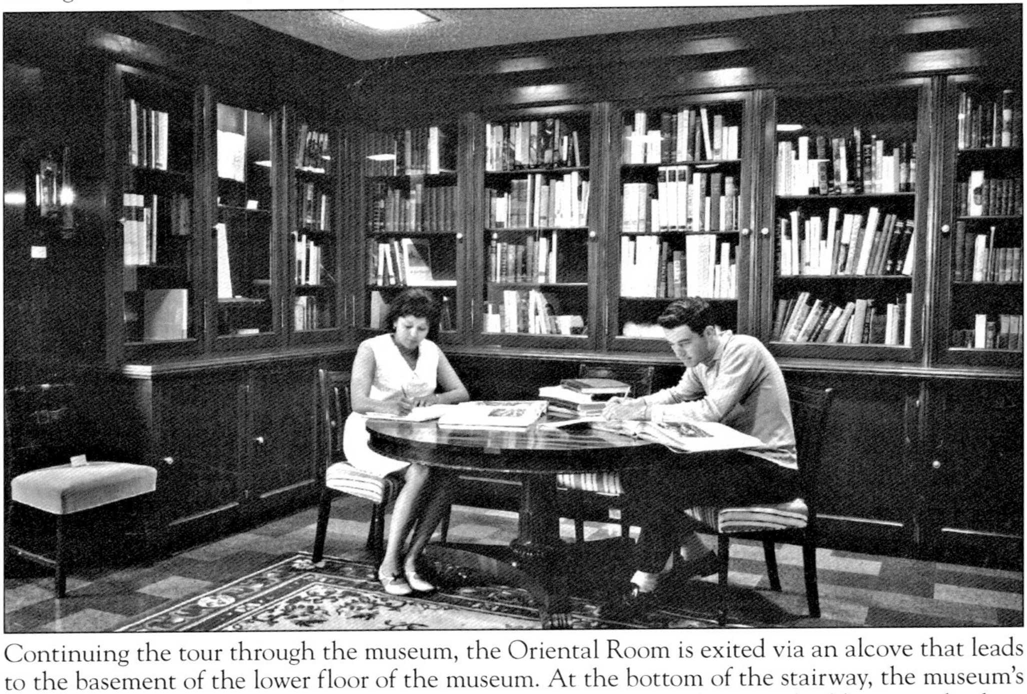

Continuing the tour through the museum, the Oriental Room is exited via an alcove that leads to the basement of the lower floor of the museum. At the bottom of the stairway, the museum's library can be entered. Two students are seen in this photograph using the library to do their research. Next to the library is the Oak Room. (Courtesy of EDM&G.)

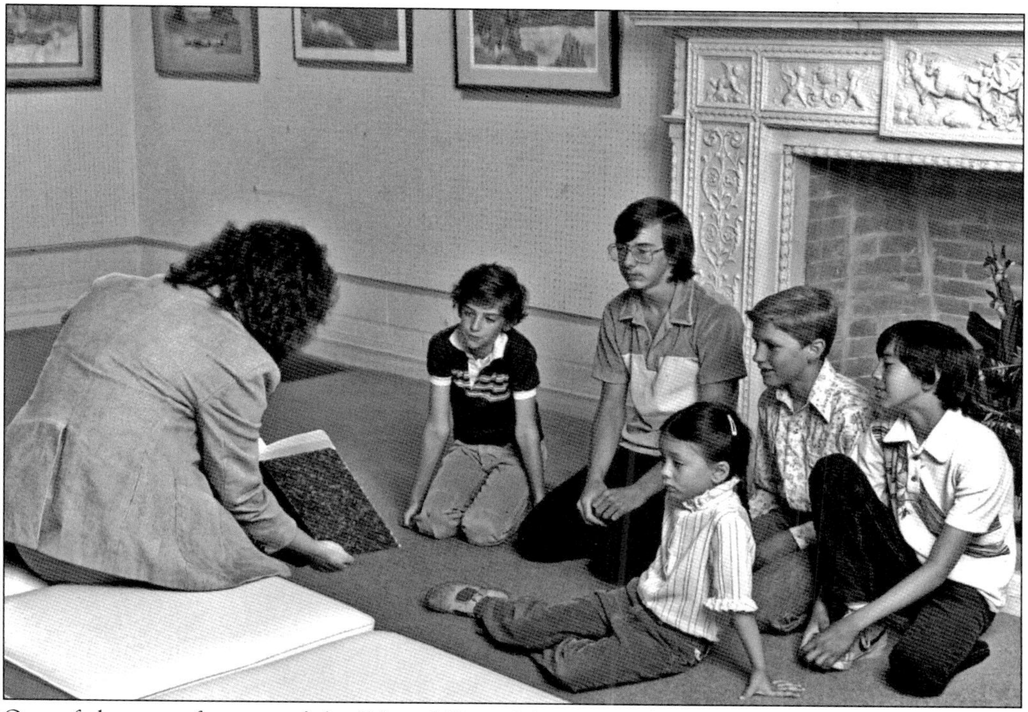

One of the great features of the Edward Dean Museum and Gardens is their strong approach toward education for children. Pictured is a group of students who have visited the museum. School tours are held every Wednesday and Thursday, 9:00 a.m.–12:00 p.m., and the community compliments the museum's efforts in this respect. (Courtesy of EDM&G.)

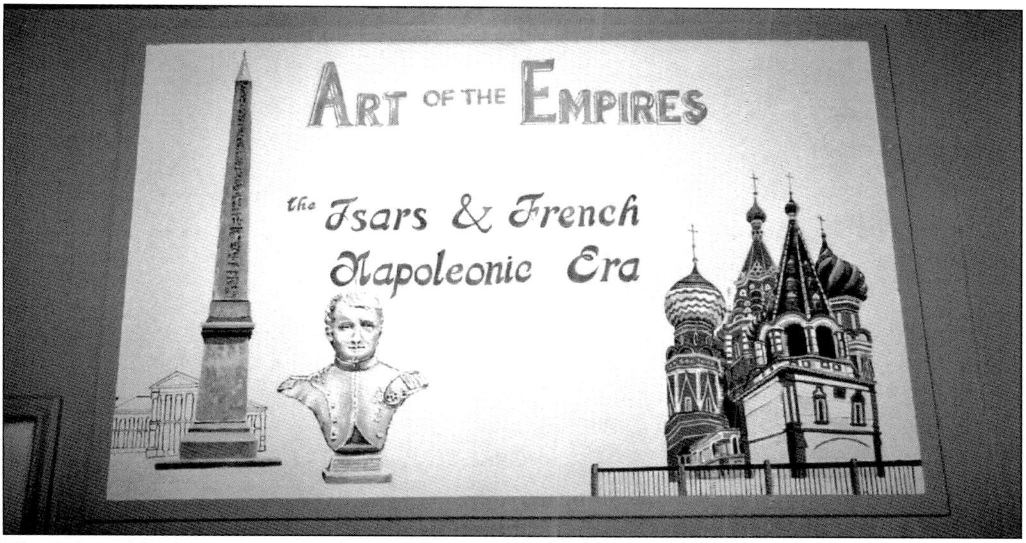

The Edward Dean Museum and Gardens maintains the Benjamin J. and Mary A. Rabe Gallery, an exhibit room where special exhibits are routinely held. Most recently, the museum hosted exhibits called Art of the Empires and the Tsars and French Napoleonic Era. The museum was honored to display artwork of renowned artists of the Soviet Union—Pavel and Nataly Tikhomirov. (Courtesy of EDM&G.)

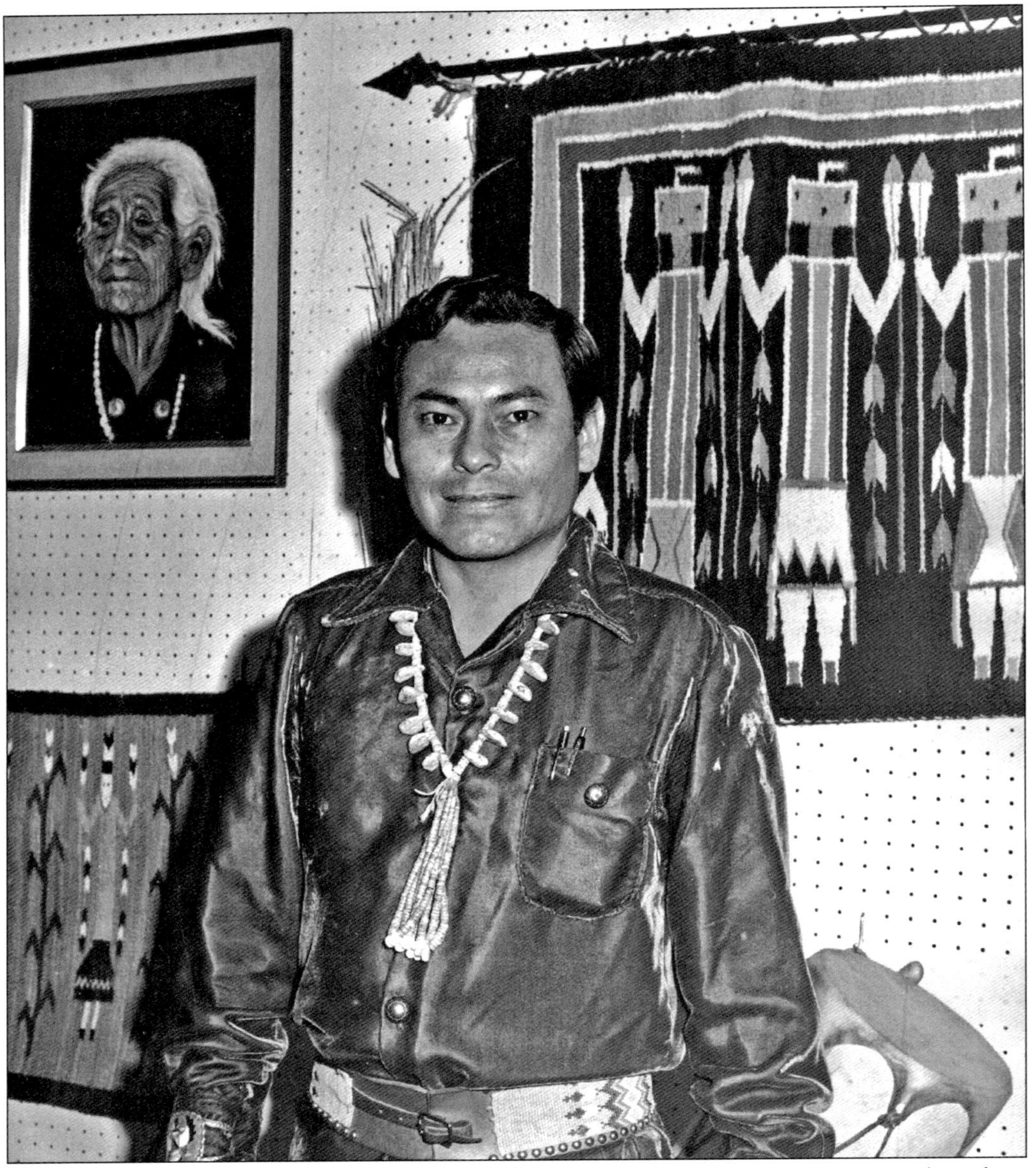

Crallie, a local Native American artist, stands before some Native American art and artifacts that were exhibited at a past special exhibit in the Benjamin J. and Mary A. Rabe Gallery in the Edward Dean Museum and Gardens. It is an opportunity for local artists, as well as some from abroad, to display their artwork. (Courtesy of EDM&G.)

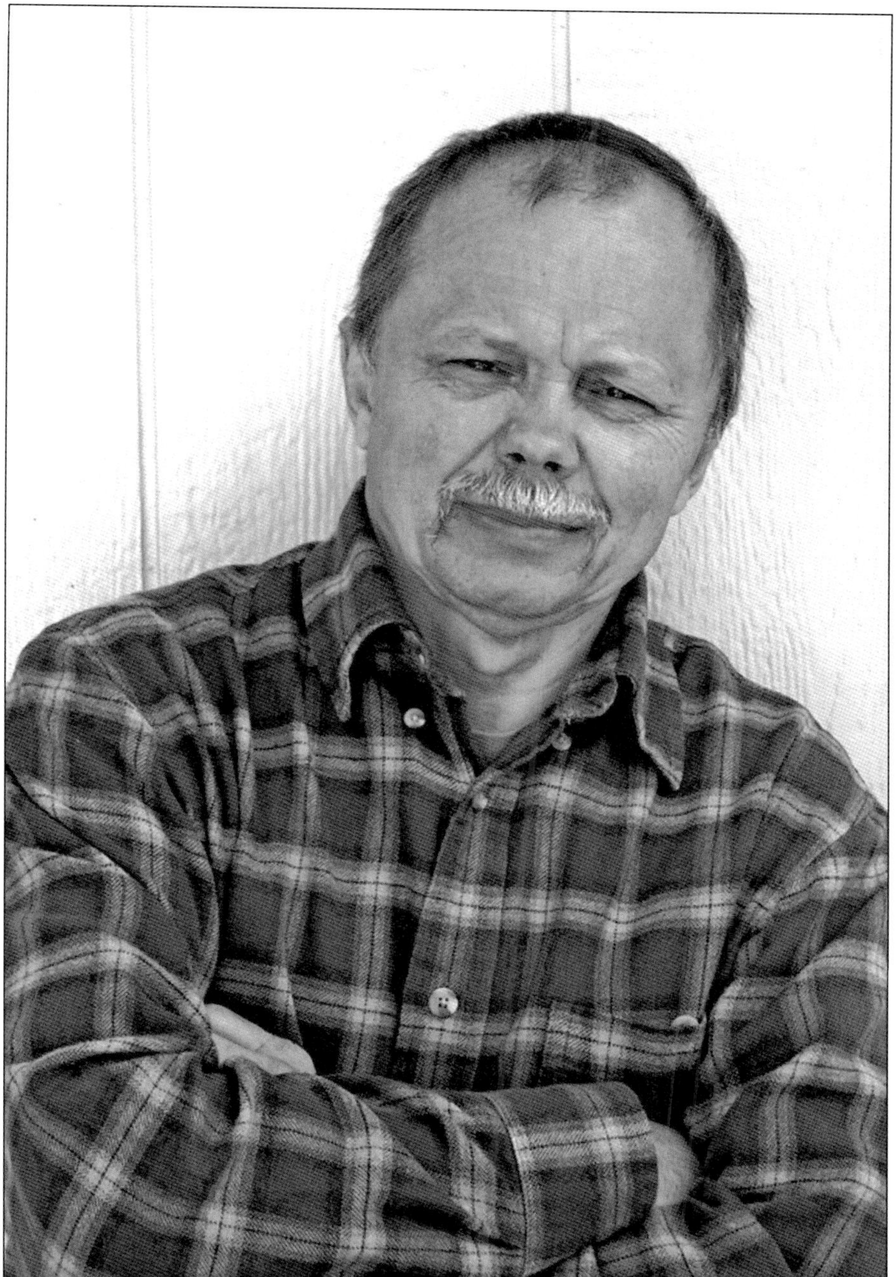

Pictured here is honored artist Pavel Tikhomirov. He and his wife, Nataly, were born in Russian villages near the Volga River and met while attending the Kholui Art Academy. Until relations between the church and state improved in the Soviet Union under Mikhail Gorbachev, they worked covertly on the restoration of ancient church art and the creation of icons. The Tikhomirovs were commissioned on many occasions to create icons and lacquered art for dignitaries, including Leonid Breshnev and former-president Ronald Reagan and his wife, Nancy. (Courtesy of Pavel Tikhomirov.)

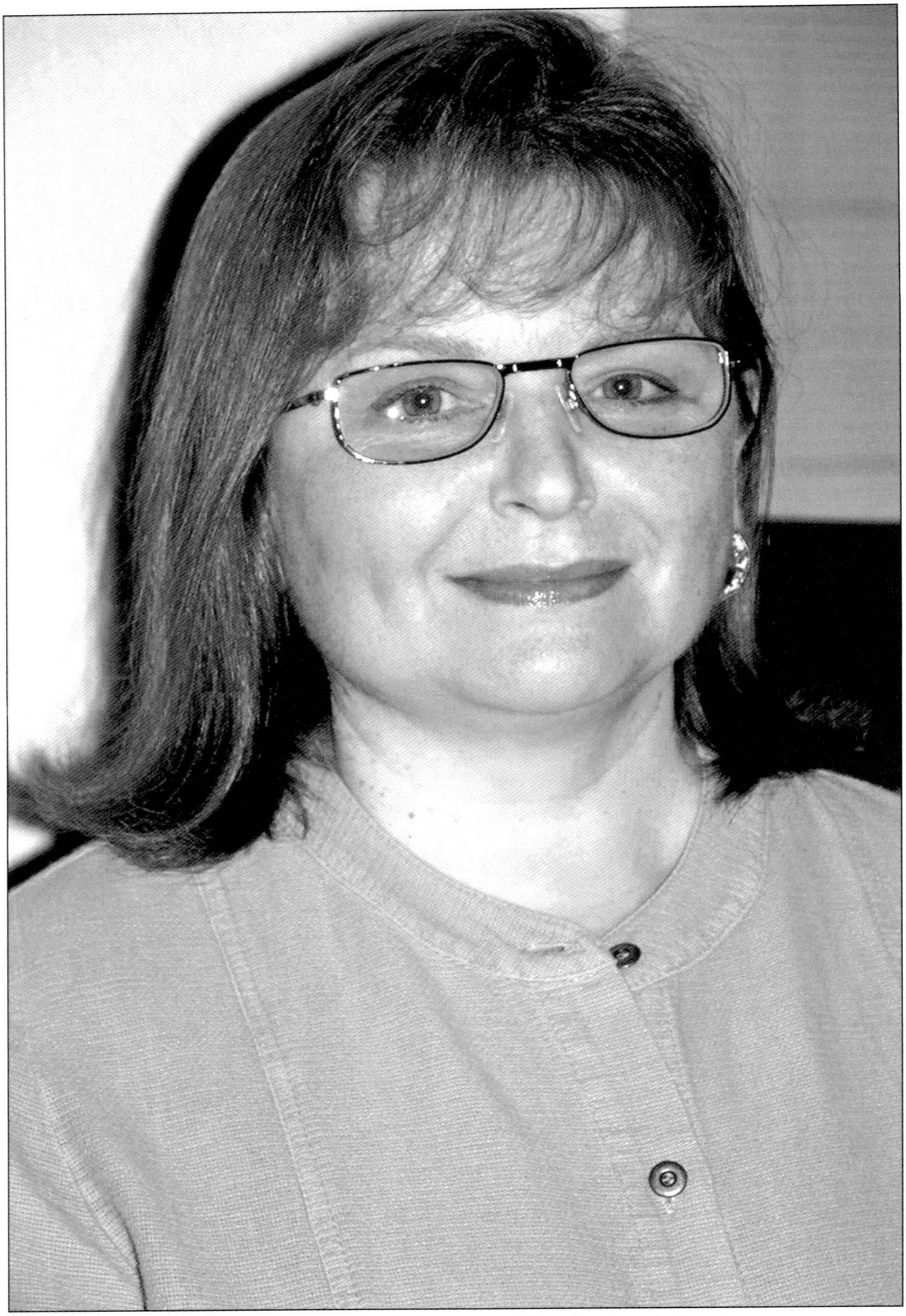

Eventually, Nataly Tikhomirov, pictured above, and her husband, Pavel, were recognized as Honored Artists of the Soviet Union. Their works were designated National Treasures of Russia and were forbidden to be taken out of the country. Their lacquered art has been awarded Best of Show in Russia and other international competitions exhibited in Paris, Tokyo, New York, Los Angles, and Washington, D.C. (Courtesy of Nataly Tikhomirov.)

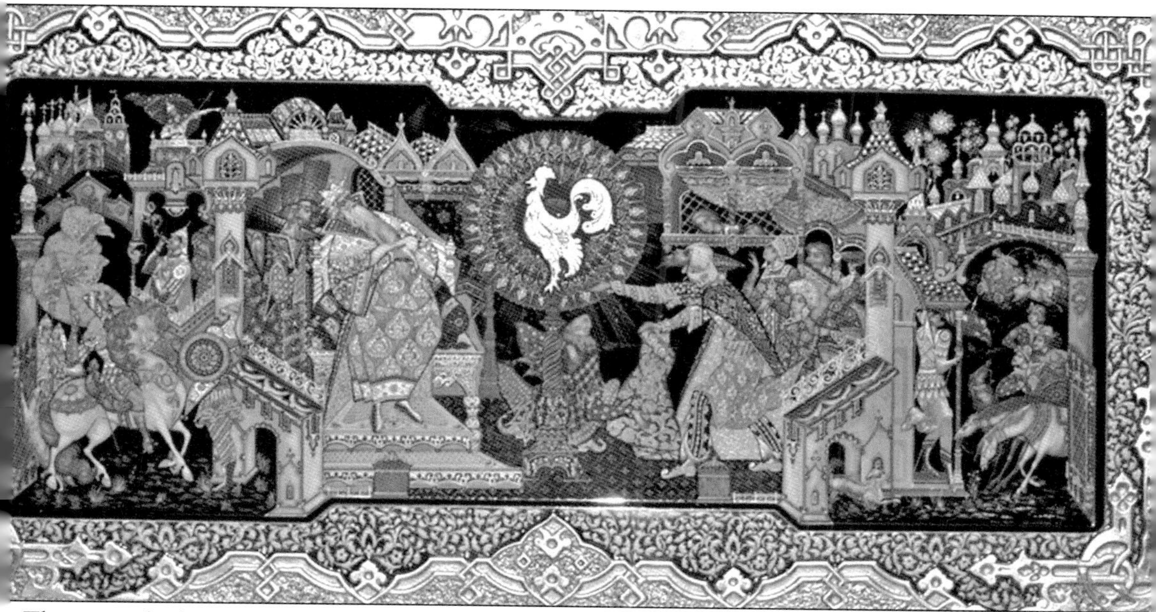

The artwork above, the Golden Cockerel, was hung on the wall of the Benjamin J. and Mary A. Rabe Gallery's exhibit room in the Edward Dean Museum from January 27, 2008 to April 23, 2008. It is a prized, egg-tempera and gold-lacquer artwork of the Tikhomirov Collection, created by renowned artists Pavel and Nataly Tikhomirov. (Courtesy of Pavel Tikhomirov.)

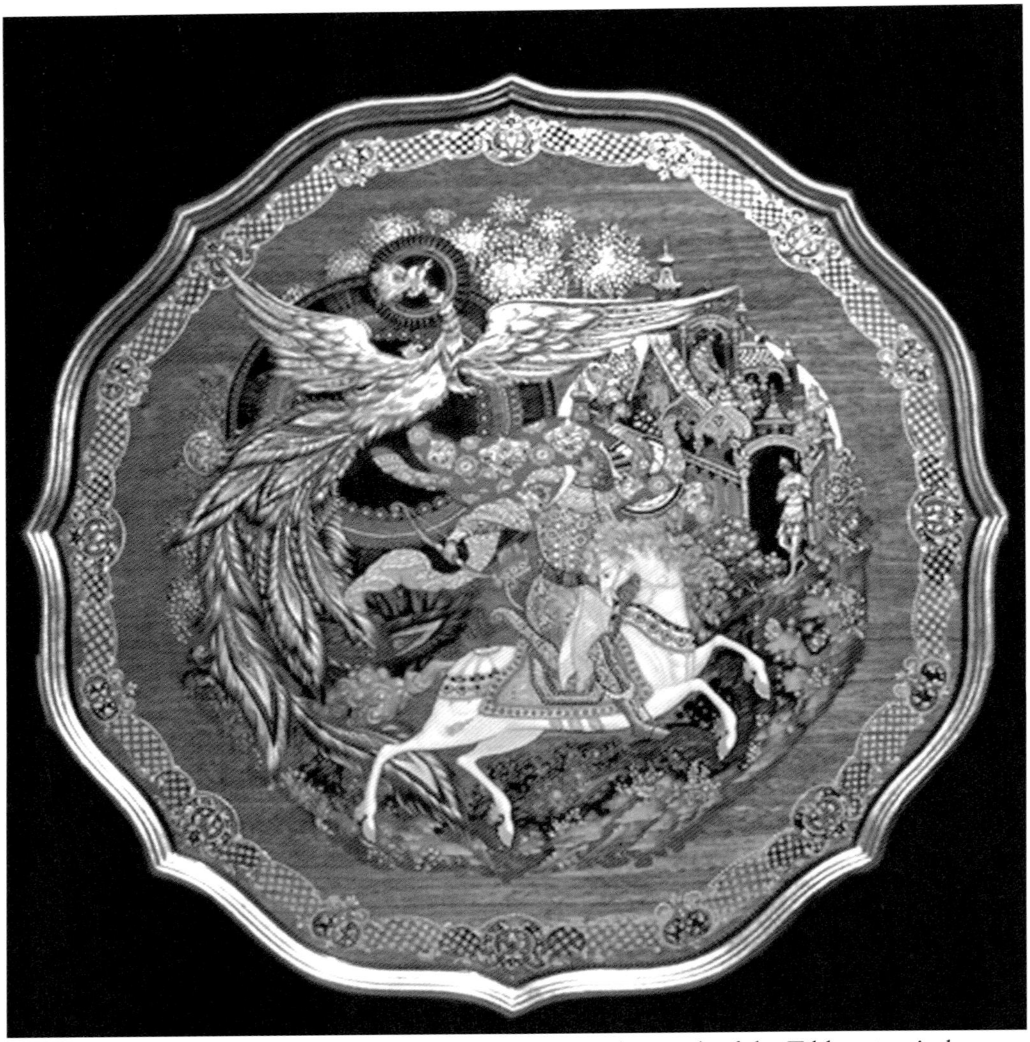

The firebird wall panel, shown here, was another piece of artwork of the Tikhomirov's that was shown in the Benjamin J. and Mary A. Rabe Gallery. Museum assistant Bahjit Toor's nephew married artist Pavel's niece, probably the impetus that brought his artwork together for introduction into the 2008 exhibit in the Dean Edward Museum. (Courtesy of Pavel Tikhomirov.)

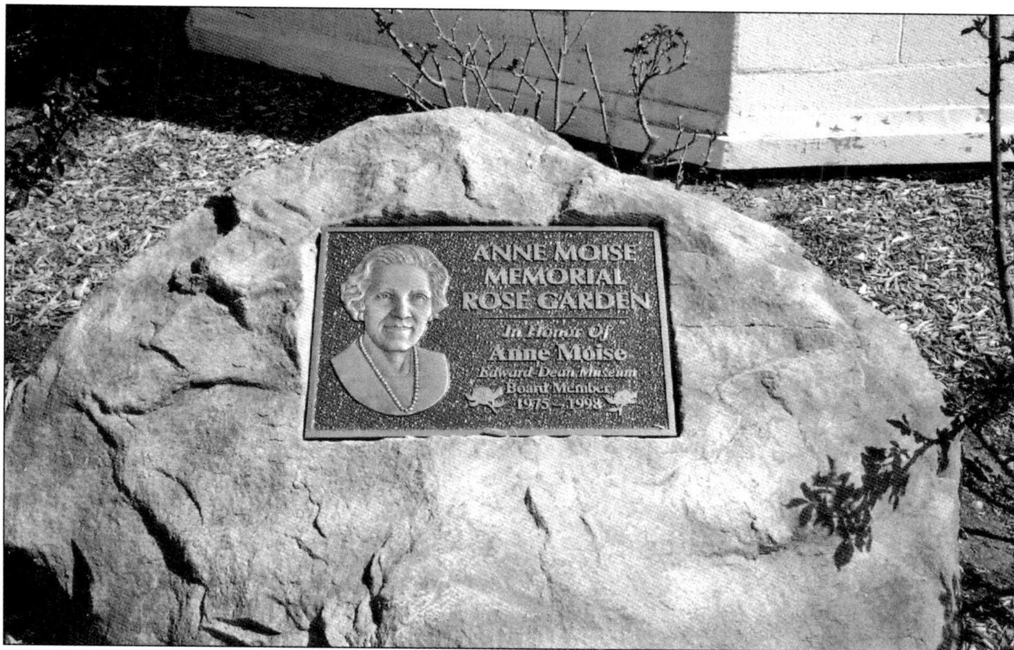

A rose garden has recently been added to the Edward Dean Museum's grounds. A memorial plaque imbedded on a large stone sits near the entrance to the rose garden. It memorializes Anne Moise and honors her devotion to the Edward Dean Museum as a board member, 1975–1998. (Courtesy of EDM&G.)

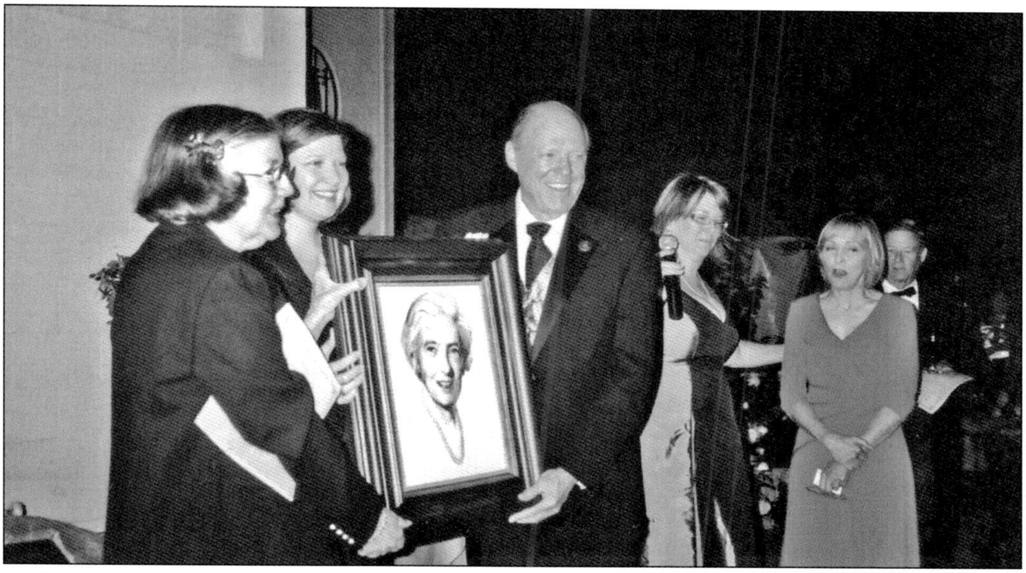

Each year, the Edward Dean Museum and Gardens promotes a fund-raising gala event. Marion Ashley, supervisor of Riverside County 5th District, joins in the event. He is holding the portrait of Anne Moise that is being presented to Sarah Mundy. Participants pictured from left to right are Sarah's mother, Jody Severkrup; Sarah Mundy, deputy director of the Economic Development Agency (EDA); Marion Ashley; Terri Bowen, assistant museum manager; and Robin Zimpfer, assistant county executive officer, EDA.

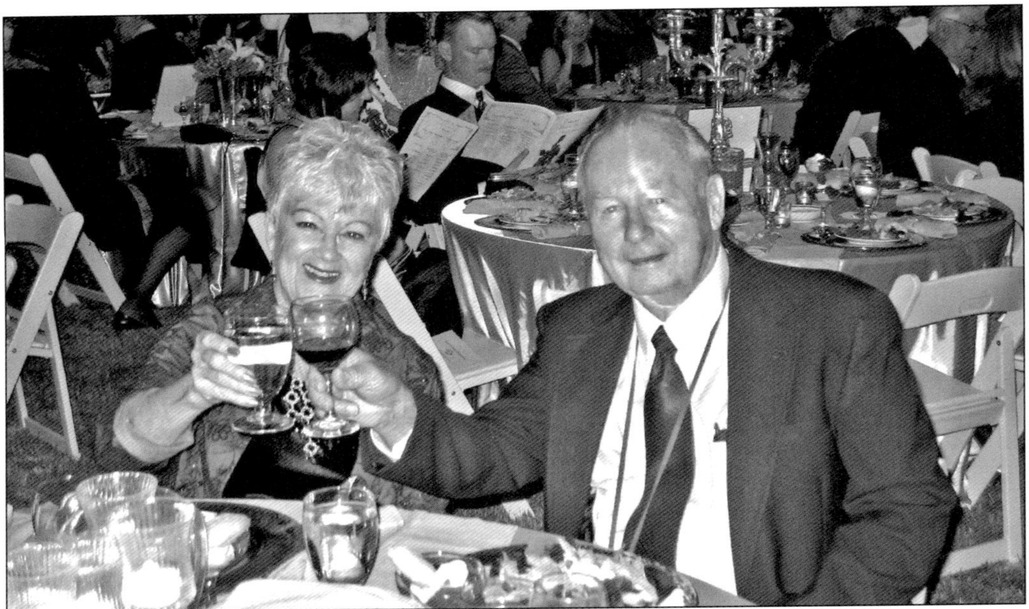

A recent gala event was held under a large tent that had been installed on the grounds of the Edward Dean Museum. Pictured at the Edward Dean board member's table are Evelyn Hawkins, board member of the Edward Dean Museum, and the author. The event was a great success and was enjoyed by a large group.

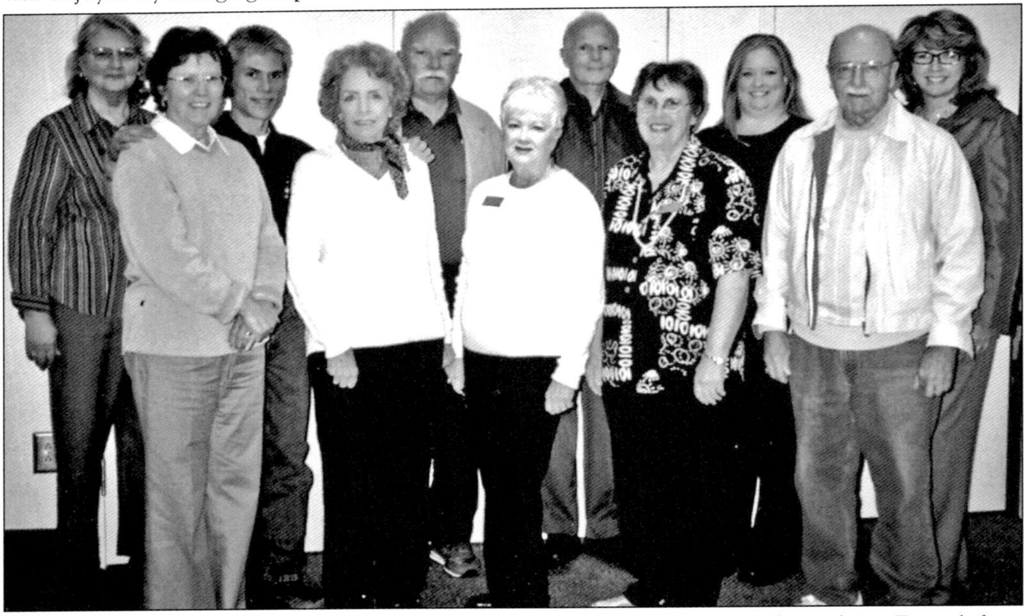

Pictured are board and staff members of the Edward Dean Museum and Gardens. From left to right are (first row) Sharon Rachal; Pat Siva; Evelyn Hawkins, vice president; Nancy Hippert, president; and Wes Laws, treasurer; (second row) Virginia Ross, secretary; Jeff Elser; George Gendarme; Dr. Stan Kormacher; Christie Burton, museum curator (staff); and Teresa Gallaven, Riverside County EDA (staff). Board members not present were Pat Herron, Dewey Jacobs, Peggy Kissach, Reg Shaleski, and Claire Wallace.

Five

Highland Springs

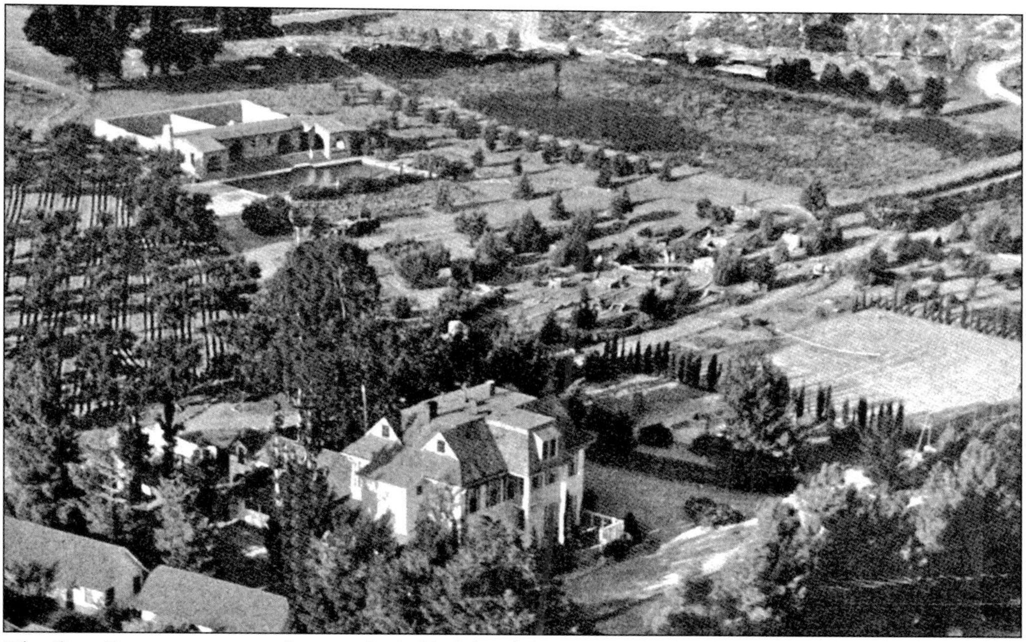

The first Caucasian to settle in today's Highland Springs was Dr. Isaac Smith. He followed some of his stray cattle in 1853 and was impressed enough with the surrounding countryside to build a new ranch here. The original Smith residence stood about where the existing swimming pool stands today at the resort. Smith was from Maine, and here he raised cattle, sheep, vegetables, and planted a fruit orchard with a small vineyard. He also raised 11 children who helped him develop his property and surrounding lands. They spread his farm and ranch operation as far as Whitewater and Big Bear Valley. Smith's ranch was dubbed Smith's Station in 1862 and was turned into a stagecoach stop. The Butterfield Overland Stage Line ran coaches from San Bernardino and stopped here before continuing on the Bradshaw Trail to Yuma, Arizona. In 1884, the Smith property was purchased by a Los Angeles company that built a three-story hotel, shown in the foreground of this photograph, called the Highland Home. (Courtesy of Steve Lech.)

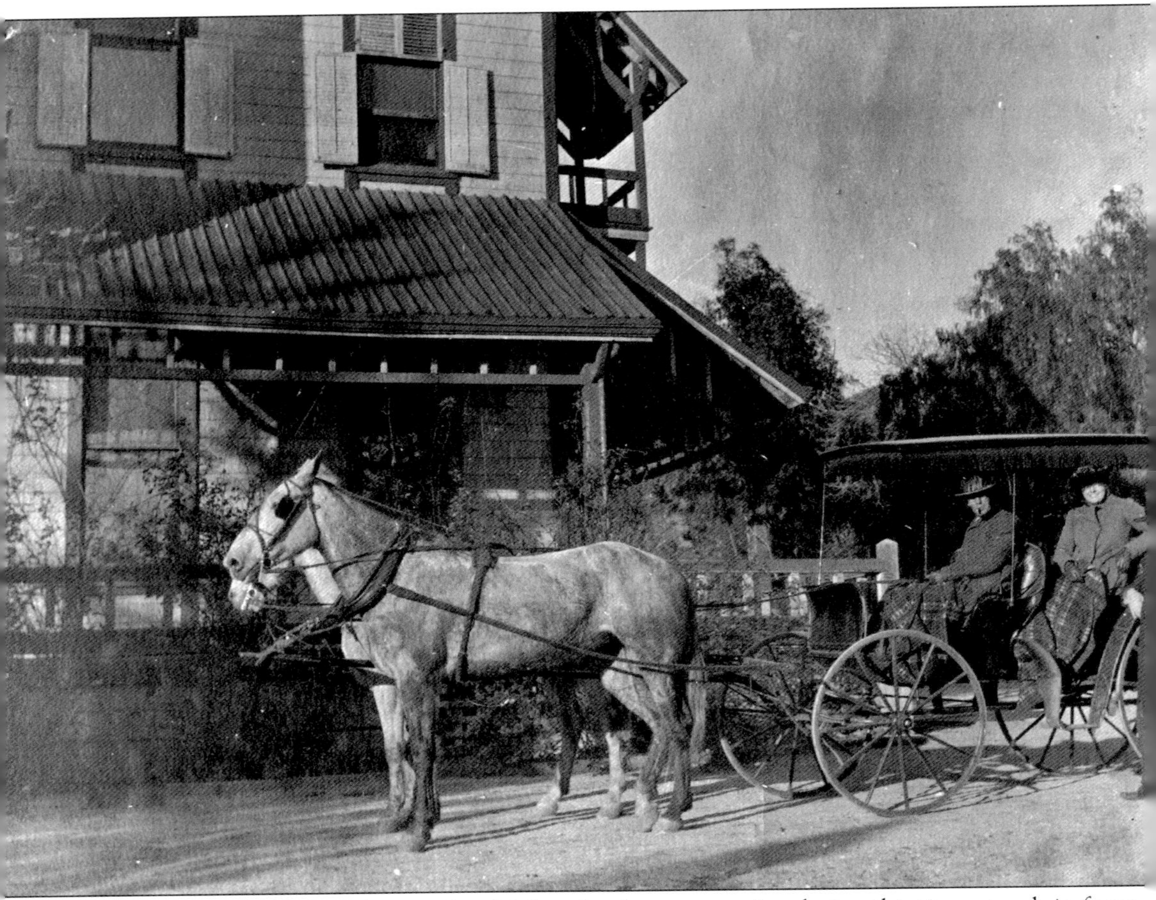

A buggy pulled by two horses, the chief mode of transportation during this time, stands in front of the Highland Home in 1905. These people are unidentified, but are not alleged to be of the Smith family. Dr. Isaac Smith had sold the property 21 years prior to this date. (Courtesy of Steve Lech.)

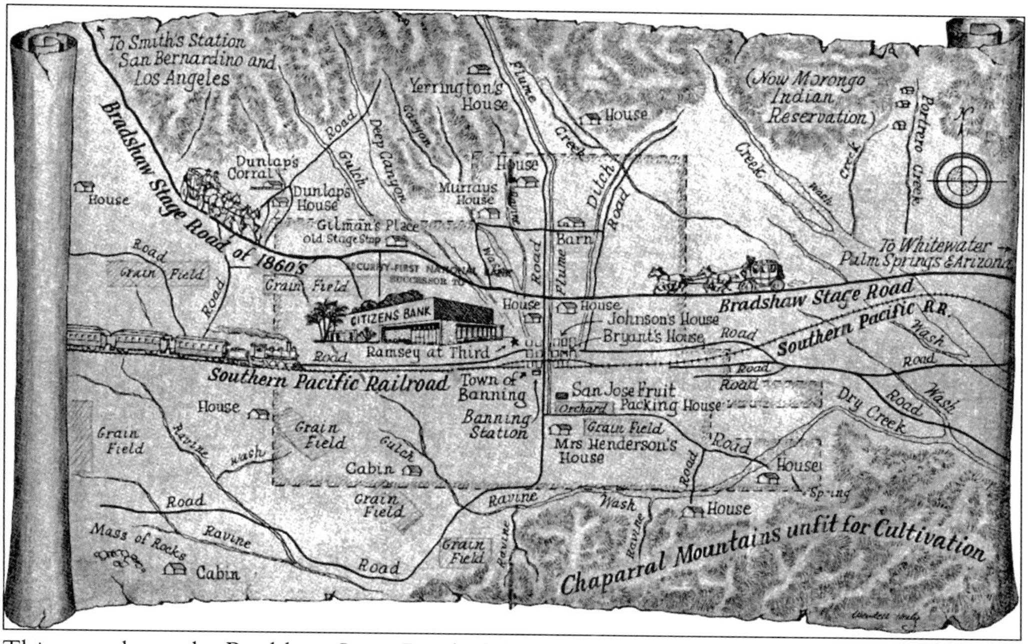

This map shows the Bradshaw Stage Road of the 1860s passing through Cherry Valley and the stage stop at Dr. Isaac's place. To the west, the stage route ran to San Bernardino and Los Angeles, and to the east it went to Whitewater, Palm Springs, and Arizona. The next nearest stage stop to the east was at the small community of Whitewater. (Courtesy of Steve Lech.)

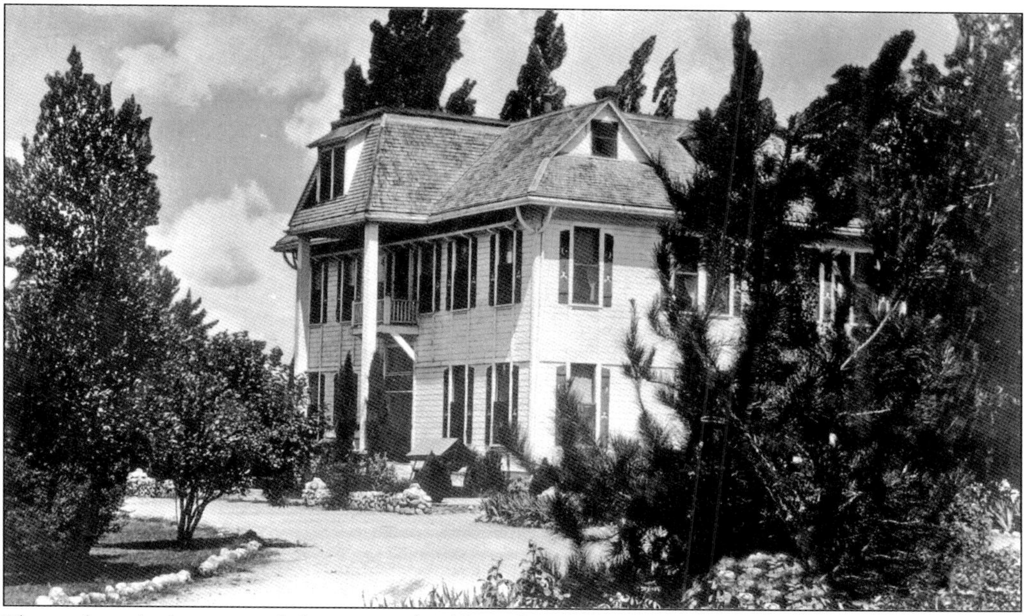

Shown here is the original three-story building that was constructed by a Los Angeles company that purchased the property in 1884. It was called Highland Home. A passenger railroad arrived in 1876 and traffic through the area began to increase. The railroad, after 23 years, became a reality and brought a new era to the region. (Courtesy of Steve Lech.)

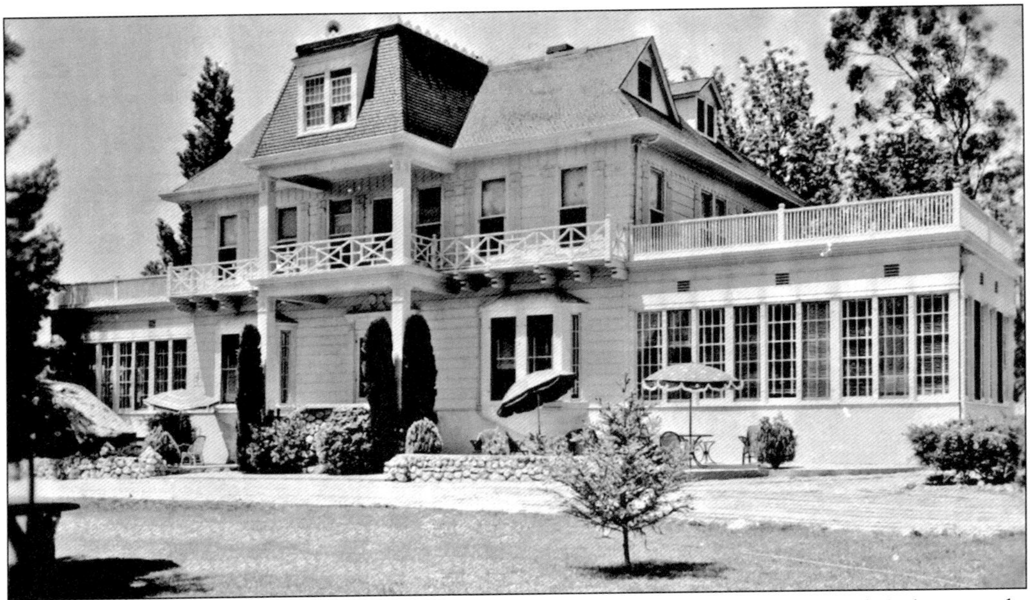

Years later, the Highland Springs Home was remolded and it appeared as shown in this photograph; an attractive place where many wanted to visit and stay for a while. It was much larger now and could accommodate more visitors. Note the two wings that are spread on each of the sides. (Courtesy of Steve Lech.)

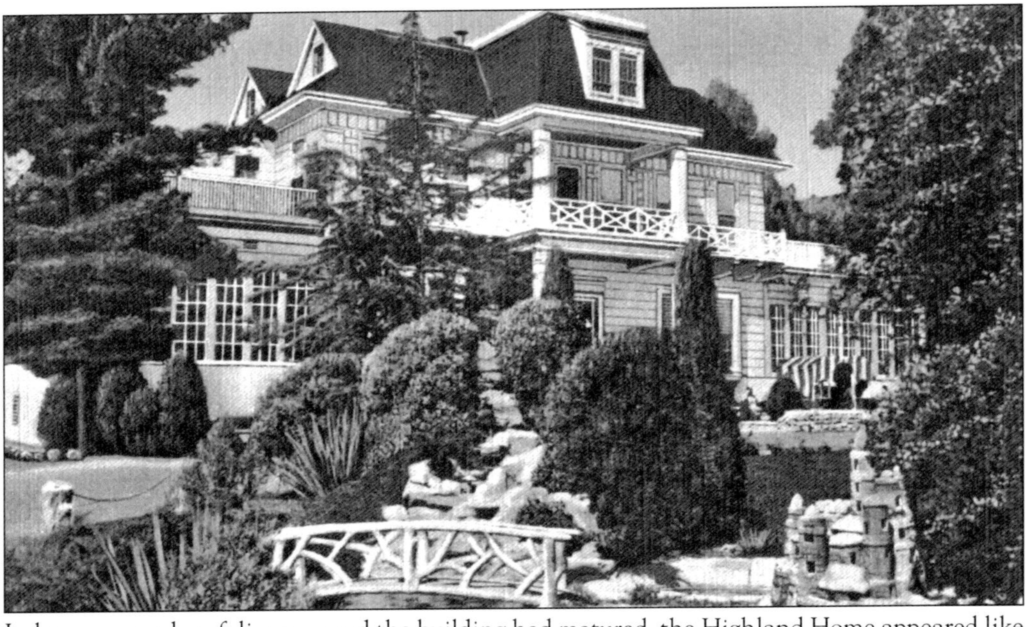

In later years, when foliage around the building had matured, the Highland Home appeared like it is shown here. During this era, it became ever so popular, and many people came here for a short stay. It was a unfortunate day when this beautiful building burned to the ground and never was replaced. (Courtesy of Steve Lech.)

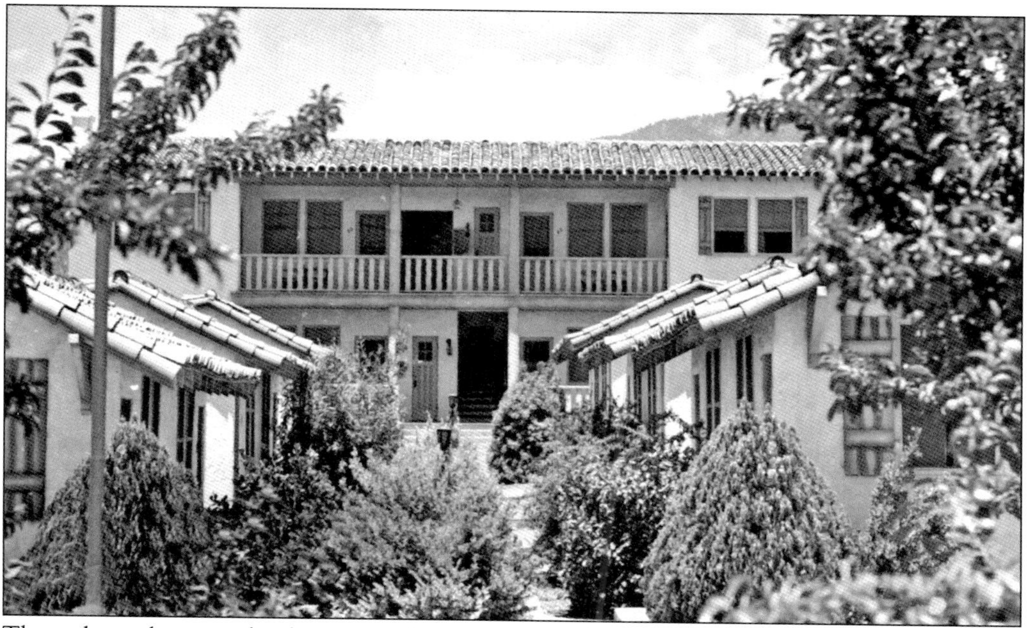

Throughout the year, the demand for housing at Highland Springs increased, and cottages like the ones shown here were built to accommodate visitors. It is interesting to note that the same cottages that were built back then are used today and are still quite adequate. (Courtesy of Steve Lech.)

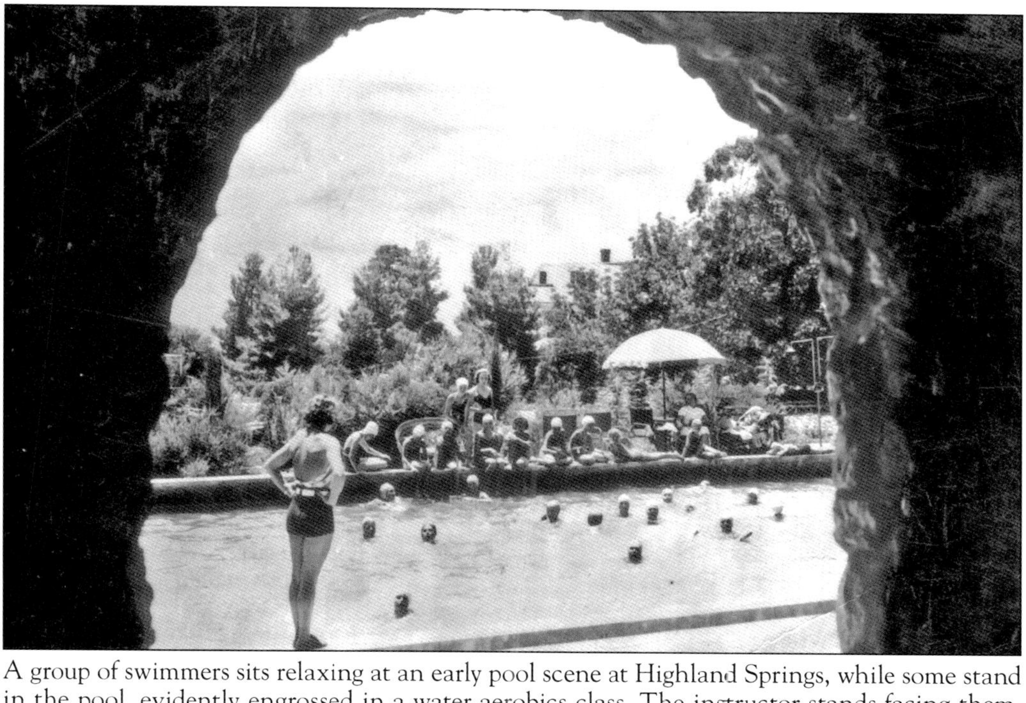

A group of swimmers sits relaxing at an early pool scene at Highland Springs, while some stand in the pool, evidently engrossed in a water aerobics class. The instructor stands facing them, apparently giving instruction. The pool at Highland Springs was a popular attraction on the resort's grounds at this time. (Courtesy of Steve Lech.)

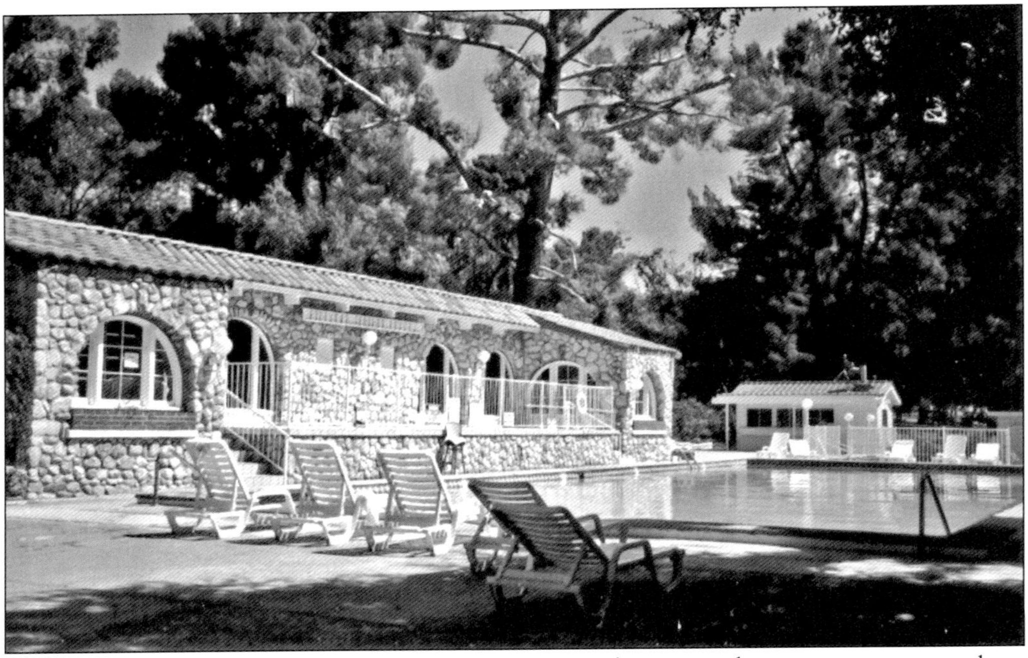

The modernized pool that exists at Highland Springs today sits on the approximate spot where the original home of Dr. Isaac Smith was built. When his house burned to the ground, this place was later chosen for the beautiful pool site. The pool resides here today and is cherished by many visitors that come to visit the resort.

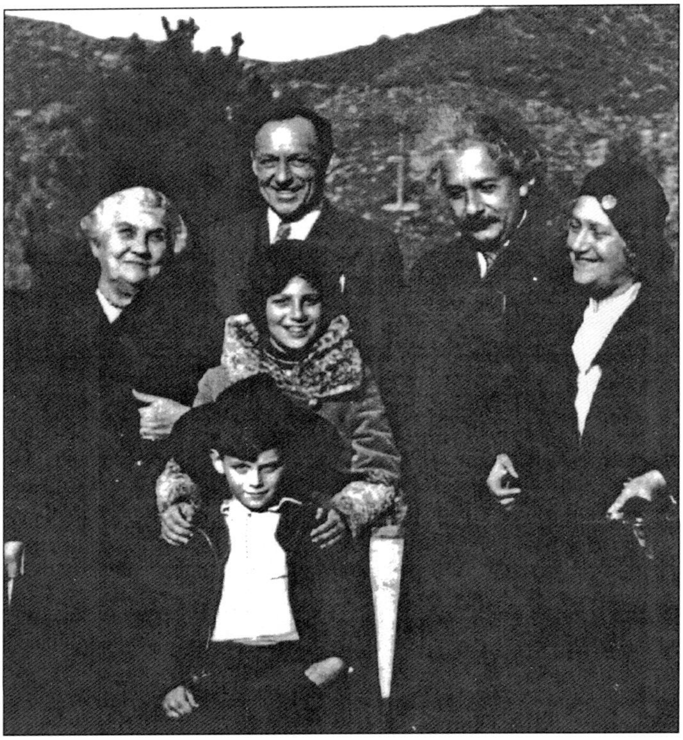

Fred Hirsch and his family are gathered at the left of this photograph, beside professor Albert Einstein and his wife (right). The photograph was taken during the 1933 visit Einstein made to his friend Fred Hirsch, who owned large real estate holdings in the area, including Highland Springs Resort in Cherry Valley. (Courtesy of SGPHS.)

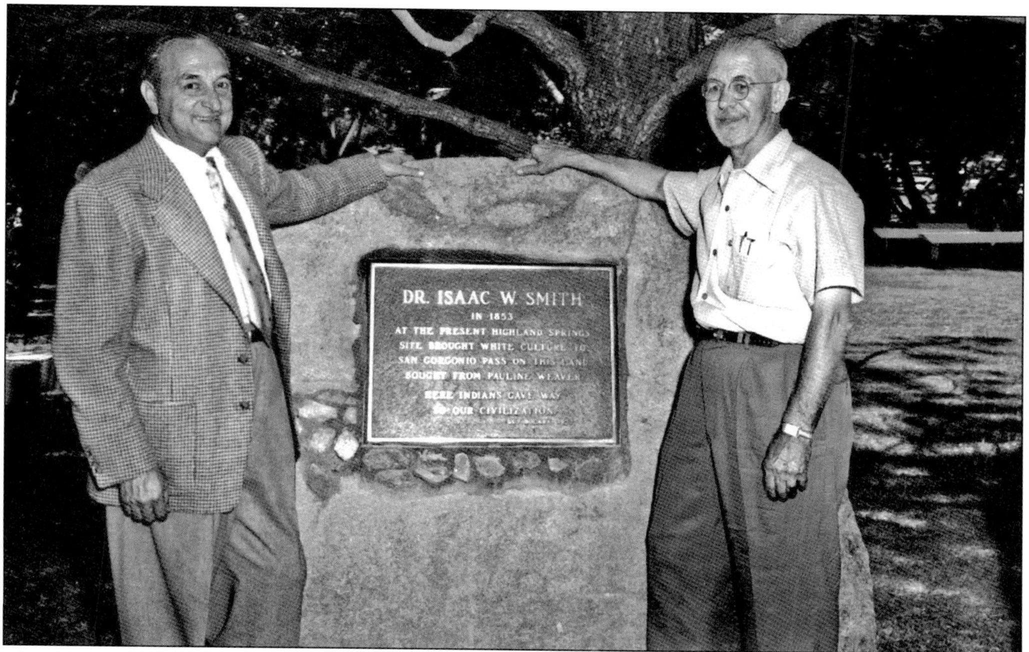

Elmer Rosin (left) and Guy Bogart (right) stand next to a large granite rock at Highland Springs during a presentation of a plaque in honor of Dr. Isaac Smith. It reads, "Dr. Isaac W. Smith in 1853, at the present Highland Springs site brought white culture to San Gorgonio Pass on this land bought by Pauline Weaver. Here Native Americans gave way to our culture." It was dated 1953. (Photograph by Leonard McCulloh; courtesy of SGPHS.)

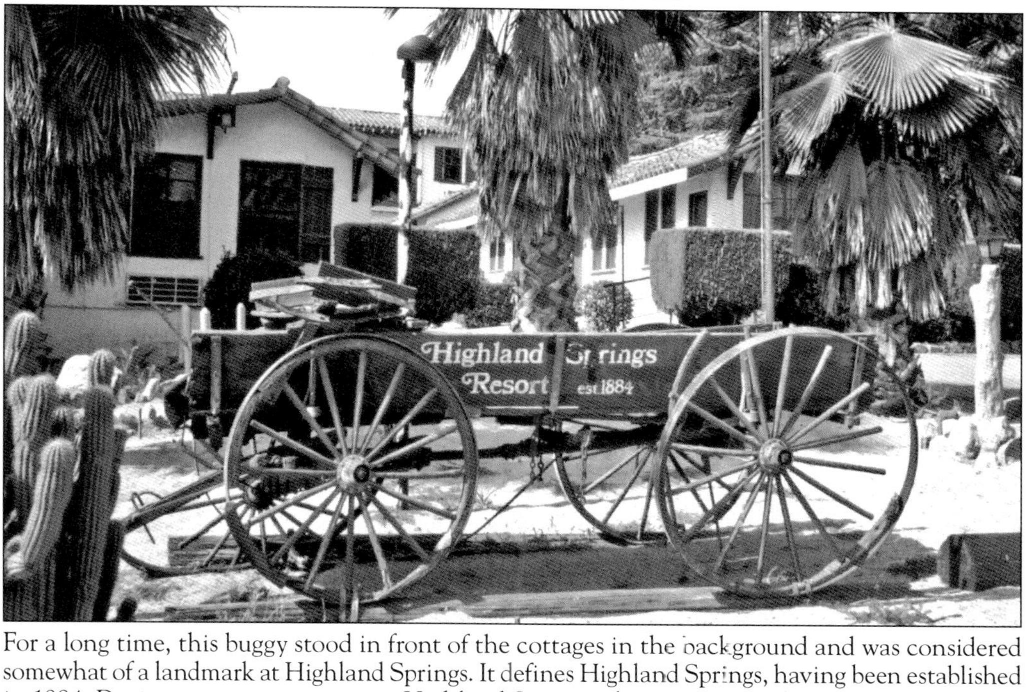

For a long time, this buggy stood in front of the cottages in the background and was considered somewhat of a landmark at Highland Springs. It defines Highland Springs, having been established in 1884. During recent renovation at Highland Springs, this picturesque buggy was removed.

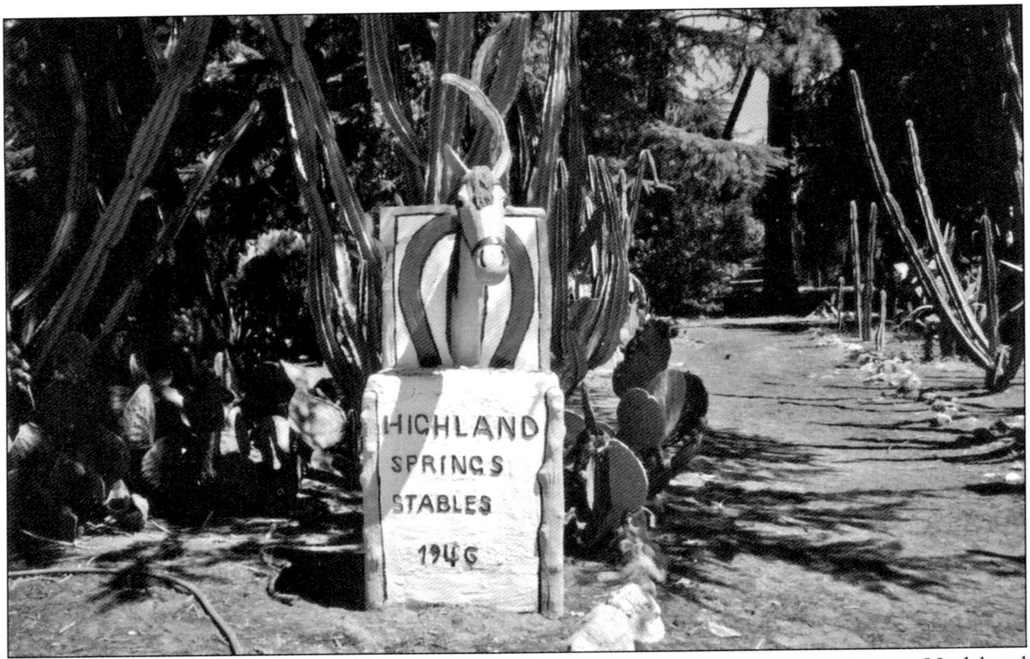

A horseshoe hangs over the neck of a horse at this sign stand, inviting a visitor to Highland Springs Stables in 1946. Horse riding was quite popular during these early years at Highland Springs Resort, and the horse stable maintained on the grounds was a delight to many visitors.

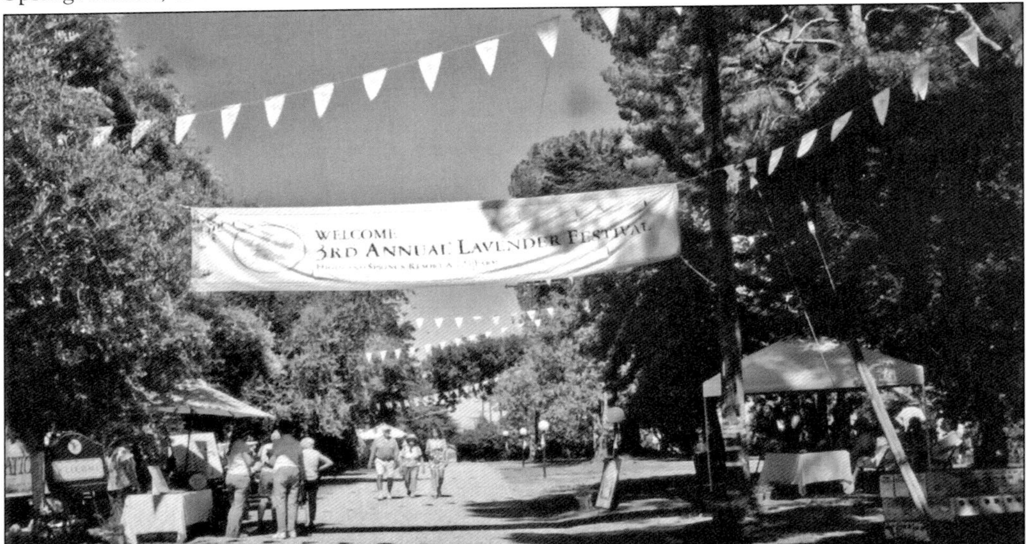

This photograph was taken during the 3rd Annual Lavender Festival at Highland Springs in 2007. The Lavender Festival has become a major, yearly event at Highland Springs and attracts more visitors each consecutive year. Not only are acres of colorful lavender to be enjoyed during this time, but also cherished is the serenity found among the tall pines throughout the grounds.

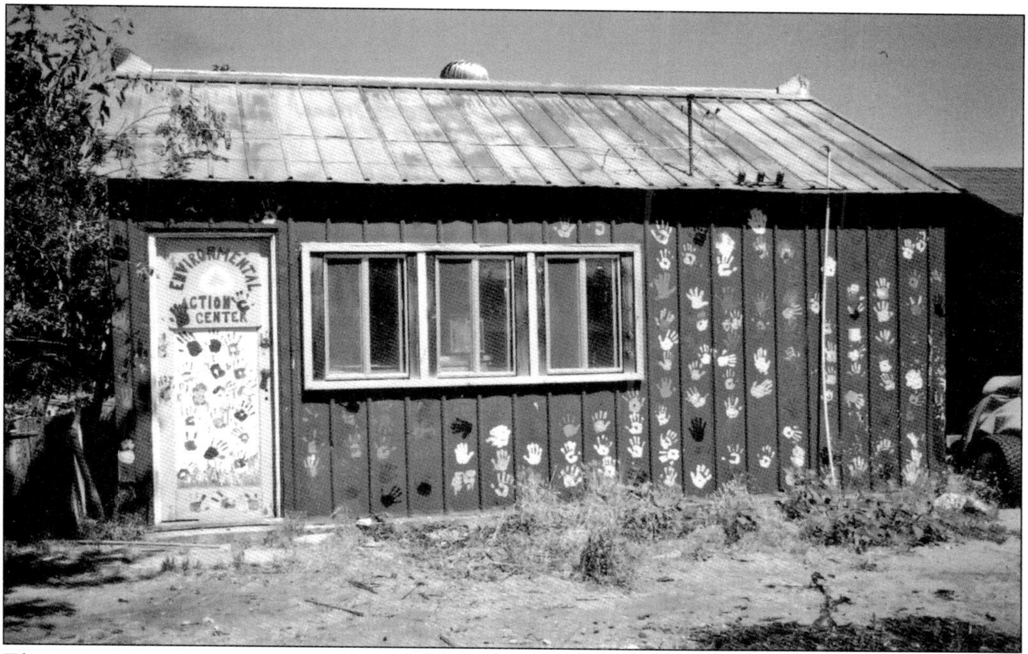

There are numerous buildings throughout the grounds of Highland Springs Resort. The small building pictured is the Environmental Action Center and was designed by students concerned about the environment. The management of Highland Springs Resort is very ecologically oriented and does a great job, in this respect, at their resort.

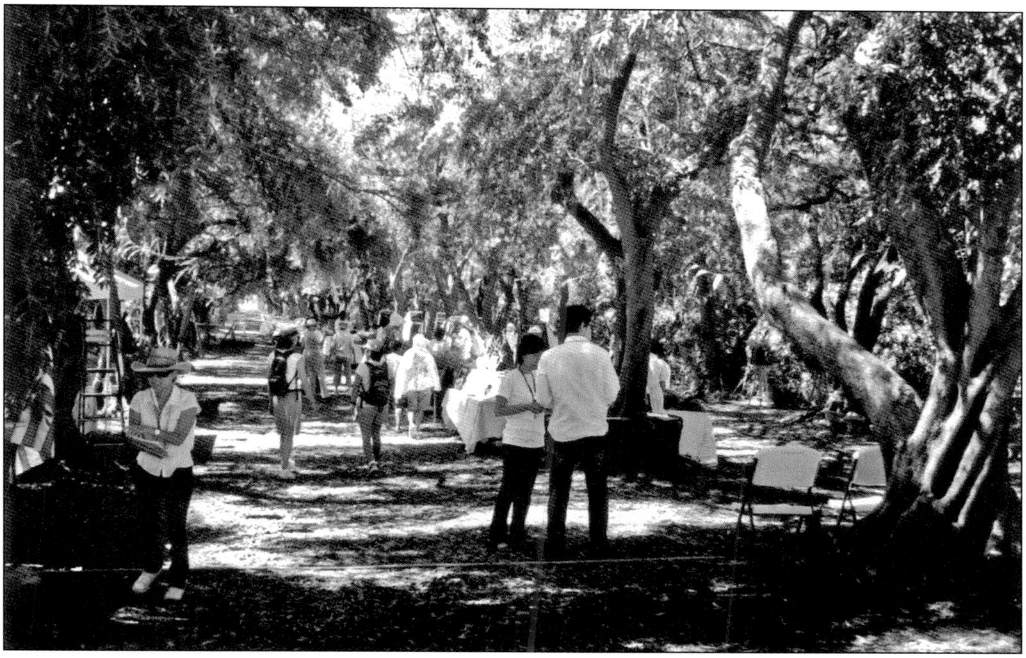

Visitors casually stroll down the alcove of very old olive trees during the 2007 Lavender Festival. It is one of the walkways at Highland Springs Resort that is a real delight to experience. It is quite evident that these groups of strollers are completely enjoying the walk.

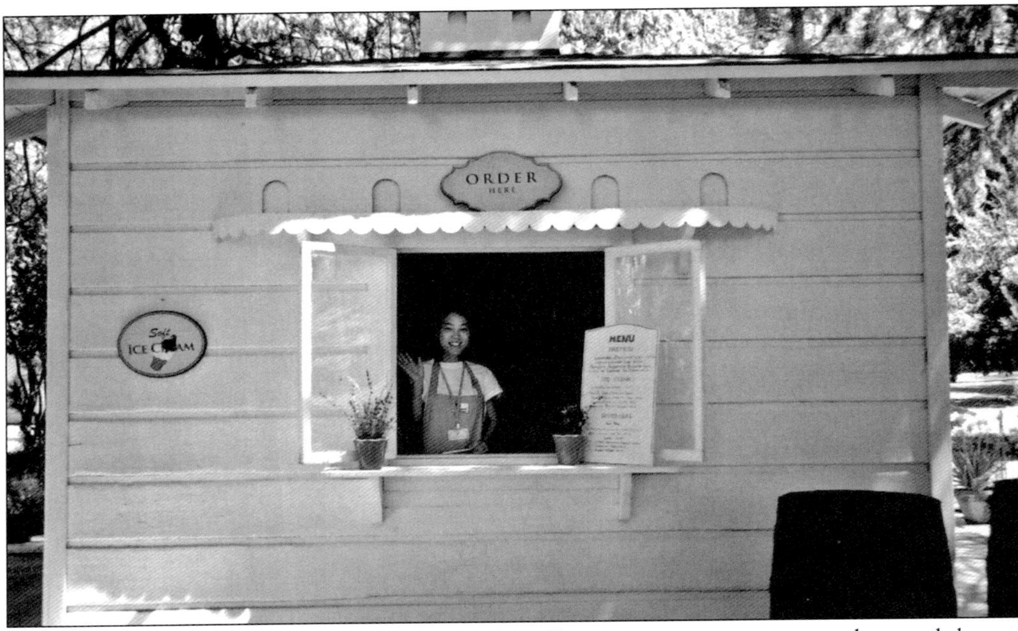

During the 3rd Annual Lavender Festival, a friendly server greets a visitor at the snack bar on the festival grounds. Of course, the specialty served at this little stand is lavender ice cream, a flavor that many people have not tasted and want to sample. Other healthful foods are served here as well.

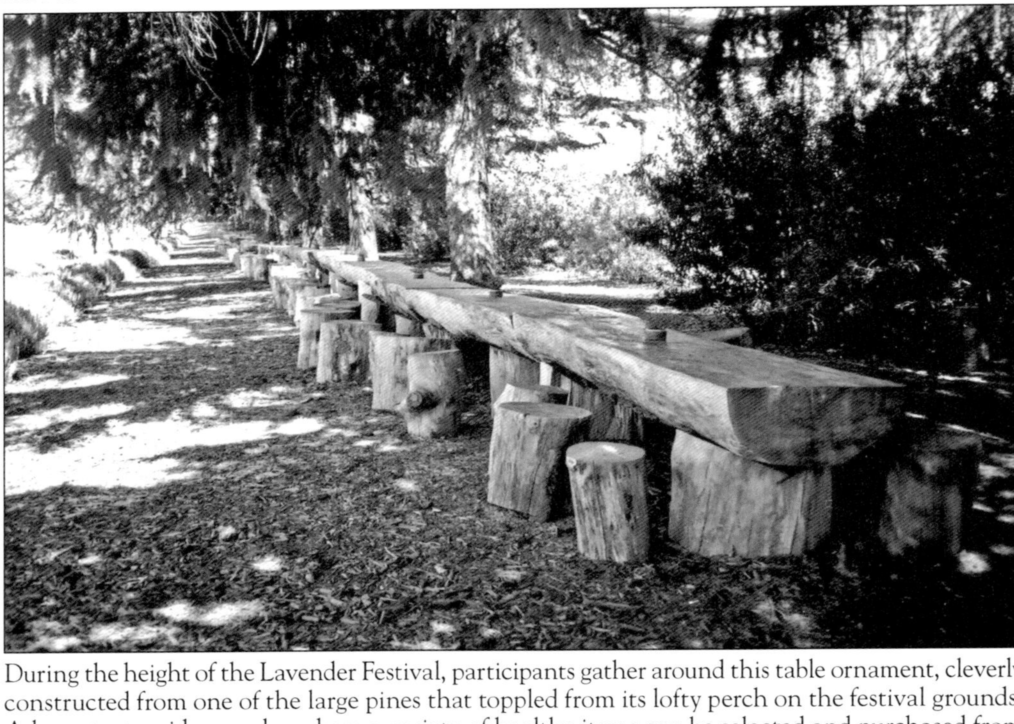

During the height of the Lavender Festival, participants gather around this table ornament, cleverly constructed from one of the large pines that toppled from its lofty perch on the festival grounds. A large tent resides nearby, where a variety of healthy items can be selected and purchased from an appealing menu.

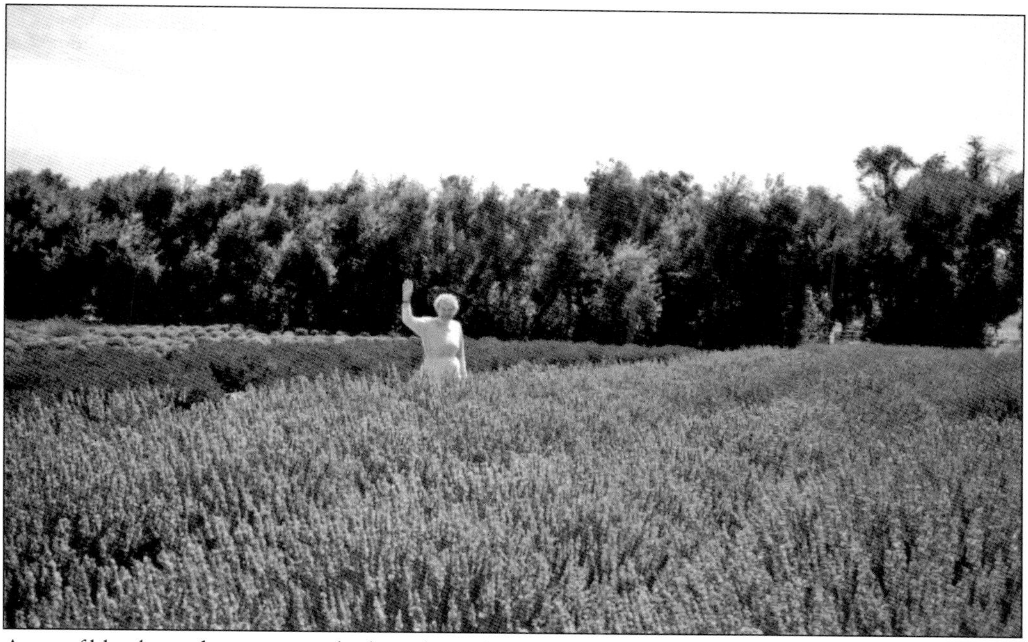

A sea of blue lavender grows on the large lavender farm at Highland Springs Resort and Convention Center. The author's wife, Margaret, is engulfed in this canopy of lush lavender. It is one of the highlights during the resort's annual Lavender Festival. It rolls back like a beautiful carpet, reaching the rows of extremely old olive trees in the background.

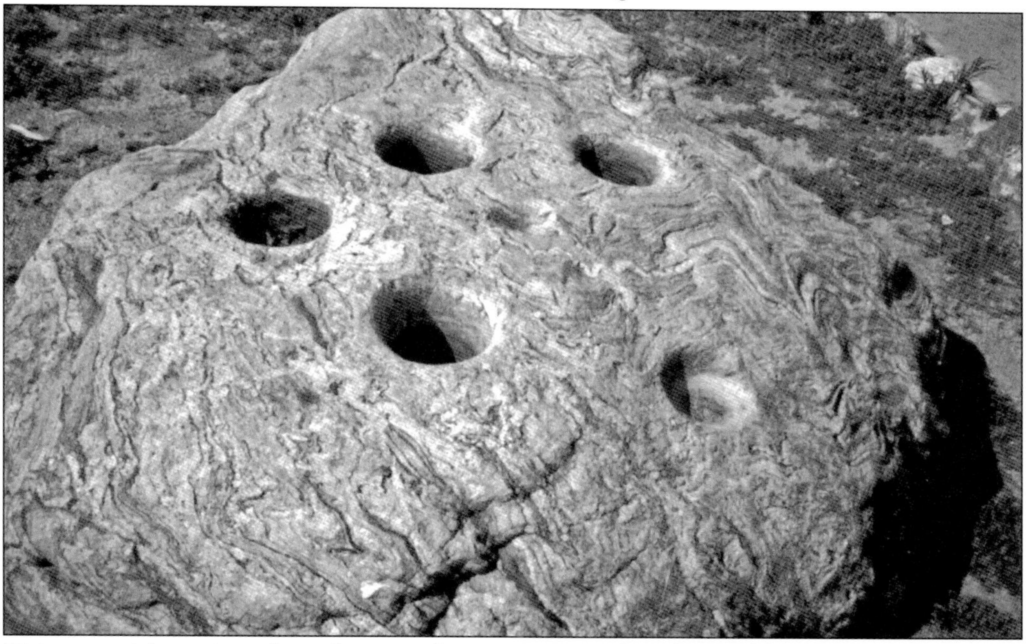

This stone slab was brought in from nearby mountains and used at Highland Springs Resort and Convention Center as one of their displays. Mortars like this were used by local Native Americans to successfully grind acorns, grains, and plant materials. Sites of other mortar findings have been located elsewhere in the area.

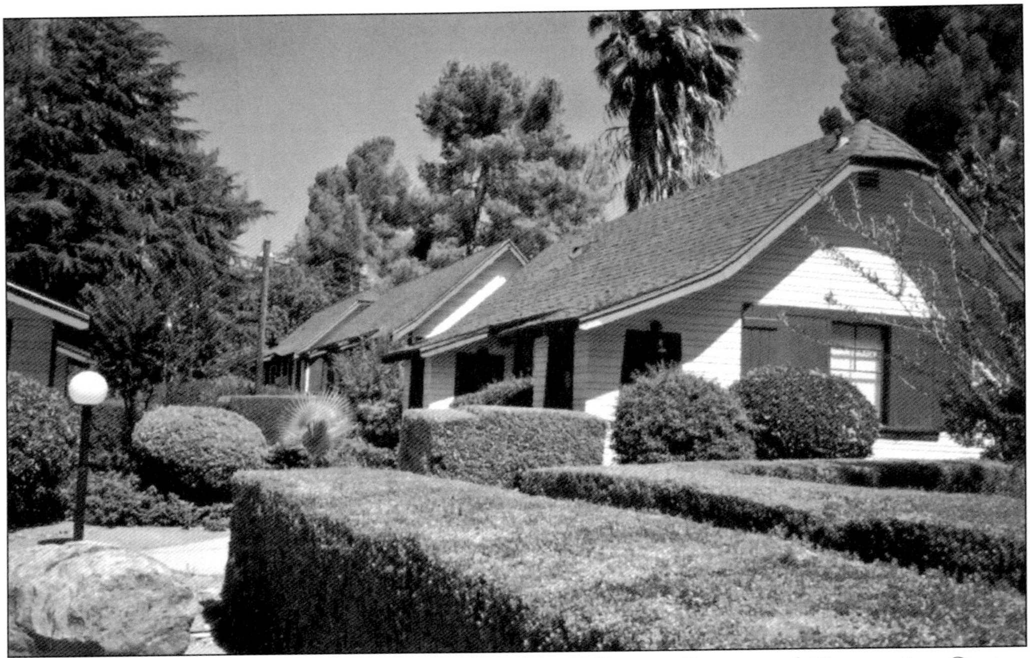

Several bungalows enhance the grounds of Highland Springs Resort and Convention Center. There are numerous ones on the premises like these pictured, some dating back to when it was built years ago. All still provide a fanciful atmosphere in this remote and quaint tree enclosure, where the visitor can be close to nature.

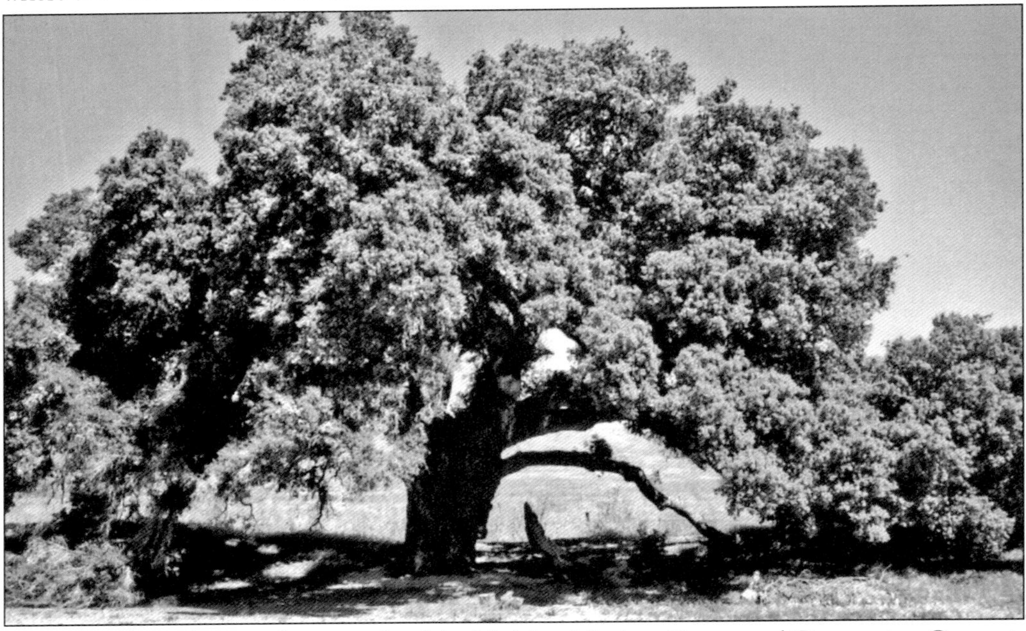

Proudly still standing on the grounds of the Highland Springs Resort and Convention Center is this old oak tree, allegedly believed to be over 1,000 years old. The author rounded the big oak with six out-reached arm lengths, circling the circumference of the tree. The rough calculation of which is believed to be around 30 feet.

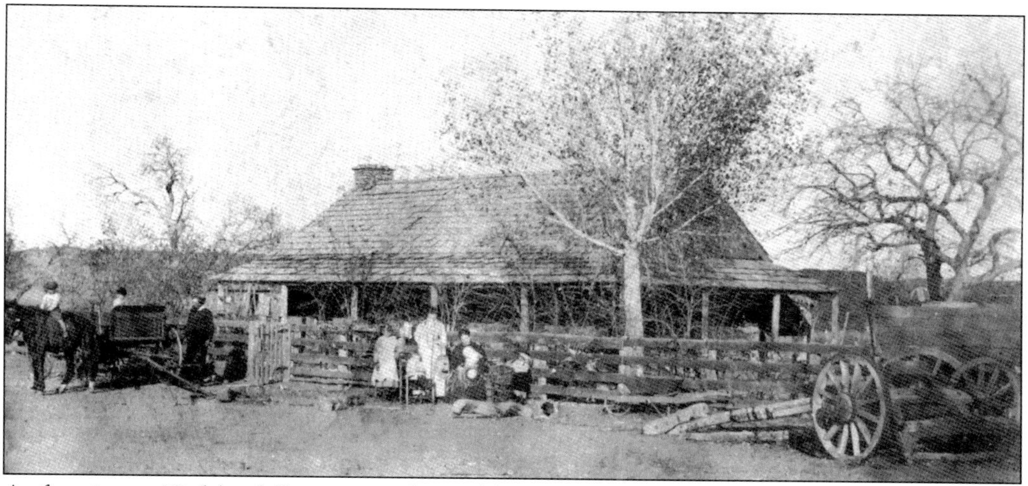

As farming at Highland Springs was limited because of available land, Dr. Smith's eldest son, Frank, filed a claim and received a patent on the property to the east, which soon became known as the Whitewater Ranch. Pictured is the ranch adobe. Like Highland Springs, it operated during the stagecoach period as a stage stop along the Bradshaw Trail. Dr. Smith died at Whitewater Ranch on March 7, 1878. The ranch at Highland Springs was sold in 1884. Oliver M. Smith, Dr. Smith's son, the first white male born in Cherry Valley, farmed the acreage at Whitewater Ranch and summered his cattle in Big Bear. (Courtesy of Joan Coombs.)

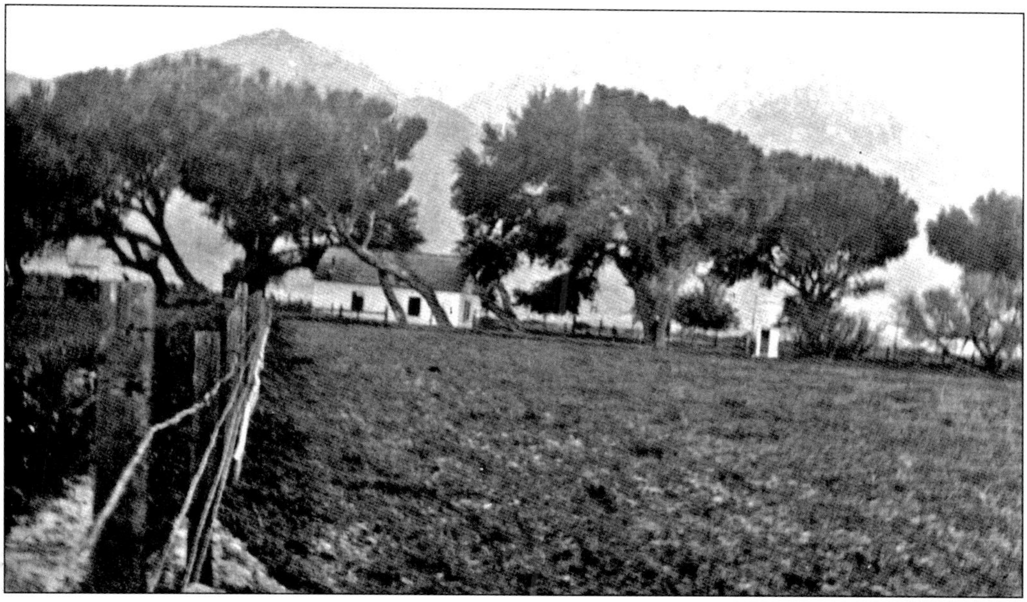

Pictured is the Whitewater Ranch adobe, probable in the mid-1970s, many years after the farm's operation ceased. The old adobe was torn down in 1981. The fireplace chimney on the building, normally seen, is not visible in this picture; the image was taken at the back of the property, placing the chimney at right instead of left and obscured by the trees at the right side of the adobe. (Courtesy of Joan Coombs.)

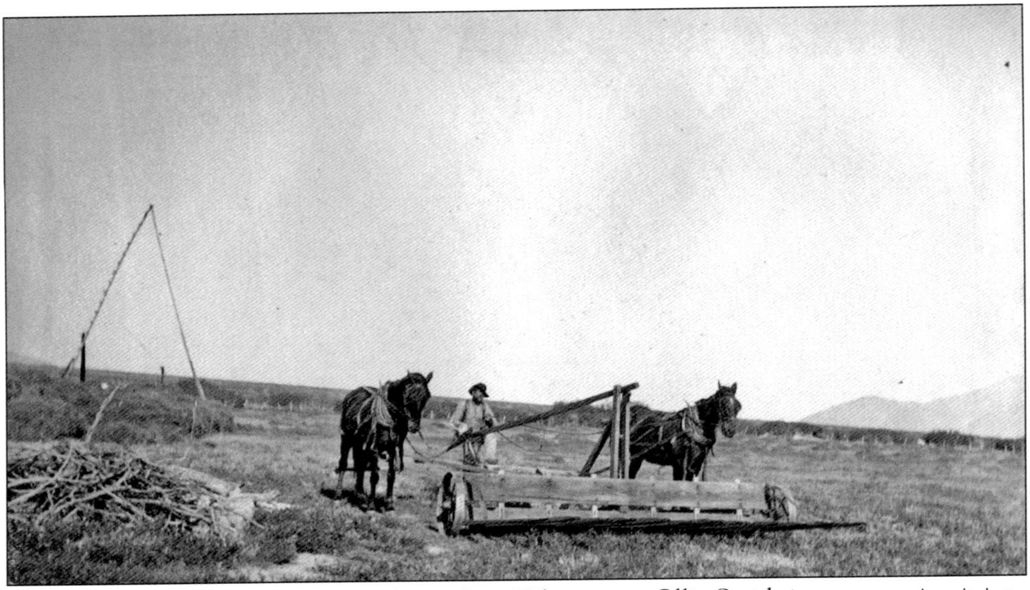

This hay rake was used on the Smith ranch in Whitewater. Ollie Smith is maneuvering it into place in the field where hay has been cut. It collects the harvested hay by being pushed along, collecting the hay as the teeth of the equipment moves under the straw. Note the lever held by Ollie that controls the angle of the teeth. (Courtesy of Joan Coombs.)

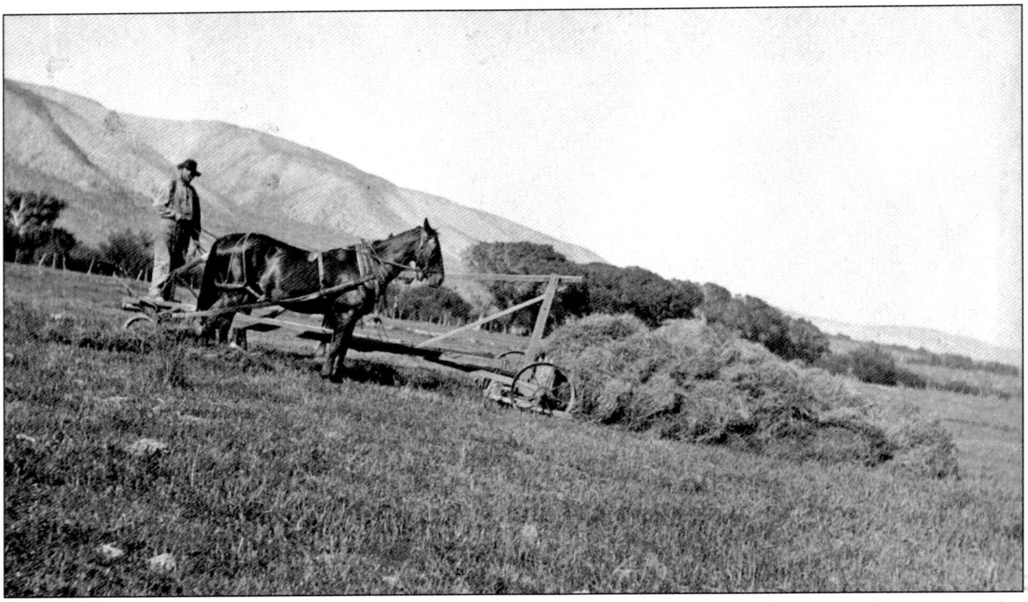

This is an example of the method used to collect the cut hay in a field into a pile so it can be picked up conveniently. Ollie Smith is standing on the apparatus that was used on his ranch for this purpose. It is tied to the horse in such a manner that when the horse moves forward, it then moves ahead of the horse and pushes the hay together. (Courtesy of Joan Coombs.)

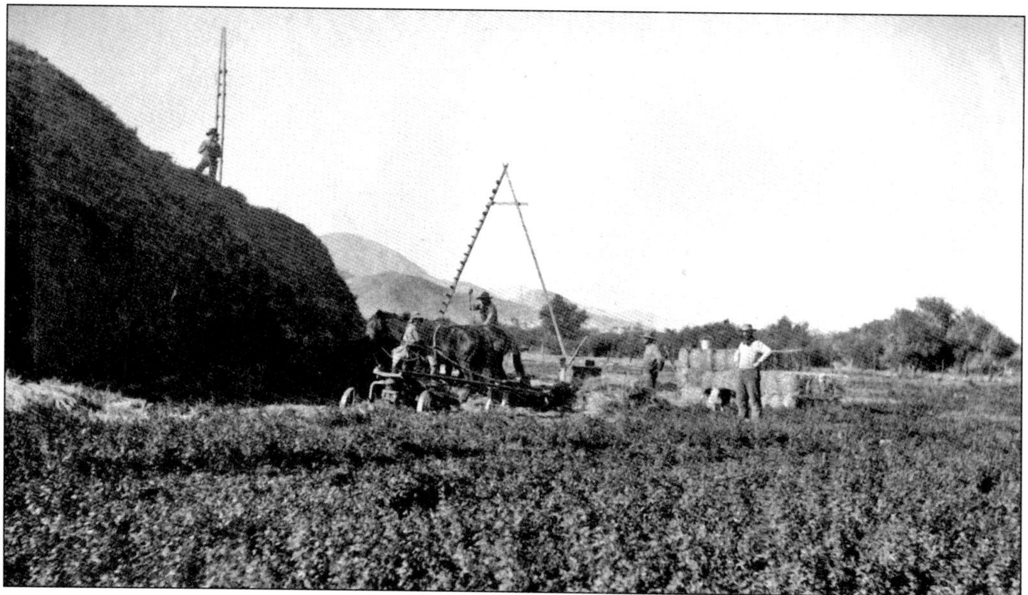

At left is a worker standing on a large pile of hay collected on Smith's Whitewater Ranch. He appears to have a pitchfork in hand and is probably tossing hay down to the work crew below who are preparing to accept it for bailing. Bailing hay during this time was a laborious task, quite unlike the mechanized methods of today. (Courtesy of Joan Coombs.)

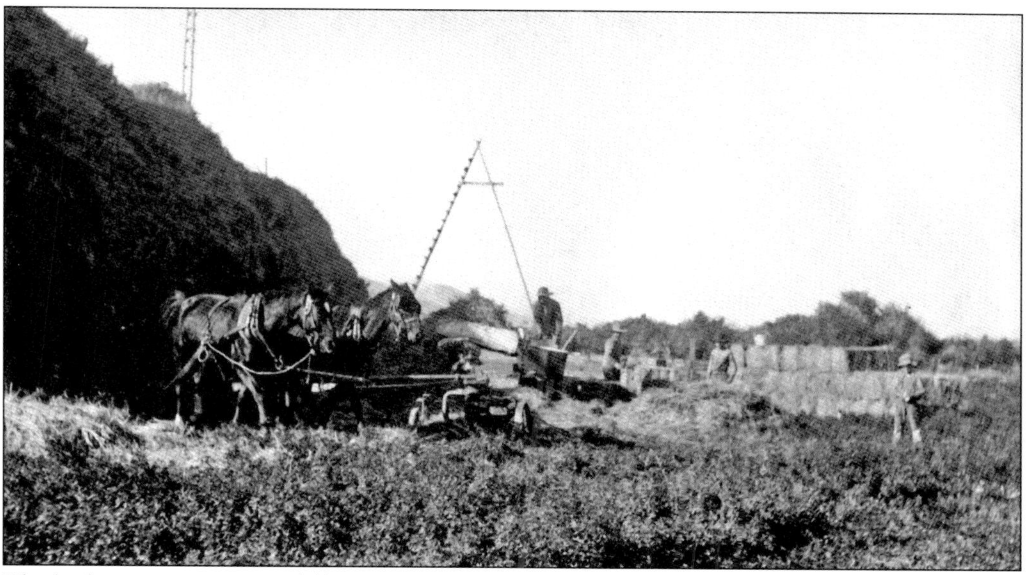

The bailing operation is in full motion. Hay is being fed into a compactor by hand by the worker at center. Then the hay that has been compacted into a standard bail is moved over to the crew that ties the bails with bailing wire and stacks the finished bail at the side (shown at right). (Courtesy of Joan Coombs.)

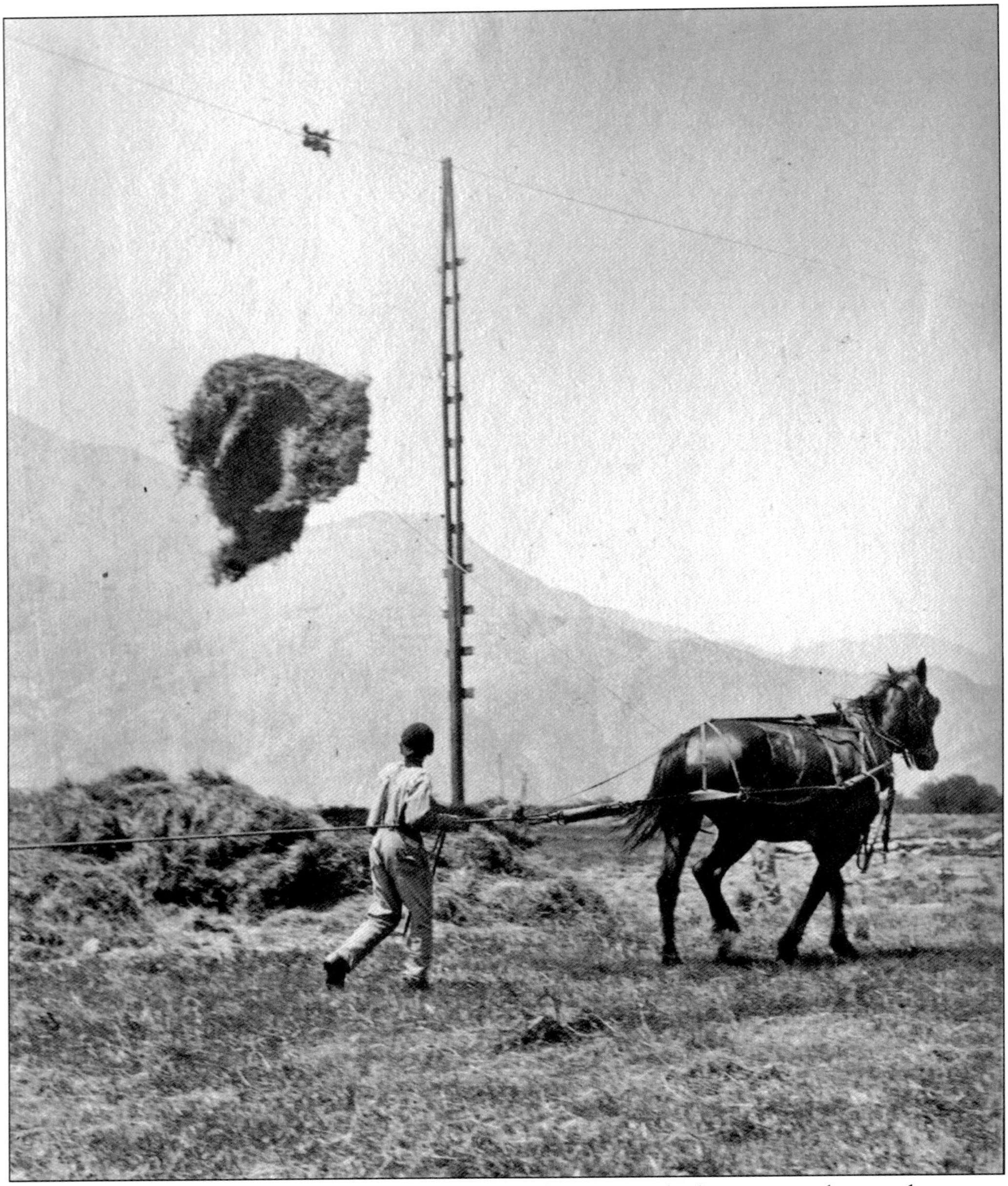

A portion of the derrick that is used for hoisting and swinging the hay into a pile is in the center of this picture. After the hay rake has collected the hay into individual piles, then these piles are brought nearby the derrick to be piled into a large haystack. The hay then waits in the stack, either to feed Smith's farm animals from the bulk stack, or to be bailed for sale to the market. (Courtesy of Joan Coombs.)

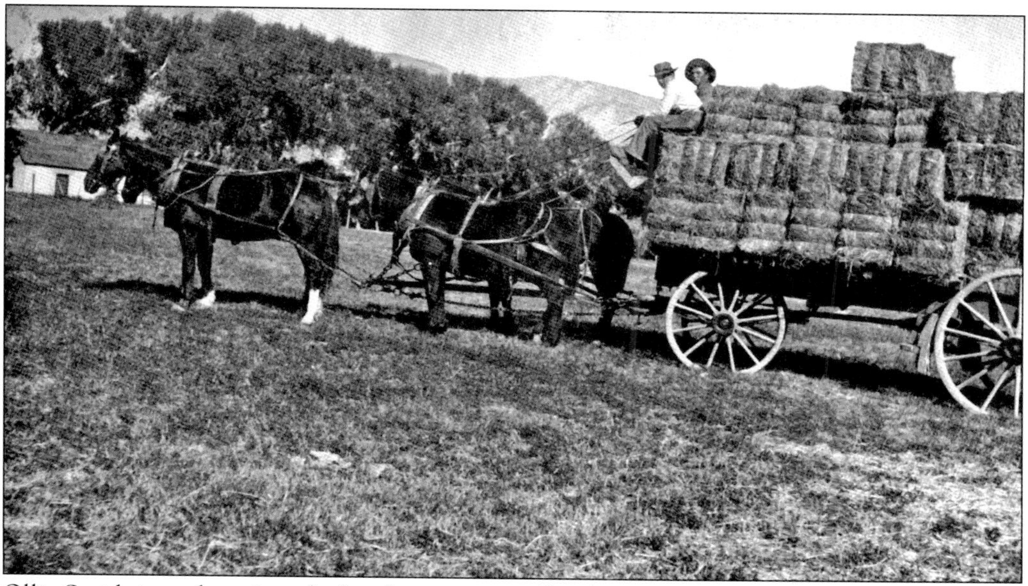

Ollie Smith is at the reins of a four-horse team pulling a newly bailed load of hay grown on his ranch. Robert Coombs (Bert) is sitting beside him on his left. Robert is the father of Phil Coombs, who later farmed in Banning. Note the old original farmhouse in the background on the left. (Courtesy of Joan Coombs.)

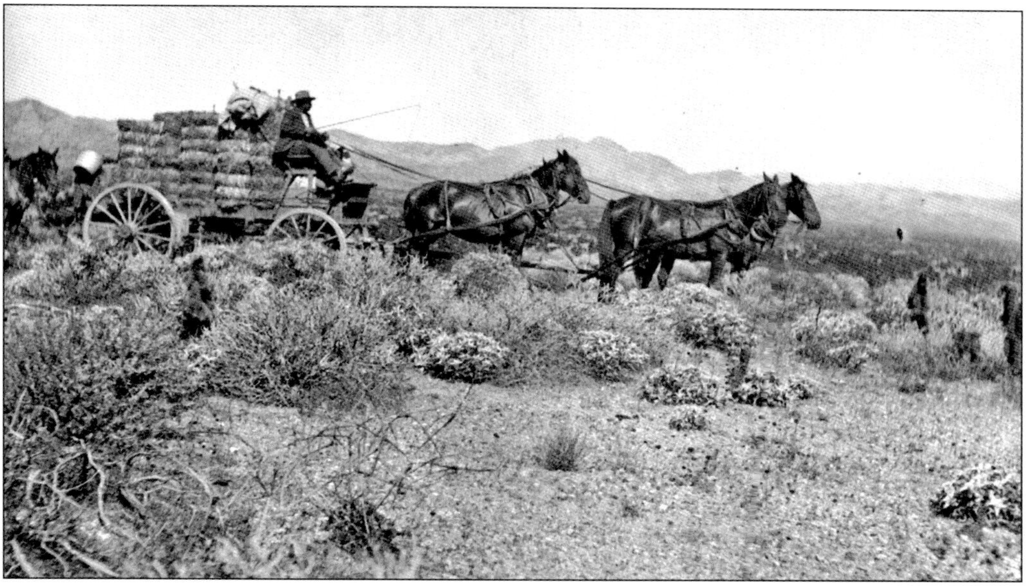

Ollie Smith is driving this loaded wagon of hay, crossing a stretch of desert between his ranch and an area where he is delivering the hay to market. Note the glimpse of the horse in the rear of the wagon, which may be the lead of another wagon. It was a tedious task getting the hay to market on hot summer days in the desert. (Courtesy of Joan Coombs.)

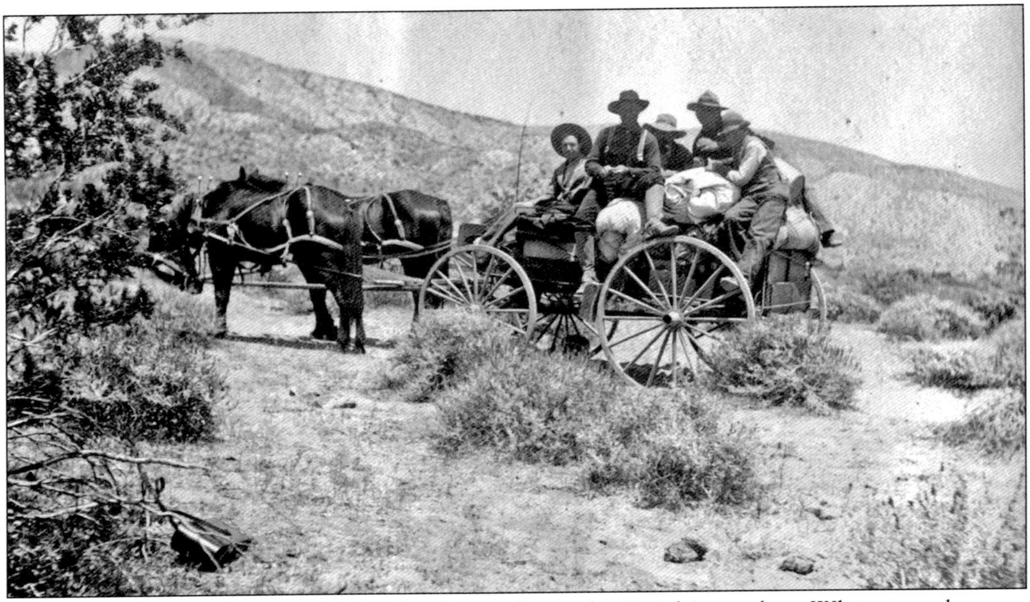

In the dry summer months, grazing for the cattle on the Smith's ranch at Whitewater became limited. Therefore, the cattle were herded some distance away to the plains of Big Bear Mountain where grazing land was still good. Here Ollie Smith and some of his ranch workers are pictured en route to their second ranch home in Big Bear. (Courtesy of Joan Coombs.)

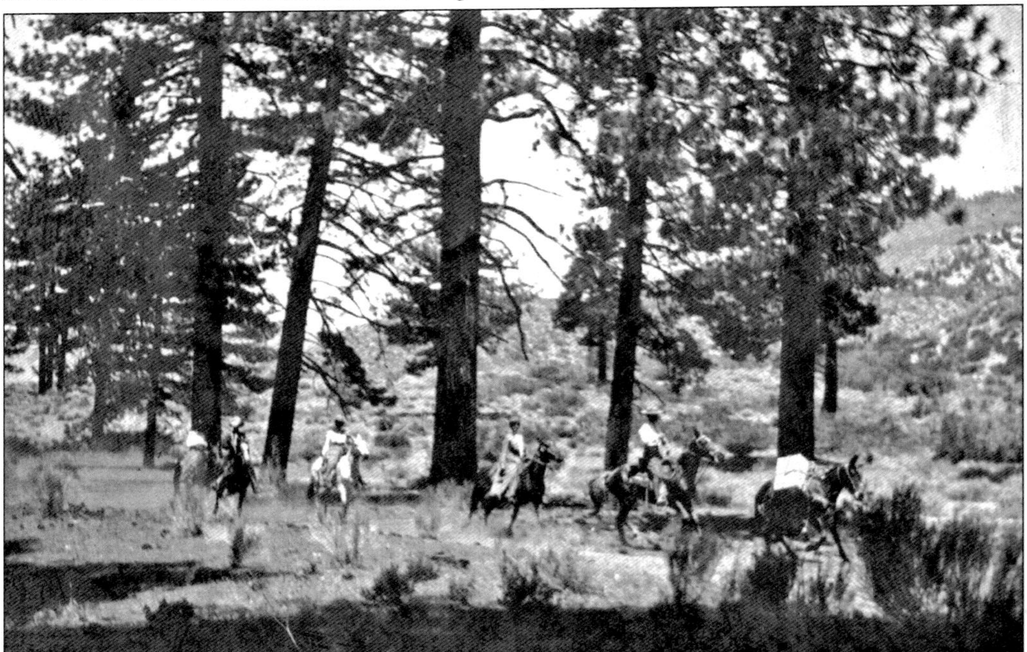

Some of the Whitewater Ranch hands preferred riding their horses to Big Bear instead of traveling by buggy. Note the donkey loaded with cargo at the head of the traveling group. By now, they have reached the pine trees that are common around Big Bear and riding is much more pleasant. (Courtesy of Joan Coombs.)

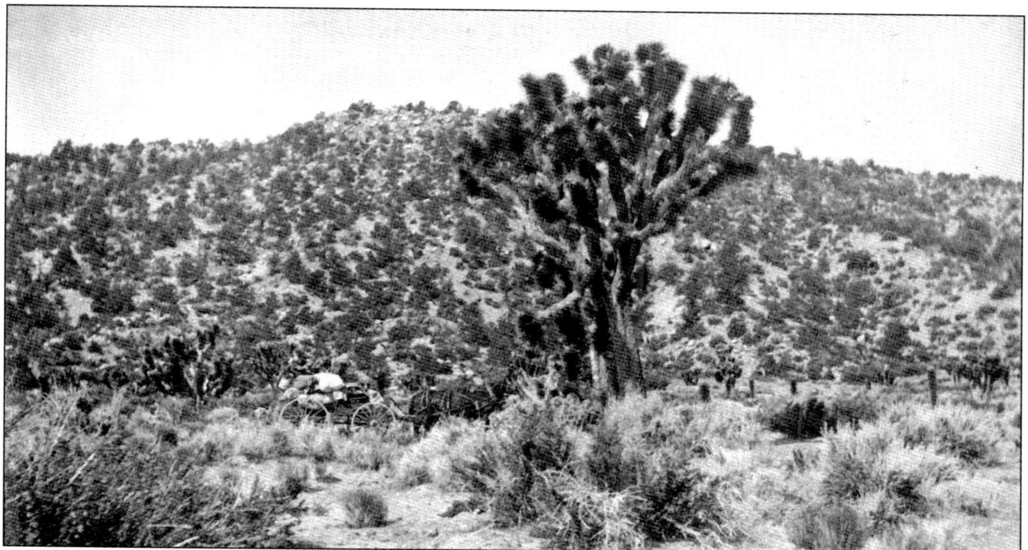

During the hot summer weather in the desert, it was a lonesome trek between Whitewater and Big Bear. Often the only reprieve from the heat was a stop beside a large cactus plant like the one pictured here. The group could stop for lunch and make a rest stop during their travel at a convenient spot like this. (Courtesy of Joan Coombs.)

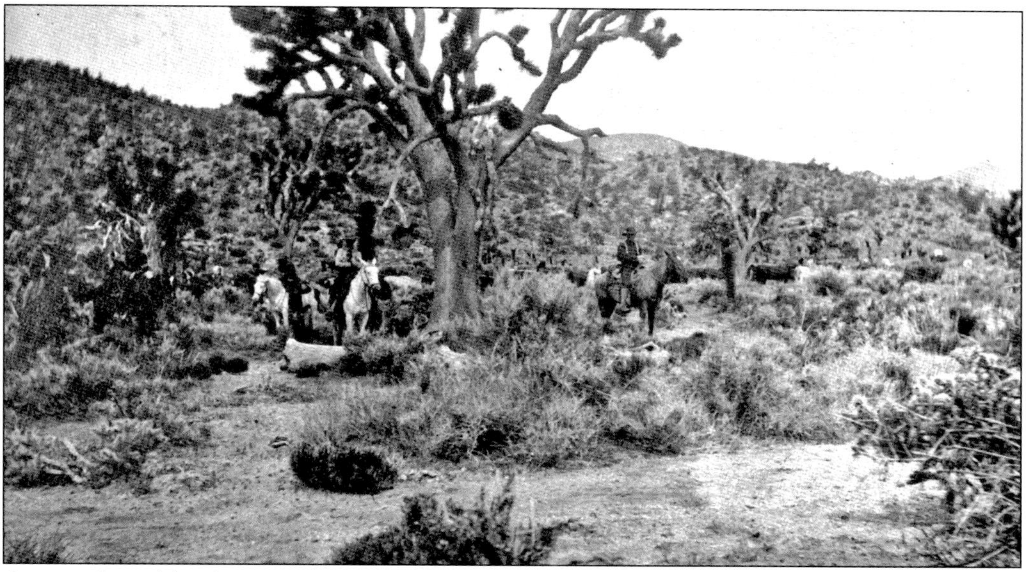

Cactus plants like this one were a welcome resting place for the ranch hands during the cattle drive to Big Bear. Both men and cattle welcomed such sights along the way and found places like this ideal for rest stops. The group of cowherders in this picture appears to be welcoming one of the big cacti along the way. (Courtesy of Joan Coombs.)

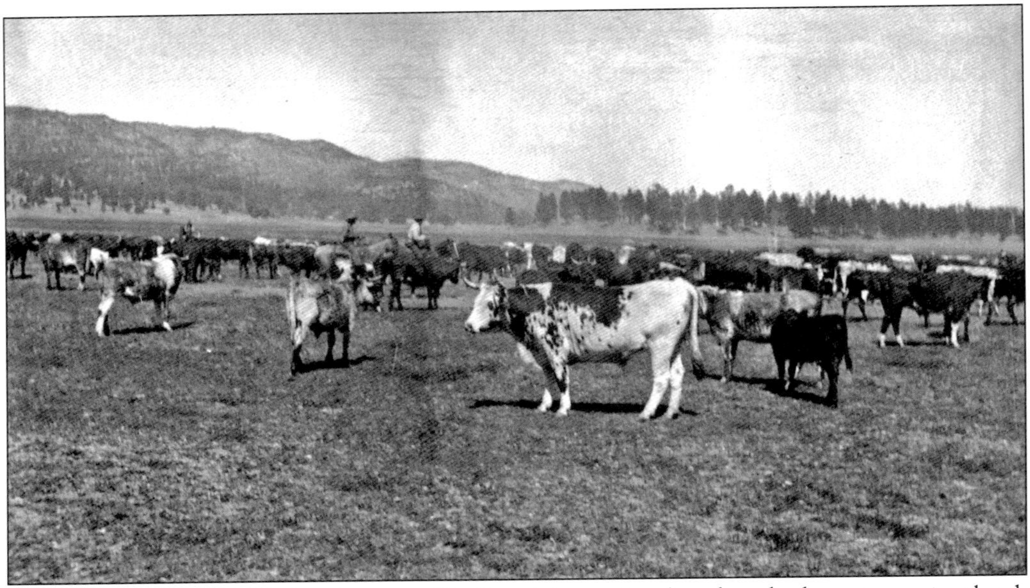

Once the cattle reached the plains on Big Bear Mountain, they found adequate grazing land. They appear to be quite content as they arrive at their new quarters. This was a great place for the Whitewater Ranch to bring their large herd of cattle in the summer. Notice the backdrop of small pines where the cattle can find shade during the heat of the day. (Courtesy of Joan Coombs.)

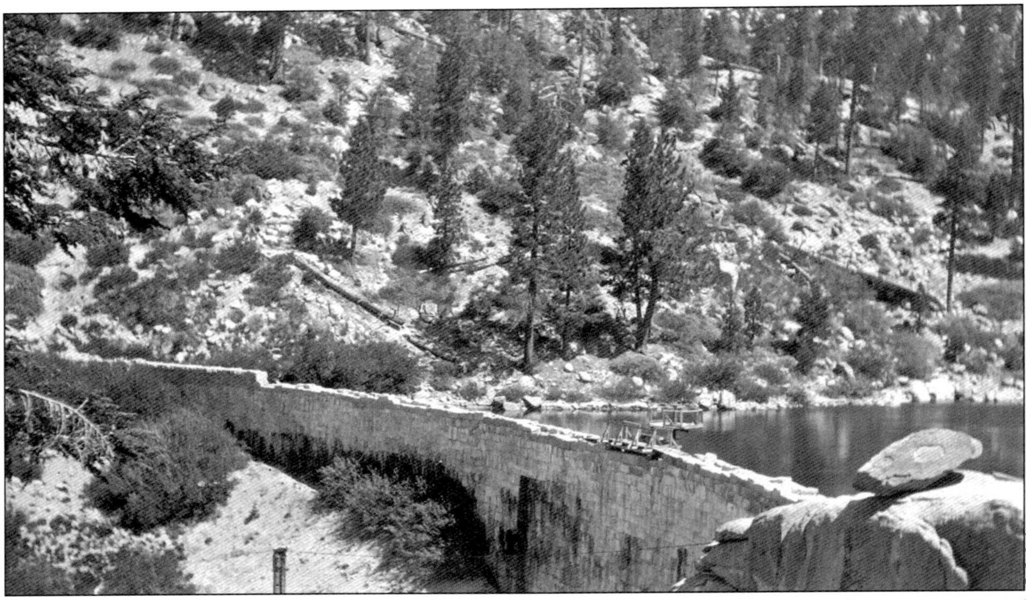

This scene shows the dam as seen from an area below the lake. The dam was the inspiration of Frank E. Brown. The dam greatly increased the area of Big Bear Lake and enhanced the area as a popular resort. The water that was taken from Big Bear Lake traveled numerous miles to Moreno Valley to irrigate the many acres of citrus that had been planted there. (Courtesy of Smiley Library.)

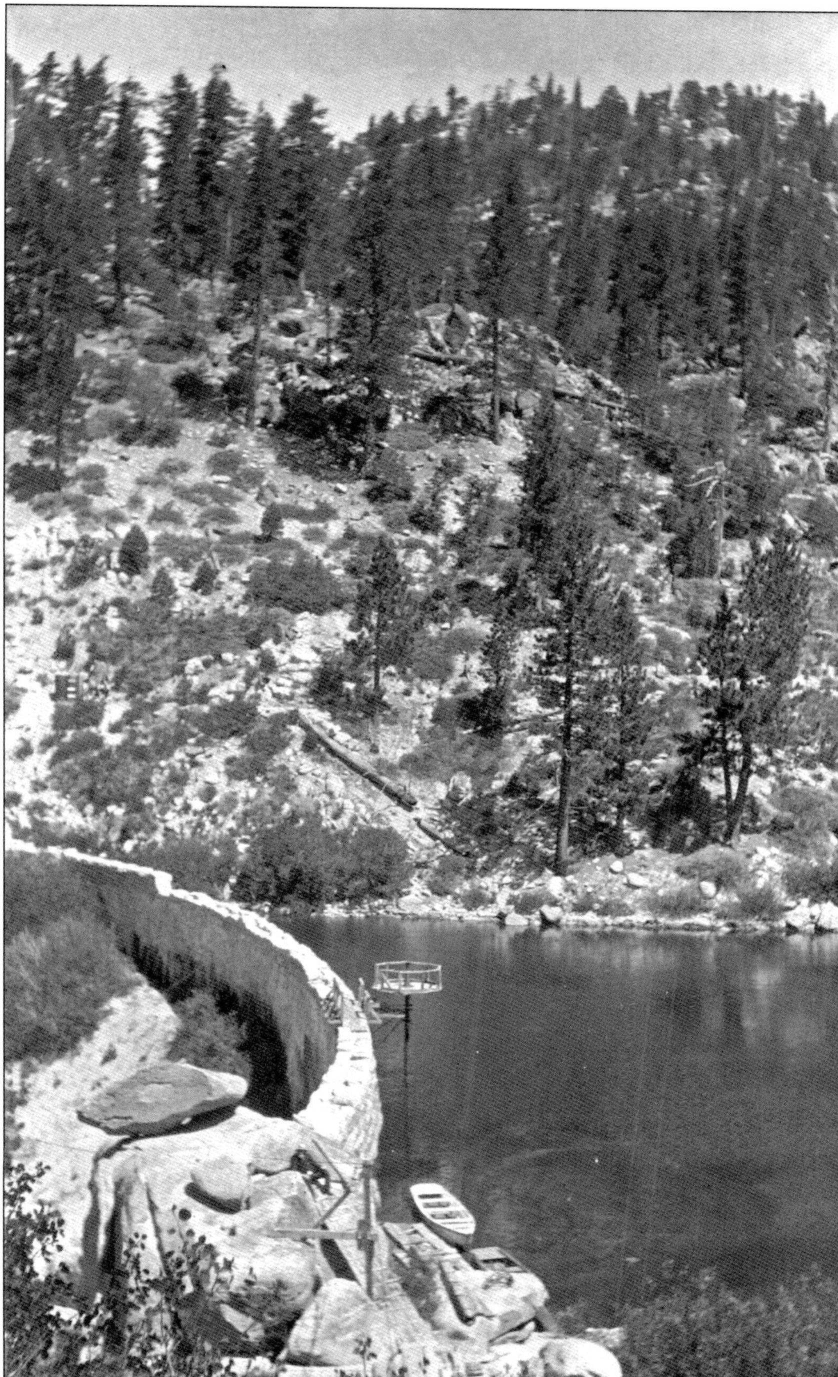

During this period in time, a dam had already been built at Big Bear Lake and plenty of water was available. The picture shows a cement block dam, but previously the dam was made of logs. Note the quietness of the scene, just a couple of boats for fishing, and the stillness of the lake water. (Courtesy of Joan Coombs.)

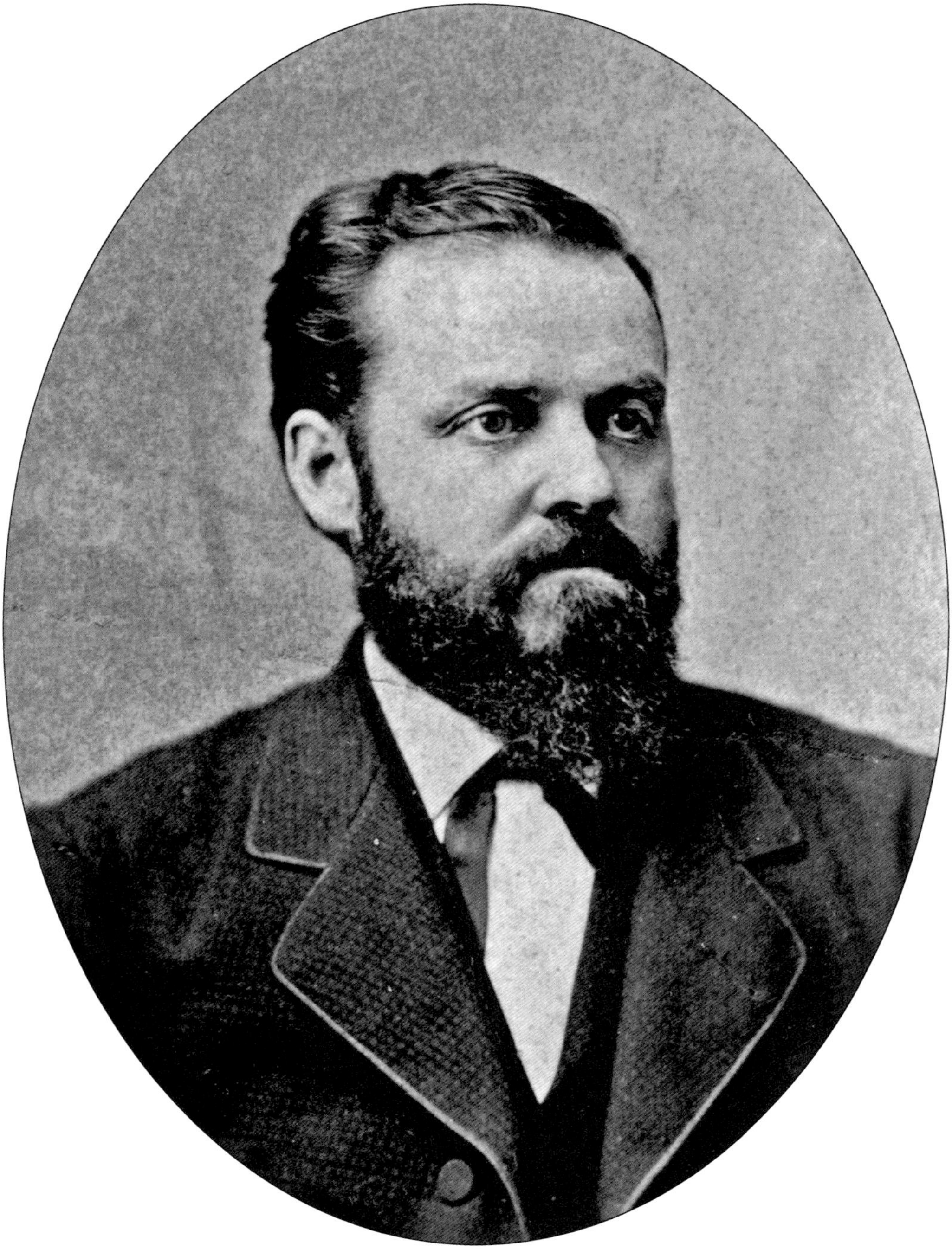

Frank E. Brown was the cofounder of Redlands and responsible for the construction of Big Bear Dam. He believed that if he could bring water from Big Bear Dam to Moreno Valley across the Badlands from Redlands, then it could become a utopia. The Bear Valley and Alessandro Development Company was formed to bring the water, initiating the future formation of Moreno. (Courtesy of Moreno Valley Historical Society.)

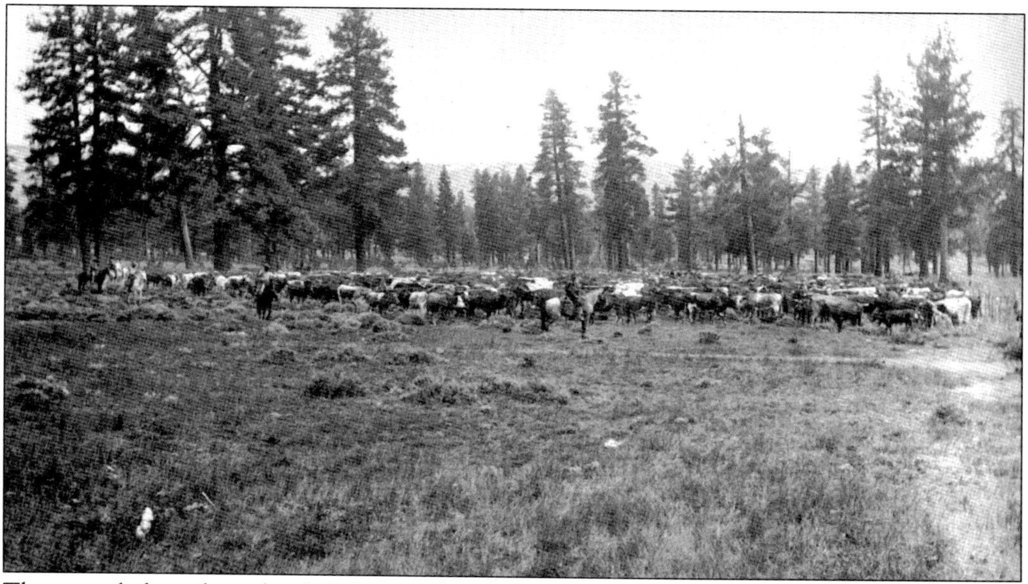

These cattle have been herded to a nearby plain in Big Bear among the pines for grazing. The foliage for the cows appears quite available. Both cowhands and cows appear to be content in this setting among the tall pine trees. It is certainly a reprieve from the heated desert below from which they arrived. (Courtesy of Joan Coombs.)

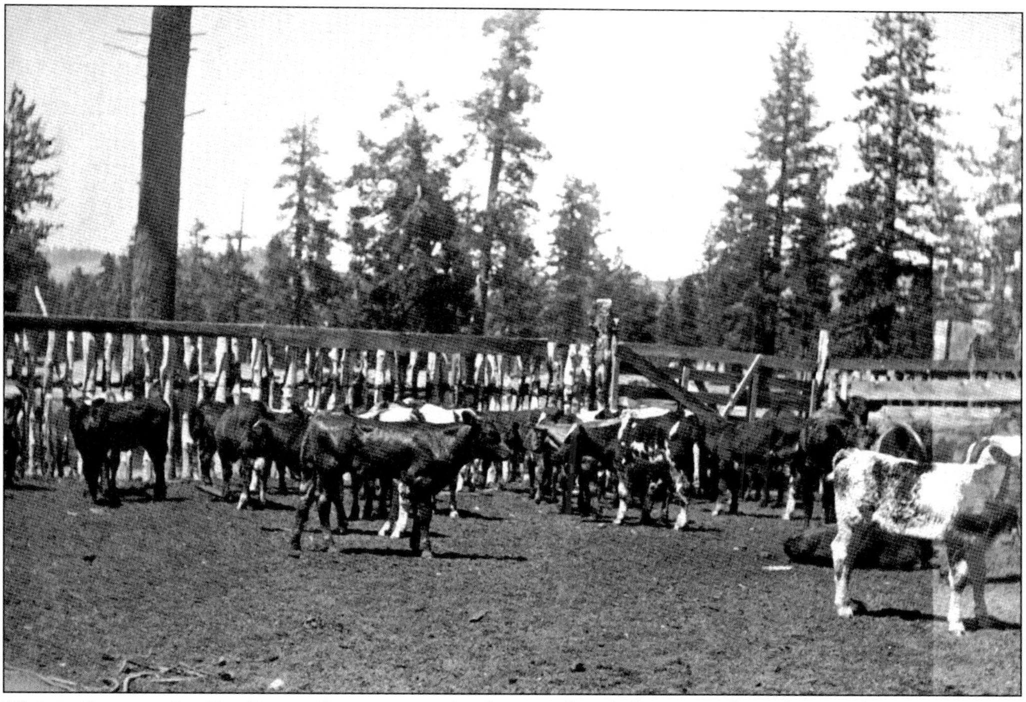

This is the corral at Big Bear, where matured calves are herded to await branding with a Whitewater Ranch brand. The season's crop of new calves has grown to a size ready for branding. This is just one of the many tasks that are required to maintain a large herd of cattle. (Courtesy of Joan Coombs.)

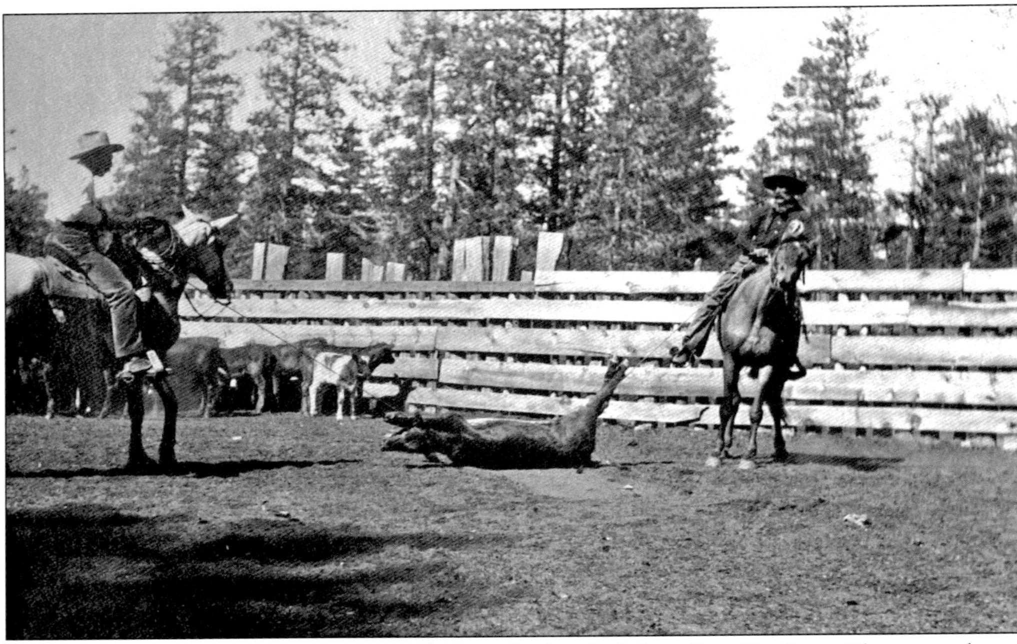

It was time for branding the growing calves in the herd while still at Big Bear. The young breed was herded into the corral and individually tied, like the one pictured. They were then branded with the Smith's Whitewater Ranch brand. Returning home after their stay at Big Bear, they are well marked, a precaution if they should stray when returning. (Courtesy of Joan Comes.)

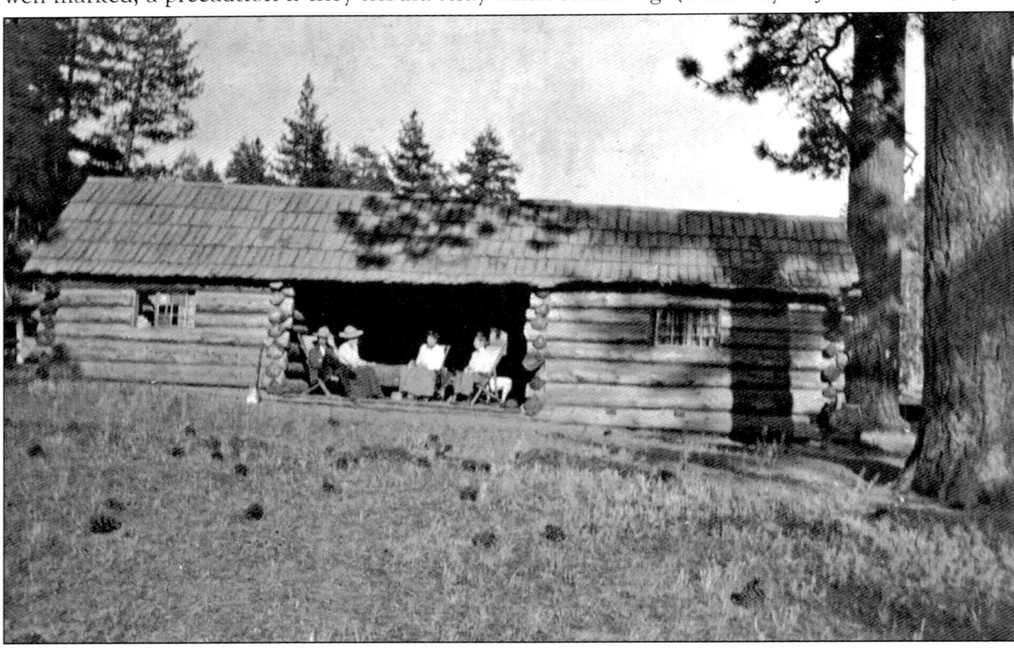

This is a scene from sometime after the Smith family left the Whitewater Ranch and arrived at Big Bear. They settled here in their summer ranch house. Living in the rustic log cabin during the summer months was looked forward to because it was a welcomed break away from the desert heat that engulfed the Whitewater Ranch in the summer. (Courtesy of Joan Coombs.)

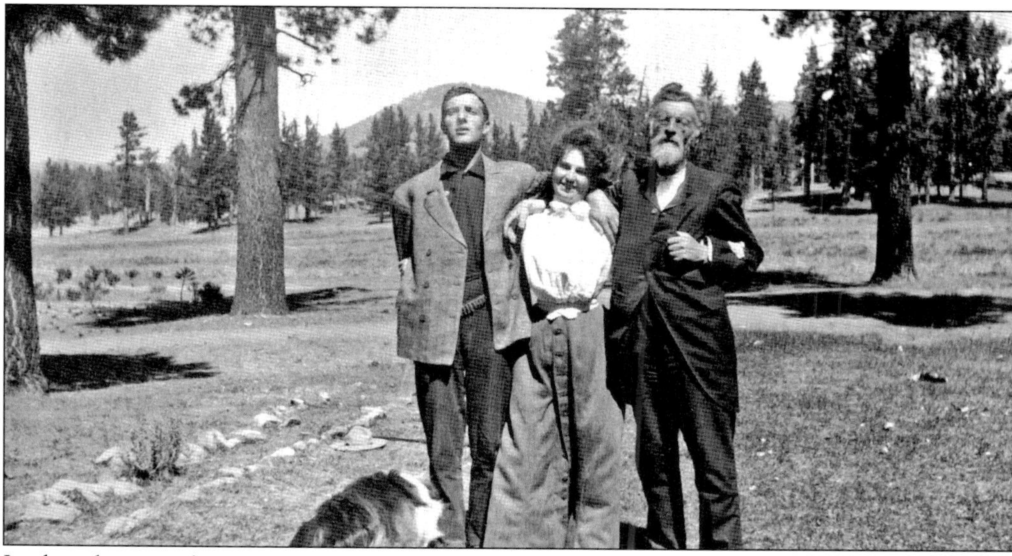

In this photograph are, from left to right, Bert Coombs, an unidentified lady, and Bert's father, Robert Coombs Sr. from London, England. He was visiting at this time. Bert Coombs and Ollie Smith were partners of the Whitewater Ranch. Bert's brother remained in England, never wanting to get involved in ranching. (Courtesy of Joan Combs.)

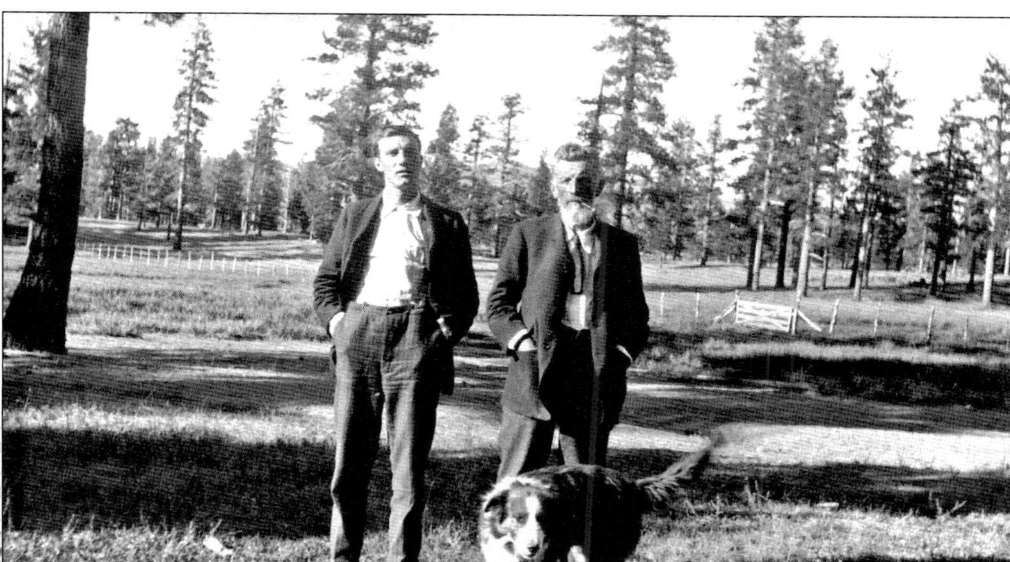

Robert Coombs (Bert) is at left with his father Robert Coombs Sr., who was visiting from London, England. This photograph was taken during his visit to California. Bert was the father of Phil Coombs, who arrived here from Chicago with his mom and dad when he was only 10 years old. Phil grew up and later began farming in Banning, the community west of Whitewater. (Courtesy of Joan Coombs.)

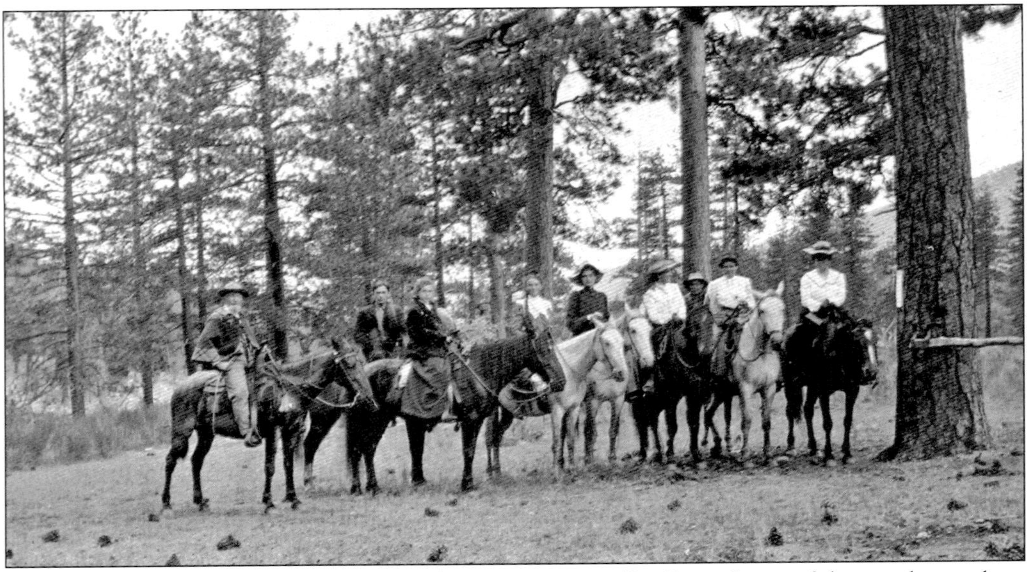

It was not all work and no play for the Whitewater gang at Big Bear. Some of the ranch members pictured here are saddled and ready for a horseback outing among the pines of Big Bear. It can be noted that many of the group are women. They often enjoyed horseback riding while their husbands were attending the cattle. (Courtesy of Joan Coombs.)

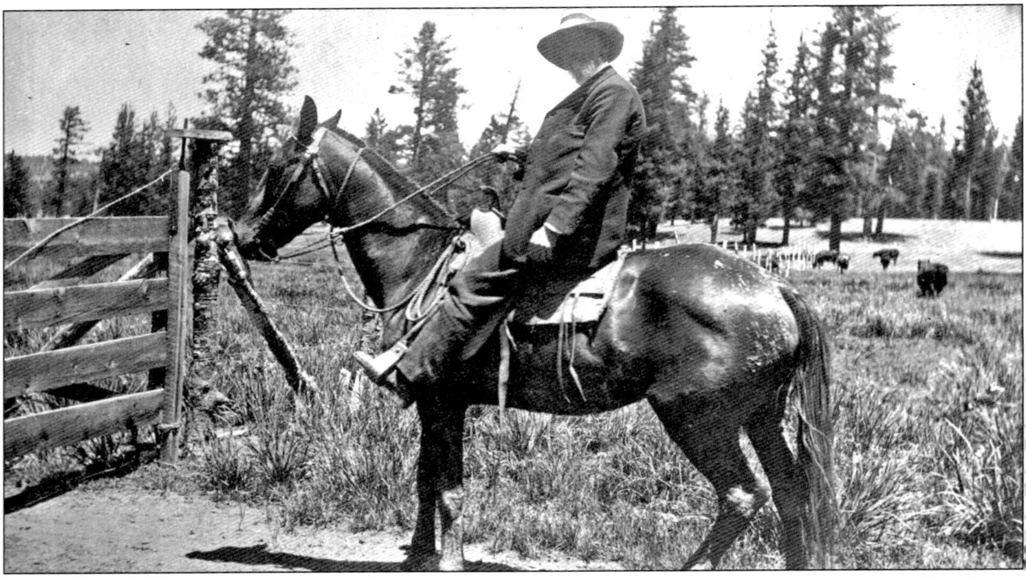

Bert Comb's father, Robert Coombs Sr., is seen mounted on a horse on the range at Big Bear. One reason he liked coming to visit his son Bert during the cattle season at Big Bear is that he could participate in this activity. Another reason for visiting was to see his grandson Phil. (Courtesy of Joan Coombs.)

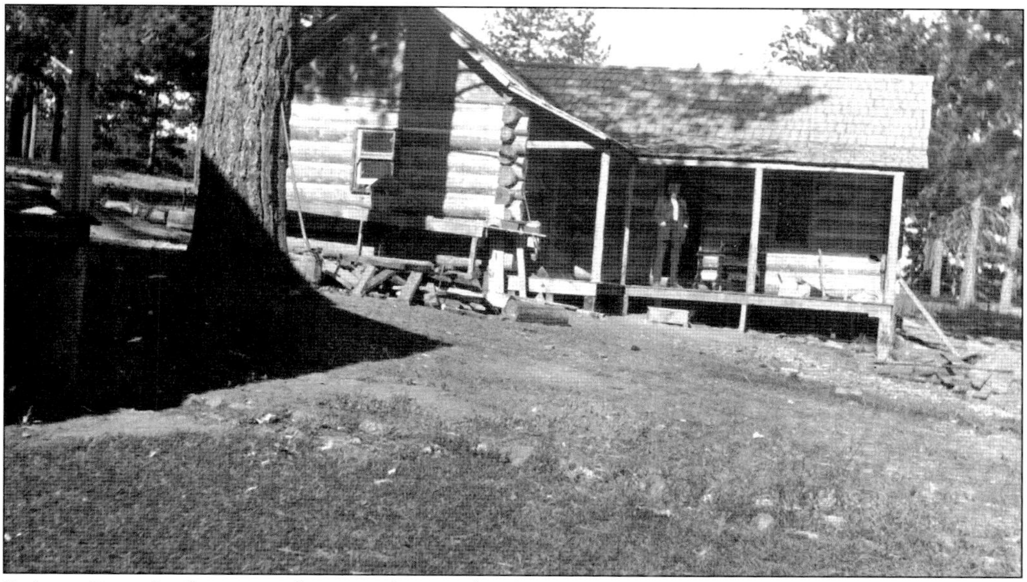

Robert Coombs Sr. is standing on the porch of one of the small log cabins that encompassed the grounds of the ranch at Big Bear. This was a far cry from the hustle and bustle of London. He enjoyed the remoteness and serenity of the mountains when he visited here. (Courtesy of Joan Coombs.)

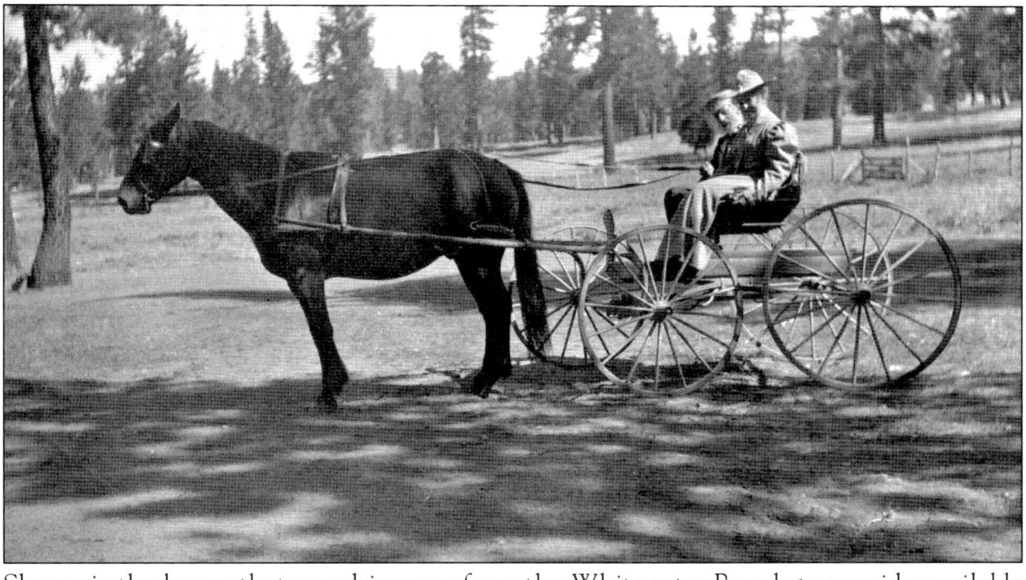

Shown is the buggy that was driven up from the Whitewater Ranch to provide available transportation around the ranch at Big Bear. The unidentified pair pictured have commandeered the buggy at this time and appear quite leisurely in command. There were many places to visit at Big Bear, including Big Bear Lake. (Courtesy of Joan Coombs.)